ECONOMICS & FEMINISM

Disturbances in the Field

The Impact of Feminism on the Arts & Sciences

Claire Sprague, General Editor
New York University

History & Feminism
Judith P. Zinsser

Biology & Feminism
Sue V. Rosser

Philosophy & Feminism
Andrea Nye

Classics & Feminism
Barbara McManus

Political Science & Feminisms: Integration or Transformation?
Kathleen A. Staudt and William G. Weaver

ECONOMICS & FEMINISM

Disturbances in the Field

Randy Albelda

Twayne Publishers • New York
An Imprint of Simon & Schuster Macmillan

Prentice Hall International
London • Mexico City • New Delhi • Singapore • Sydney • Toronto

Twayne Publishers
An Imprint of Simon & Schuster Macmillan
1633 Broadway
New York, NY 10019

Library of Congress Cataloging-in-Publication Data

Albelda, Randy.
    Economics & feminism : disturbances in the field / Randy Albelda.
       p.   cm. — (The impact of feminism on the arts & sciences)
    Includes bibliographical references and index.
    ISBN 0-8057-9759-9 (alk. paper)
    1. Feminist economics.   2. Sexual division of labor.   3. Women—
Employment.   I. Title.   II. Series.
HQ1381.A43   1997
306.3′615—dc21   97–12263
                                                                        CIP

10 9 8 7 6 5 4 3 2 1

Printed in the United States of America

For Beto Albelda

CONTENTS

FOREWORD

The contemporary women's movement has entered its third decade. We can now take a longer and larger look at what has been happening to traditional modes of research and evaluation in the universities. The Twayne series on the impact of feminism in the arts and sciences represents a unique contribution toward such a look, toward such an assessment. It addresses the complex questions as well as the uncertainties and possibilities that are raised by the meaning of feminist impact. Which disciplines can claim to have been altered as a result of feminism? Which cannot? How can we measure feminist impact? What biases or gaps in scholarly thought are still there? Are we creating new ones? Has a gendered approach developed in the field? What are the major areas of resistance to change?

The scope of the series is ambitious. Over the next several years, we envision the publication of individual volumes on anthropology, art history, bioethics, biology, classics, drama, education, economics, film, history, law, literature, music, philosophy, political science, psychology, and sociology. The decision to have one volume for each field rather than an anthology or anthologies means that each author will have the opportunity to develop a position in some detail. The series will not follow a uniform format or approach. The belief behind this approach is that feminism is a plural adventure. There are feminisms; there is no single feminism. We anticipate that each volume will combine the virtues of accessibility with original interpretations of central issues of gender, genre, methodology, and historical perspective. These are the areas that feminism has explicitly and implicitly unsettled in every field of knowledge, forcing us all to reconsider how we learn, how we choose what we learn, and how we change what and how we learn. We hope that the series will be both charting change and making it happen.

In this sixth volume in the series, Randy Albelda unearths for her readers the impact of feminism on economics. Her witty subtitle points more to the future than to the present, for feminism cannot be said to have significantly disturbed the field of economics. The last five years, however, have seen a raft of feminist publications that suggest that the disturbances in the field may become measurable, if not seismic. The percentage of women choosing to earn higher degrees in economics has increased since the 1970s after a significant decline from a high point in the 1920s. Women who stayed away from even attempting to earn higher degrees in economics for some five decades must be experiencing a warming trend. Although we have learned that evolution is not an uninterruptedly onward and upward phenomenon, let us hope that the productivity and influence of feminism in economics in the last five years will continue its rising motion.

Like the previous volumes, biology, history, philosophy, political science, and classics, the economics volume denies disciplinary assumptions that objectivity and reason characterize its theory and methodology. This social science, considered the most male dominated of all the social sciences, appears to be the most insulated from the influence of the other social sciences. Perhaps it has needed to hold onto its "hard" image as the social science most like "a real science," one that should avoid contamination from the "soft" sciences.

Not surprisingly, this "hard," "male" field has not welcomed diversity. Its neoclassical paradigm, despite competition from other paradigms, has dominated the profession in all areas—from graduate curriculum to journal publications to teaching appointments. Despite so many closed doors, feminists have managed to make their presence felt. Perhaps their efforts have begun to be heard more because women are now statistically so large a part of the paid labor force. Women economists have for long been visible in labor economics. Other feminist economists have managed to broaden the scope of neoclassical economics from within and are creating models of unequal power relations and including in those models the role of domestic violence in marriage. This is a significant echo of an earlier era that understood economics to include subjects like currency, trade, poverty, child labor, women's wages, and the role of government and education. These areas have moved to other social sciences like sociology, psychology, social work, and home economics. Economics came to concentrate on economic activity outside the home.

Feminist change has also developed from within neoclassical economics by feminists who have tried to enlarge conceptions of work. What is called "new household economics" was developed by a male scholar in the 1970s. Although his approach has been important, his approach, according to Albelda, "plagues" most feminist economists because it rationalizes rather than explains women's unequal economic status; the phrase "new household economics" inevitably reminds us that the root meaning of economics is household management. That is a neat recovery of origins.

Most feminist economists have found Marxist models more congenial than neoclassical ones. That choice has its problems, as the perfectly turned phrase "the unhappy marriage" of Marxism and feminism reflects. Although the neoclassical model in effect asserts that women's status is unequal because women freely chose inequality and Marxism asserts the pull of economic and historical forces, neither model has shifted away from an outdated conception of the family unit. Both models developed out of a capitalist context and sought to explain market-based behavior. The concept of unpaid work outside the marketplace was inevitably trivialized if not altogether ignored. Today we have a new phenomenon—a great number of women who regularly perform both paid and unpaid labor.

Randy Albelda's study of the impact of feminism on economics is exceptional in its thoroughness and its sensitivity to weak spots in the profession's theory and practice. In a social science extremely resistant to change, change has begun to happen. Albelda herself characterizes the changes in the last five years as "exponential"—and she is not given to overstatement. Will these changes solidify into long-term change in economics? Feminists have effectively challenged many assumptions of neoclassical economics in recent years. They have helped to broaden its scope. They now have an organization and a journal and an internet list (FEMECON-L). They have a public voice. These changes may make the development of an alternative paradigm a fact in the future. Solidifying change and creating a new paradigm will not come about, to use Albelda's last sentence, "by exchanging pronouns, but by reformulating economic models to integrate what economists never measured or theorized but the world has always expected—the production, allocation, and organization of time and care in the household."

Claire Sprague
Series Editor
December 1996

ACKNOWLEDGMENTS

This book took longer to write than I ever intended. As a result, there are many people to acknowledge. For their patient support, I thank my editors at Twayne, especially Claire Sprague and Margaret Dornfeld, who put up with me never meeting my deadlines, and my family—especially my partner, Mary—who lived with this book and too many promises of its near completion for a long time. For their very able research assistance, I want to thank Sonia Jorge, Christa Scharfenberg, Nicole Manning, and Tiffany Manuel, all students (and some now alumnae) at the University of Massachusetts–Boston. Their help in finding library and statistical materials, inputting survey results, summarizing data, and thoughtfully carrying out miscellaneous research tasks was invaluable. I want to thank the various chancellors, provosts, and deans at the University of Massachusetts–Boston who provided summer stipend money so I could pay Sonia, Christa, Nicole, and Tiffany for their work. I also thank the members of the economics department at the university for their continued support of this work from the beginning.

This book took so long for two good reasons. The first is that the other books and articles I wrote in the intervening years—all coauthored—took a good bit of my time. It was easy to put other writing before this book because the personal and intellectual gratification of working with my coauthors was so compelling. Chris Tilly, Arthur MacEwan, Bob Drago, Steve Shulman, and Nancy Folbre at some point in our collaborations all provided suggestions and comments on this book, and I thank them for their support and friendship over the years. A second reason is my rather extensive commitments to two separate organizations—*Dollars and Sense* magazine and IAFFE (International Association for Feminist Economics). My efforts in these groups have most certainly lengthened the time it took to write this book, but both organizations have provided me with an enormous amount of pleasure, a feeling of accomplishment, and a sense of belonging as a feminist economist. I extend my appreciation to the members of both groups for their commitment to a common vision.

Finally, I want to thank the friends and colleagues who have provided advice and feedback on a variety of subjects that have helped shape many of the ideas in this book over the years. They include: Teresa Amott, Lee Badgett, Radhika Balakrisnan, Lourdes Benería, Jim Campen, David Colander, Mary Ellen Colten, Richard Cornwall, Bob Drago, Mary Eich, Lou Ferleger, Nancy Folbre, Sue Himmelweit, Mary King, June Lapidus, Meg Lewis, Catherine Lynde, Martha MacDonald, Arthur MacEwan, Elaine McCrate, John Miller, Manuel Pastor, Janet Seiz, Jean Shackelford, Mary Stevenson, Myra Strober, Chris Tilly, and Rhonda Williams.

This book is dedicated to my father, Beto Albelda, who died in October 1991. He was a just and thoughtful man who taught me, through his example, how to value fairness, independence, and hard work. They are lessons that have served me well in everything I do. He would not have been very patient waiting for this book to be done, but he would have been extremely proud. I'm sorry he is not here to see it.

TABLES AND FIGURES

TABLES

FIGURES

I

REPRESENTATION OF WOMEN IN ECONOMICS

1

ECONOMICS AND FEMINISM: BEYOND THE PALE?

If you were to ask the average neoclassical economist to explain the economic basis of gender stratification, you would be directed, in all likelihood, to the sociology department.... If one went instead to the average nonorthodox economist (an eclectic set of institutionalists, radicals, etc.) hoping for a more weighty response to the same question, one would in all likelihood be directed to their women's caucus.

—Penelope Ciancanelli and Bettina Berch[1]

IN THE BEGINNING

When first asked to write this economics volume of the Twayne Publishers' series of books on the impact of feminism on various disciplines in the arts and sciences, I was convinced it would be the slimmest volume of the set. As other accounts of feminism and economics had already suggested and my casual observation (actually more of a complaint) as a feminist economist since the early 1980s confirmed, there has been little room for feminism and feminists in economics.[2]

After a much more careful analysis of the subject, I can report that feminism has had little impact on economics since the modern women's movement of the 1970s. But, despite this rather disheartening conclusion, there is good cause for hope on the future of feminism and economics. First, women and economics have a rich history, which is only now being uncovered, that can serve as a foundation for feminist claims to a role in the profession's past, present, and future.[3] Second, since 1991 there has been an organization dedicated to feminist economics that has begun publishing its own journal— *Feminist Economics*—and is beginning to make some important progress in the field through a rapidly growing body of literature dedicated to developing and advancing feminist economic analysis.

Nonetheless, the main focus of this book is documenting and understanding feminism's minimal impact on economic thought, method, and policy as practiced in the United States. I was able to document this empirically using a survey I administered to a random sample of economists (and have presented in part II of this book) on the topic in 1992. By their own account, economists think that feminism has had little impact on economics. Further, many economists consider feminism and mainstream economics to be at odds, if not entirely incompatible. For the most part, economists and economic paradigms have only marginally integrated feminist analysis and insights into their research agendas.

Economics holds the dubious distinction of being the most male-dominated discipline among the social sciences and the humanities in the United States today. And although having women in a profession by no means ensures feminist analysis, it is a necessary condition. That other disciplines incorporate varying degrees of feminist theory and have more feminists suggests that there are important historical, institutional, and methodological differences in the development and reproduction of disciplines worthy of exploration. This book explores some of the reasons that the economics discipline has long remained distant from feminist demands and feminist analysis of economic, political, and social problems.

WHY NOT FEMINISM?

It is not surprising to find resistance to feminist analysis in all the disciplines. Feminism and feminist thought represent a dissenting viewpoint in the "accepted wisdom" of most disciplines by offering critical analyses of the current social, economic, and political order. Feminism argues that women face unequal opportunities and have unequal access to a host of resources compared with men. Because feminists see that systemic and individual barriers have resulted in a society in which women are generally subordinate to men, they call for a realignment of the current social relations in society as a whole. And as Thomas Kuhn's pathbreaking analysis of the development of paradigms suggests, when dissenting views are presented, they will most likely be perceived as a threat by those entrenched in and rewarded by current methods and analysis.[4]

However, economics, as a profession and a discipline, has been *particularly* inaccessible to women in general and feminists in particular. The humanities, other social sciences, and even some of the life and physical sciences have seen more inroads than economics. In that light, the inability of economists to address feminist concerns and its corollary—the lack of feminists in their field—actually turns out to be a rather remarkable achievement. Feminism's invisibility in economics, at least until recently, raises a larger question, then: What accounts for the inability of feminist dissenters to be heard and to influence any discipline? In this chapter I suggest there are three vital components: the discipline's methodologies, the relative diversity of ideas, and feminist organizational representation.

First, the degree to which a discipline's prevailing methodology (or methodologies) can interpret and integrate the dynamics of power, control, and domination will matter for feminists. Although there are many different kinds of feminism and feminist analysis, all argue that gender relations are unequal and that men wield more power both as individuals and within institutions than do women. Any discipline that assiduously avoids modeling or describing power relationships among actors will make it extremely difficult for feminists to employ established feminist methodologies to understand gender dynamics.

Second, the degree to which there is hegemonic control over a discipline's methodology and its social and intellectual institutions will shape the way in which ideas and people in the profession reproduce themselves and stave off challenges to the prevailing ideas and institutions. Disciplines in which one school of thought prevails over the production and reproduction of knowledge are likely to be more successful at marginalizing dissenters who do not adhere to the mainstream, making alliances among distinct, dissenting approaches much less effective. Paradigm shifts are most likely to take place if alternative voices and theories flourish.

Third, if the institutional basis of the group within the prevailing methodology in a discipline is left unchallenged, there will be little change. No one gives up control or power easily. The degree to which dissenting groups organize themselves and collectively struggle to secure a place in the profession will shape their ability to influence the profession.

Over the last 25 years—exactly coinciding with the development and expansion of the feminist movement and feminist thought in academia—economics has lacked all three feminist-friendly criteria just discussed. Since the 1970s neoclassical economic theorists have dominated economics rather effectively. Neoclassical economics is built on a model of the world that is ahistorical and predicated on harmonious relationships among individual economic actors. These individuals are self-satisfiers who pursue their individual interests based on a predetermined set of tastes and preferences. And although it is readily recognized that any individual's choices are constrained by such factors as family income, historical patterns of discrimination, and institutional structures, neoclassical economics offers little or no discussion of the causes or dynamics of those constraints. Constraints are assumed to be exogenously determined and typically considered to be outside the purview of economics. When it comes to policy matters, neoclassical economists usually argue the less government in the economy, the better. Governmental interference, in this theory, impedes actors' ability to act freely in the marketplace, creating distorted and often undesirable economic outcomes.

It would be hard to imagine a theory of social and economic interactions that is *less* responsive to modern-day feminist methodologies than neoclassical theory. Neoclassical economics begins with a set of assumptions about economic life (namely, that individuals act as self-satisfiers in a timeless world with no nonmarket power relations) that are difficult to reconcile with the starting point for many strands of feminism. With only a few exceptions—discussions of labor supply and noncapitalist development theory—women and women's work are assumed to be indistinguishable from men and men's work or are made invisible. Women are most often relegated to the home in economic analysis, but neoclassical economic theories of home production are modeled as an extension of marketplace production even though the motivations and conditions of work in the home are vastly different. And when the neoclassical model does explicitly analyze women's paid labor, the bottom line conclusion is that women deserve the low wages they get.

Despite the presence of alternative economic theories with equally long (or longer) traditions in economics, the neoclassical paradigm and articles that use its assumptions about economic behavior and the role of markets have reigned supreme since the 1970s. Most of the leading economic journals, organizations, and graduate programs in the United States are neoclassically based. The lack of diverse approaches was obvious to the blue-ribbon panel of economists that recently examined graduate education in economics. W. Lee Hansen, who served as the executive secretary of the American Economic Association's Commission on Graduate Education in Economics, noted in his study of graduate programs: "The most striking result to emerge from examining the descriptive brochures, course syllabi, and comprehensive Ph.D. examinations provided by departments is not their diversity but rather their great similarity."[5] He went on to state that not only are the required course offerings in the first year virtually identical across graduate programs but also that the content of the courses is very similar.

Women surfaced as the objects of economic analysis in the most prestigious economics journals in the 1970s, as the modern-day women's movement was taking hold in U.S. society. However, the most widely published and cited authors of these articles were among the staunchest observers of the neoclassical paradigm—those affiliated with the University of Chicago. Feminist critiques of neoclassical work on women appeared soon after their publication, but few paid attention.[6] These neoclassical treatments of women's work in the home and marketplace soon found their way into economics textbooks and graduate course syllabi and have become standard fare.

Until very recently little effective feminist organizing has occurred inside economics. One reason is that there have been few women, let alone feminists, in economics. Feminists who did enter the economics profession (or "came out" as feminists later in their careers) have not been afforded much prestige or security in the profession. Still, the economics profession is not bereft of feminists or feminist analysis. A group of feminist economists were successful in establishing the Committee on the Status of Women in the Economics Profession (CSWEP) in the early 1970s. CSWEP still serves as a standing committee of the main economics professional organization—the American Economic Association (AEA)—but it lost much of its feminist fervor and flavor in the mid-1980s when it diverted attention away from interpretations of the overall economic status of women to documenting and promoting women's standing in the economics profession. Many feminist economists have worked in nonorthodox paradigms within economics since the late 1960s and early 1970s and have been instrumental in developing feminist economic analysis in those paradigms. The strongest feminist presence in these traditions is in Marxian economics. But rather than putting their energies into organizing feminists within the mainstream economics profession, most Marxist feminist economists waged internal struggles: They organized women's caucuses in radical economics organizations and built alliances with Marxist feminists in other disciplines. Since alternative economic paradigms have also been marginalized within the profession, this strategy served to keep the impact of feminist analysis muted in the profession.

There is reason to believe there is now an opening up of the three criteria for feminist impact in economics. Neoclassical economic methodology shows signs of change and a weakening grip on the profession. The failure of distinctly neoclassical policies in the 1980s to revive an ailing U.S. economy, as well as the ever-apparent failures of neoclassical market-based strategies in developing and former socialist economies in the 1990s, has worn some of the luster from neoclassical economics' shine. Further, there is an increasingly loud drumbeat of criticism of neoclassical method from within its own ranks. Finally, many neoclassical theorists have begun to explicitly model power relations and to make the historical development of institutions more central in their analyses.[7] Although still largely individualist in their approaches, these two latest developments provide more space for feminist economic analysis.

There also has been a strong wave of activity in feminist economic analysis independent of any particular existing economic approach. In 1991 a new organization dedicated to feminist economics developed—the International Association for Feminist Economists (IAFFE). It has sponsored summer conferences and organized scores of panels dedicated to presenting feminist economic research and topics at international, national, and regional economics and women's studies meetings and has begun to receive some attention in the profession.[8] In 1995 IAFFE launched a new journal, *Feminist Economics,* devoted to publishing and furthering feminist economic analysis. This new organization has successfully brought together feminist economists from mainstream and nontraditional paradigms and has the potential to make a substantial impact on economic thought.

THE PLAN OF THE BOOK

At least until very recently, feminism has made few inroads into economics. This comes as no surprise, since any profession with so few women would clearly lack feminist voices. But why are there so few women in economics? To answer this question I began by exploring the history of women in the economics profession and compiling data on women's representation in economics over the last 30 years. Those findings (along with this introduction) comprise part I of this book.

As is the nature of much research, I found what I was not looking for—a remarkably rich history of women in the early economics profession. In fact, the percentage of female Ph.D. candidates in the 1920s surpassed those of the following five decades, only again reaching those levels in the late 1970s. At the turn of the century, women were quite attracted to economics. A brief history of why women entered and then left economics is reported in chapter 2.

Data on women economists in the United States since 1970 are reported in chapter 3. It is in counting the women where one finds the largest impact of feminism in economics. As elsewhere in society, economics and economists have been affected by the modern-day U.S. women's movement's demands for access as a means to gender equality. Despite its mostly male composition, economics has seen an increase in women's representation, especially in academia. The percentage of women in economics has doubled since the early 1970s when 5.6 percent of all Ph.D. economists were women to close to 12 percent in 1990.[9] Further, economists have explored areas that feminists have called attention to in their political struggles. The most notable example of the expansion of economic inquiry into a typically feminist subject area is the "new household economics" pioneered by University of Chicago economists and 1992 Nobel economics prize winner Gary Becker.[10]

To test the claim that feminism has had little impact on economics, I needed empirical evidence, so I devised a survey on the topic. In the spring of 1992, I mailed the survey to a random sample of AEA members. The results of the survey are presented in part II of this book. Chapter 4 details the demographic information obtained from the survey and provides a rich profile of economists. Chapter 5 analyzes the results from the survey that deal with the impact of feminism on economics and, for the first time ever, empirically documents feminism's marginal impact on economics. Chapter 6 focuses on the only qualitative response in the survey, which illuminates economists' perceptions of the uneasy relationship of feminism to economics.

Because the historical richness of women's participation in the early economics profession contrasted with the dearth of women economists in the current period and the survey results, it became obvious that I needed to ask a broader set of research questions. Why hasn't feminism made more of an impact in economics? What is it about the economics discipline that has made it more resistant to women scholars than most of the social and behavioral sciences and even some of the natural sciences? What is it about modern-day economics that either repels or does not attract feminists? These questions could only be answered by looking at economic methodology and the reproduction of ideas in economics, discussed in part III of this book. Chapter 7 looks at neoclassical economics and feminism, and chapter 8 discusses Marxian economics and feminism. Chapter 9 further explores the problem with most economic thinking as it concerns gender and how feminist economic analysis provides the potential to redefine the economics discipline.

This book is written with an audience of feminists *and* economists in mind. However, the intersection between those two groups is not large, which means that some readers will be unfamiliar with economics while others might be unfamiliar with feminism. And although the language and analysis used is intended to be accessible and informative for feminists and economists, economists may want to skip the rather brief overview of neoclassical economics in chapter 7 while feminists may choose to skim the discussion of ordered probit regressions in chapter 5.

WHAT'S AT STAKE?

Economic analysis is absolutely critical to feminism and feminists. Without an adequate understanding of the material basis of women's inequality, there is little hope for achieving gender equality. Unfortunately, women's equality and feminist analysis have never really been a central part of the discipline's agenda. The distinctly androcentric nature of economics has important implications for women's lives. Economists and economics seem to hold a special place in the policy-making world, with more influence than almost any other discipline. Women's economic interests, however, are not adequately represented in much policy research and implementation. Indeed, one of the most important contributions women make to any economy—their work in the household—is not even included in measurements of labor force participation or indicators of total economic output.[11] As a result, policy solutions to persistent economic problems of particular importance to women and feminists, such as the widespread poverty among single-mother families and women's low wages, reflect male biases.[12] Arguably, mainstream economics has probably done more to undermine gender equality than to improve it.

The stakes are high for feminist economists and women's economic equality, and the barriers to change in the profession seem almost insurmountable. Until feminists and others are successful in fundamentally changing the nature of economic analysis, it is very likely that the discipline will continue to work against women's economic interests. At a minimum, to push the profession to take feminist concerns into account, there must be feminist economists. This simple proposition, however, is not so easily accomplished. To become an economist, one must first get a Ph.D. in economics. Graduate education in economics is highly theoretical and technical. Those who have excellent quantitative skills, a solid belief in economics as an objective science, and little interest in applied work have a much better chance of not only surviving but also succeeding in the profession than those who do not.[13] Graduate training in economics tends to be difficult and unsatisfying for many, but for feminists it is an inordinately alienating and hostile environment.[14] As one of the respondents to the survey noted about being a feminist in economics: "It takes a special person to want to run uphill all day."

Women, let alone feminists, are rarely hired and retained in those prestigious universities where economic theory is shaped and reproduced. Academics working in economics graduate programs who develop neoclassical economic theory are considered the "high priests" of the profession. Being tenured at one of the economics departments in the top-tiered schools, to carry the analogy a bit further, is like being a "cardinal." The economics profession has more women in the top hierarchy than does the Catholic Church, but not very many more. As of 1993, 3 of 150 of the tenured faculty in the six schools ranked in the top tier of economics programs were women.[15]

The project of transforming economics to embrace the fight for women's economic equality will not be easy as long as neoclassical economics prevails. But without an understanding of why women and feminists are missing from economics, it will be even harder to make any forward motion. It is my hope that this book furthers the goal of establishing a feminist economics that will work toward and succeed in achieving economic justice for all men and women.

2

AT THE THRESHOLD:
WOMEN, FEMINISM,
AND ECONOMICS
BEFORE 1970

INTRODUCTION

From a statistical standpoint alone, the more women there are in a profession, the more likely there will be feminists. And the more feminists, the more likely there will be feminist challenges to prevailing "wisdom." Therefore, a precursor to discovering and interpreting the impact of feminism on economics must start with finding the women.

The economics profession has always been a male-dominated field and remains so today, with 12 percent of Ph.D. economists being female.[1] Although many professions and most academic disciplines are male dominated, economics is especially so. Since women have been opening the doors to all the professions and academic disciplines over the last 25 years, their paltry representation in economics cannot be considered coincidental. It suggests an aversion on the part of women to enter the discipline relative to other fields and/or a concerted reluctance by those in the field to integrate women.

The dearth of women economists that was obvious to me as an undergraduate and graduate student in economics led me to assume that there had *never* been many women economists. But as I began to look for historical forerunners in the U.S. economics profession before World War II, I uncovered some rather unexpected findings. The percentage of female doctoral candidates in the 1920s surpassed the percentages of the 1930s, 1940s, 1950s, and 1960s, only to be eclipsed in the late 1970s. Looking closer, I discovered a history of women entering and then leaving economics in the first 30 years of the twentieth century, a phenomenon that is hardly conventional wisdom in the economics profession.[2] I found the names of feminists like Crystal Eastman and Charlotte Perkins Gilman participating in the American Economic Association's annual meetings. Women economists were gathering and analyzing data for think tanks and government bureaus. For its first 40 years, the economics profession was keenly involved in, if not devoted to, the social and economic debates of the day caused by the tremendous economic dislocation of the emerging economic order: poverty, change in family structure, urbanization, corporate greed and expansion, international trade, and economic reform. The voices of women economists, as well as their expertise, were included—albeit as minority participants—in these debates.

I found a profession, though still deeply sexist and overwhelmingly male, seemingly more conducive to and comfortable with women's and feminists' participation at the turn of the century than it was in the 1970s and arguably even than it is today. It soon became obvious that women's societal role in the early 1900s and the development of economics as a social science in the United States were linked. Each played an important part in the social and economic reform debates that so characterized the Progressive Era. However, as the economics discipline became more developed in the United States, academics seeking to secure their newly developed professional status severed the link between feminine pursuits and the study of economics. Thereafter women's participation was substantially reduced, not to reemerge until the modern-day feminist movement.

In one of only a few references to women in her comprehensive book on the development of social science in America, Dorothy Ross notes: "Women, already deeply involved in charitable and reform activities, were a natural constituency for the social sciences, but one that could threaten the masculine image of the social scientists' effort to achieve realism, science, and professional standing."[3] Ross never tells the story, however, of *how* social scientists, particularly economists, were so effectively able to eliminate the feminine (and the feminist) from their science and profession. In this chapter, I try to fill in parts of that story.

The relatively small number of female economists and the barriers to feminist analysis in economics today can be traced to three related changes in the study and understanding of social and economic phenomena in the United States that developed from the 1860s through World War II. Each of the three developments was linked to the professionalization of economics, a goal of the middle-class academic reformers at the turn of the century. These three changes and their role in pushing women out of the profession are (1) the establishment of academics as social science experts employed in graduate departments, which served to effectively bar women from becoming experts; (2) the adoption of positivist methodology in the form of marginal analysis, which made almost all types of feminist (and left) analysis incongruous with economics; and (3) the move toward specialization, which served to segregate women into particular fields and eventually move questions concerning women and even women economists out of the economics profession.

Professionalization was important because it established academic social scientists into their distinct disciplines, which gave them some control over the terms of the debate in the production of social science "knowledge" and its uses in the United States. The process concurrently served to exclude women, blacks, and radicals who during the Progressive Era were each struggling to stake out social, political, and economic claims on the rapidly encompassing capitalist relations. Social science and social scientists would not face as serious a challenge to their established positions until the late 1960s with the resurrection of precisely the groups that had been shut out earlier—radicals (students associated with the left antiwar movement), black nationalists, and feminists.

The development of the social sciences, and especially economics, has been extensively documented and researched, but little (if any) attention has been paid to women's changing role in the social sciences.[4] Margaret Rossiter provides an excellent historical record of women in the natural and physical sciences but does not address the social sciences.[5] And although Rossiter's analysis provides an invaluable starting point for understanding women's place in economics, it is not always applicable. Her focus is on the natural sciences, which, in the United States, were always defined as "masculine" endeavors. What makes economics a compelling historical exception is that its initial mission included "feminine" pursuits. Economics emerged as a discipline devoted to reform, which was one of women's accepted spheres of activity. Tracing the historical record of women in economics in a comprehensive way is a task waiting to be done. Still, the available histories of women in academia and of the development of social sciences make it possible to piece together the beginnings of an analysis of the history of women in economics. From that history, some explanations for the dearth of women and feminist analysis in mainstream economics emerge.

THE RULES OF THE GAME: ESTABLISHING THE ECONOMICS PROFESSION, 1865–1920

Economics developed as a distinct discipline in the United States in the last two decades of the nineteenth century, just as a new economic order, industrial capitalism, was generating a host of new problems. One of the most pressing problems was the growth of an impoverished working class, largely made up of immigrants who were subjected to the vagaries of market production without the benefit of government "safety nets." The change in the economic conditions warranted a study of social and economic conditions and the development of proper reforms intended to soothe the growing pains of a society rapidly undergoing urbanization and increasingly becoming a national industrial-based economy.[6] Social science was such a study. It was shaped primarily by U.S. academics who wished to break with the religious roots of academia by building more secular institutions and more structured theories of social behavior and change.[7] Historian Mary O. Furner argues, "Ministers and moral philosophers still taught people how to behave ethically in their personal and civic affairs, but they seemed no better equipped than their fellows to explain the baffling new economic relationships. In an age that honored science above other sources of wisdom, it became clear that people who established their ability to study society scientifically would command attention and influence the course of events. The modern social science professions were the product of that need and opportunity."[8]

But establishing the definition and method of social science did not come without fights. The main battleground for the fights over the nature of social sciences and who was best suited to do it was in the largest organization dedicated to social science study: the American Social Science Association (ASSA), founded in 1865. The ASSA attracted a wide array of literary and political figures, industrialists, and social reformers, as well as academics. The membership drew heavily on those previously active in the abolitionist movement.[9] Leaders of the ASSA came primarily from the Northeast and most were professionals (doctors, clergy, journalists, lawyers, and college professors) and the sons of families who were long settled in North America.[10] The statement of purpose in ASSA's constitution declares the organization's aim as bringing "together the various societies and individuals now interested in these objects [amendment of laws, education, reformation of criminal, economy, trade and finance, sanitation regulation, and pauperism], for the purpose of obtaining by discussion the real elements of Truth; by which doubts are removed, conflicting opinions harmonized, and a common ground afforded for treating wisely the great social problems of the day."[11] The ASSA divided social sciences into four departments: education; public health; economy, trade, and finance; and jurisprudence. Although ASSA's goal was never to transform the system, the organization was established in part to advocate for legislation and promote educational instruction on occupational health and home safety for the poor. Leaders argued that social scientists needed to engage in agitation, education, and state administration.[12] In short, the early notion of social science was reform through knowledge. The appropriate training for that knowledge, however, was contested.

As early as the mid-1870s, academics—mostly those trained in the historic school of thought in Germany—had gained control of the ASSA.[13] Academics employed in institutions steeped in religious origins found themselves in a precarious position when they argued that social science dedicated to the systematic understanding of social phenomena should not resort to religious arguments and moral persuasion. To be convincing, academics had to define their study as distinct from both moral philosophy and mere public advocacy and they needed to be backed by authority. Most academics, despite their professional backgrounds, were not descendants of the ruling class and had little personal claim on productive resources. Hence, they soon realized they needed to appeal to their specialized knowledge and expertise to establish not only their authority but their employment security as well.[14] Professionalization, then, was vital for the academics among the ASSA members. They argued that the collection of pertinent facts and the skills needed to interpret those facts could be attained *only* through specialized and technical study offered by advanced degrees. Professional social scientists, they agreed, needed to be qualified "experts." Academics, then, worked to define their role in social science as training experts and engaging in the debates of the times. To that end, universities began to offer advanced degrees in economics (called political economy at the time) in the 1870s, with Johns Hopkins, Yale, and Harvard being the first U.S. institutions to award Ph.D.s in the field.[15] Soon thereafter, Columbia, Princeton, and the universities of Pennsylvania, Chicago, Michigan, and Wisconsin also awarded degrees in political economy and began to attract larger and larger enrollments in their graduate political economy programs.[16]

Promoting the other side of the debate over the expert in social science within the ASSA was a group of nonacademics Dorothy Ross refers to as the "gentry activists."[17] This group claimed that "professionals were regarded as men and women of broad general culture and wide-ranging ability. They were knowledgeable and reliable model citizens who could be trusted to manage affairs. Essentially their competence was the product of individual character and class privilege, not esoteric knowledge or technical skill beyond the laymen. They conceived problems in practical terms and communicated their findings to ordinary people in everyday language."[18] Typically, this group sought to create and staff government bureaus whose primary goal was to perform scholarly investigations.

In addition to their struggle over who were the true social scientists, academics were engaged in a heated debate over social science ideology and methodology. This debate was publicly waged in a set of articles published in *Science* (the journal of the American Association for the Advancement of Science) in the early 1880s.[19] On one side of the methodology debate sat the historicist (or ethical) economists who wanted to break with the seemingly subjective and U.S. exceptionalist views of economic progress that dominated explanations of economic phenomena at the time. They supported government intervention into a variety of thorny issues of the time, such as labor and capital strife, international trade, and poverty. The ethical economists also wanted to retain the moral element of both religious and political movements of the times in their understanding of the economic condition of the U.S. population. Their vision for academic economists was to use their special knowledge to help reform society by providing economic analysis to an informed middle class. The other camp of academic economists were much more conservative and ascribed to laissez-faire views of policy. They were also interested in reform, but they saw their constituency as the elite. They looked down upon the often passionate advocacy among the historicists.[20]

In a move intended to ameliorate the increasing tensions between the academics and the gentry activists, and the controversy within the academic-leaning branch of the ASSA, the ethical economists formed the American

Economic Association (AEA) in 1885. Led by Richard T. Ely, a rather out-spoken advocate from the Midwest, 182 political economists split off from the American Social Science Association to form their own group.[21] The break from the ASSA and the explicit incorporation of scientific method served to create economics not only as a distinct field of study within social sciences but also as a distinct profession. The new association was "oriented toward the occupational needs of academic men and was the concrete expression of a community of inquiry. Its members defined themselves primarily as investigators, and collectively the community would warrant its members' performance only in the role of investigator, not agitator."[22]

Unlike the American Historical Association, which had only a year earlier split off from the ASSA, the AEA initially began with the intent of informing reform movements. To encourage the participation in the organization, the AEA allowed anyone who could pay the $3.00 membership fee to join.[23] Although the association was open to anyone, the founders and leaders were almost all academic economists, including all 6 officers and 19 of the original 24 executive council members.[24]

The AEA's first report stated its founders' desires for "a society which, free from all trammels, should seek truth from all sources, should be ready to give a respectful hearing to every new idea, and should shun no revelation of facts, but, on the contrary, should make the collection, classification and interpretation of facts its chief task. The ideal of this new society, as it presented itself to the minds of its projectors, was to seek light, to bear light, to diffuse light—ever the highest aim of all true science."[25] This statement appealed to members from both schools of academic social scientists who were in agreement about the use of statistics and data for economic analysis, the break with religious doctrine, the need for professionalization of economics, and the application of economic knowledge to reform. Ely correctly counted on the commonly held views of doing social science to attract some of the laissez-faire economists. However, under Ely's leadership, the AEA explicitly regarded the state as a positive agent of change, held that the conflict between capital and labor was the prominent social problem of the time, and denounced laissez-faire doctrine as "unsafe and unsound in morals."[26] Not surprisingly, several prominent laissez-faire political economists refused to join.

Moving the source of knowledge to academic experts was a necessary but insufficient condition for professionalization. As Furner notes, academic economists continued to face an authority problem when these new experts disagreed on such fundamental economic issues of the time as tariffs, the formation of labor unions, and the role of money and banks in an economy.[27]

Because funding for many universities was coming from the very sources that were actively advocating laissez-faire principles meant that studies which concluded that mergers must be busted and workers deserved better treatment were very problematic for academic administrators.[28] At a time when the battle lines in society were being drawn more sharply by the events of the late 1880s and the 1890s—notably, bloody labor battles like the Haymarket bombing in 1886 and the 1892 Pullman and Homestead strikes—where academics stood on such matters could have some consequences.

It seemed that academic authority would come only when the struggle to define the parameters of objective study and acceptable reform was resolved. Economists perceived as advocating on behalf of labor were seen as dangerous both by university administrations and by the newly established economists. Several famous academic freedom cases silenced the voices of several economists who promoted the profession's advocacy role and helped define the direction of academic economics.[29] The most notable was Richard T. Ely, who recanted many of his views when faced with dismissal from the University of Wisconsin in 1894.[30] Professionalization, then, also meant establishing some methodological and ideological cohesiveness in the discipline that would serve to define the difference between being objective and being an advocate. In Ross's words:

> [T]he historical economists' overt ethical stance, sympathy with labor, and tendencies toward socialism made their objectivity suspect and endangered the professional project. Professional pressures soon led the AEA to drop its statement of principles and bring in classical economists. . . . In case after case of university pressure brought against social scientists in the 1880s and 1890s, the conservative and moderate professional leaders carefully parceled out their support, making clear the limited range of academic freedom and the limited range of political dissent they were willing to defend. A degree of professional autonomy was achieved by narrowing its range.[31]

With the mainstreaming of economics, Ross argues, three distinct models of economic analysis and thought emerged. Each, however, was wedded to the notion of economics as scientific study. One strand was the historical, evolutionary, and socialist thought associated with Thorstein Veblen. However, this school never gained much ascendancy in the profession, especially after the academic freedom cases. The antisocialist Red Scare of the late 1910s purged many from academia. The terms of the economic debate in economics, then, were defined by the other two schools of thought: the nascent marginalists (now called neoclassical economics) on the one side and liberal empirical historicists on the other.[32]

The political and social atmosphere of the Progressive Era provided the historicists with considerable support, if not plentiful employment. Best exemplified by the work of E. R. A. Seligman (the father of the progressive income tax), this school sought to provide a historical dynamic to empirical analysis of the tremendous economic and social problems caused by the material conditions of the day. Applied research by trained experts provided politicians and reformers "facts" to help shape legislation. During the first two decades of the twentieth century, the historicists were the link to economics' origins in reform, even as many would come to embrace the developing ahistorical, deductive school.

John Bates Clark, more than any other American economist, helped shape the marginal school at this time. In the 1870s Clark's views of socialism were rather positive, but by the 1890s he had thoroughly repudiated them. And it was Clark's work, *The Distribution of Wealth: A Theory of Wages, Interest and Profits*, published in 1898, that initiated American economists' foray into neoclassical economics. In this work, he argues capital and labor were each paid according to their marginal contribution to production. Clark's exposition resolved two of the important dilemmas that the newly established academic economists faced. First, by employing abstract theory in the discussion of wages and profits, Clark moved economists in a direction that would make it much less applicable to real-world events and economic reform. The development of abstract theories would quickly take economics from a field that was easily understood by educated men and women at the time to one that could only be understood and debated by trained economists. Social science historian Robert Church notes, "Mastery of complex, jargonistic, and extended theory and the techniques associated with it came to distinguish the academic economists from the amateur and made his statements about economic affairs and his opinions about economic policy more accurate and authoritative than statements and opinions of those who had not mastered such a theory."[33] Second, Clark's work was a theoretical justification for the emerging capitalist order. He helped shape a theory that claimed workers and capitalists get what they deserve in the production process (i.e., their marginal product).[34] Clark's work repudiated classical economic labor theories of value associated with the work of Adam Smith, David Ricardo, and Karl Marx. Clark argued that profits were a payment for capital's contribution to production, not surplus. Similarly, workers get paid for their contribution to production and are not exploited. Clark's keen awareness of his project is obvious in the introduction to his book: "The welfare of the laboring classes depends not on whether they get much or little, but their attitude toward other classes—and, therefore, the stability of the social state—depends chiefly on the question whether the amount that they get, be it large or small, is what they produce. If they create a small amount of wealth and get the whole of it, they need not seek to revolutionize society; but if it were to appear that they produce an ample amount and get only a part of it, many of them would become revolutionists, and all would have a right to do so."[35]

By the first decade of the 1900s, the economics profession had become a well-defined "old-boys' network" whose ranks were small and members well connected with one another.[36] The leaders of the AEA used the association's publications as a forum for their work. Between 1885 and 1910, the 81 men who made up the organization's officers over the period represented 16 percent of all the authors published by the AEA but accounted for 44.2 percent of all the titles published (including monographs, articles, papers and discussions).[37] The leaders of the AEA were able to stave off the more liberal and disgruntled midwestern and western academic economists from forming regional organizations by offering key people positions in the association.[38]

By 1910 several disciplines splintered from the ASSA to form separate fields and organizations within social science. The American Historical Association, established in 1884, preceded the AEA. But three others followed: the American Psychological Association organized in 1892; the American Political Science Association and the American Sociological Society were both established in 1903.[39] Those interested in studying family life, public health, and legal reform were routed to these new specializations as each scrambled to define the parameters of their disciplines. Those interested in actually *practicing* economic reform were steered toward social work. By 1905 specialization had allowed economists to narrow their field of study, but not their role in reform.

A MISSED OPPORTUNITY: WOMEN AND PROFESSIONALIZATION

By the end of the Civil War, manufacturing was beginning to thrive in the cities established on the Northeast's major rivers and harbors and was quickly spreading west toward Chicago. As the economy was undergoing dramatic transformations, so too were the economic and social activities of women (and men) in the postbellum Northeast. For most families engaged in small-scale farming, women's and men's work was in the home. But with industrialization the goods that families had traditionally produced at home—clothing, soap, and foodstuffs—were being cheaply manufactured.[40] Farm families began to rely more and more on wage income to purchase the goods they needed, rather than making them at home. Newly arrived immigrants came to cities and had little opportunity to produce for themselves. In America, the rapid growth of waged work in manufacturing brought the separation of men's paid work from the home and with it new economic and social roles for family members based on gender and marital status. By the end of the nineteenth century, married men were seen as primary wage earners obliged to enter the labor market in hopes of bringing home incomes sufficient to support their families. Women's primary role, particularly married women, was to oversee and/or provide family care and necessary household work. If men's wages were not sufficient to support their families, as was the case for many working-class families (particularly for newly arrived and often unskilled immigrant workers and African-Americans), women and children needed to find waged work as well. Married women often earned additional income via manufacturing-based homework or by taking in boarders or laundry. For unmarried women, wages were typically earned through domestic (often live-in) or factory work.

In the new capitalist order, man's "place" was to earn a living but woman's "place" was still in the home. Even though the site of women's economic activity did not change, the ideology about women's true nature and acceptable social roles did. An ideal woman was no longer the hardy farm wife, just as the ideal parent to raise children was no longer the father. A whole new standard for gender roles in white, native-born families emerged, which feminist historians refer to as the "cult of domesticity"—true women were virtuous, pure, and pious.[41] The cult of domesticity prescribed women's home roles and their public roles in the ascending capitalist order. Women were seen as being perfectly suited to raising children and managing the affairs of home life. As such, women became the purveyors of moral and religious instruction. Who better to provide guidance and moral uplift in the economic and social chaos caused by the emerging capitalist order than women? Women who could afford to live by the ideals of the cult of domesticity also had a social responsibility (and the time) to engage in reform movements of the time.

So, like the mission of the economics discipline, one of women's prescribed activities was social, economic, and moral reform. In this sense, under early definitions of social science, economics could be considered a "feminine" pursuit. It is not surprising, then, to find that women were very attracted to studying economics. However, the successful moves toward professionalization meant that women too needed to get Ph.D.s in order to be "experts" in the field. The first hurdle for women in economics, then, was access to institutions of higher education. Fortunately, women's opportunities for obtaining degrees at institutions of higher education were expanding rapidly because of a rising demand for college-educated women. Without parcels of land to pass on to sons, families of modest means passed on to their sons and daughters the proper training and education necessary to survive and thrive in the emerging managerial and professional classes. Women, as the vessel of knowledge in families, clearly needed education as much as men did. Women's education (among those who could afford it) was almost a patriotic duty.

In the 1870s and 1880s, state universities opened their doors to women students at the undergraduate level. Of particular relevance for women academics was the establishment of women's colleges whose mission was to provide equal educational opportunities to women. Vassar College opened in 1865, followed by Smith College (1871), Wellesley College (1875), Bryn Mawr College (1985), Goucher College (1885), Mount Holyoke College (1888), and Barnard College—as a coordinated institution of Columbia (1889).[42] And although graduate programs initially did not allow women students to officially matriculate, by the 1890s most had relented on that policy. Education was still for the elite, but women had made significant inroads by 1900: 19 percent of the approximately 2 percent of the population 23 years old that were college educated were women,[43] with 6 percent of all doctorates awarded to women.[44] By 1900 five women had received Ph.D.s in economics.[45]

Professional women economists were active from the very beginning of the economics discipline, although they were a distinct minority. One of the AEA's original executive council members was Katharine Coman, the founder of the economics department at Wellesley College.[46] In the first year of the AEA's existence, 4 of the 182 members were women. Further, the AEA was explicitly concerned with women in the new economic order, as evidenced by its inclusion of the employment of women in factories as 1 of the 10 topics offered to the Chairmen of the Standing Committees as "proper subjects for reports" in the 1886 AEA resolutions.[47] Richard T. Ely boasts in his memoir: "Women have always been welcomed into our ranks, but in our early days there were few of them. When we held our first annual meeting in Philadelphia there were perhaps fifteen or twenty women present, including such distinguished women as Florence Kelly and President M. Carey

Thomas, of Bryn Mawr College."[48] This is not to say women were always treated as equals. Ely goes on to report that at the same meeting one of the Association's star members planned a reception at a male-only club, leaving the women attendees in the cold. Embarrassed, the AEA scheduled a separate reception, but the women boycotted it.[49]

In 1890 an AEA publication published its first article written by a woman. It was a prize-winning essay on child labor by Clare de Graffen-ried.[50] Mrs. John Armstrong Chanler had established a $100 prize for the best essay on women wage earners.[51] The second article by a woman, published in 1893, was written by Emily Greene Balch, who later went on to teach economics at Wellesley College for 22 years. (Balch is particularly notable because she was the first and only woman economist to receive a Nobel Prize, though not for her work in economics.)[52] The first woman to receive her Ph.D. in economics in the United States was Helen Francis Page Bates.[53] In 1896 she completed her doctoral work at the University of Wisconsin in its newly formed program headed by Richard T. Ely.[54]

Despite their minority status, women were better represented as graduate students in economics in the 1920s than they were for the next half century (see figure 2.1). The most important graduate school for training women economists was Columbia University. Almost 50 percent (26 of 53 women) did their doctoral work at Columbia between 1914 and 1919, compared with 41 percent of the men over the same period.[55] The wave of feminism at that time may help account for women's attraction to studying economics in general and at Columbia in particular. Rossiter notes that feminists were active in efforts to liberalize social thinking in the social sciences in the 1910s and that "interest in feminism was particularly intense in the liberal and intellectual circles of New York City, especially at Columbia University."[56]

Despite the continual efforts to house economics in academia, the AEA's annual meetings, where important research was shared, were still open to gentry social scientists and activists, including feminists. Proceedings from the nineteenth annual meeting of the AEA held in 1906 in Providence, Rhode Island, included the well-known social feminist Charlotte Perkins Gilman as a discussant on child labor. In 1908 Crystal Eastman delivered a paper on workers' safety and health based on a Pittsburgh survey.[57]

Women were finding themselves better situated to participate in the economics profession via more access to higher education, and the distinct gendered role for women in reform movements gave them good reason to want to become economists. Economist Claire Hammond, in her study of women in the economics profession, notes, "By 1900 women had fought the battle

Women are educated

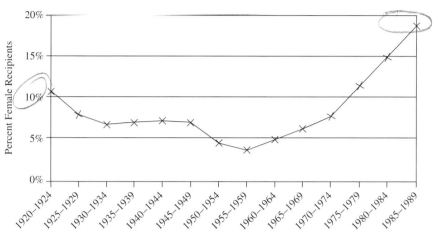

FIGURE 2.1. *Percentage of all economics doctorates awarded to women by five-year periods, 1920–1989.*

Source: For 1920–1961, National Academy of Science, *Doctoral Production in U.S. Universities, 1920–1962* Publication 1142 (Washington, D.C.: National Research Council, 1963), 50–53. For all other years, various issues of U.S. Department of Education, Office of Educational Research and Improvement, *Digest of Education Statistics* (Washington, D.C.: Government Printing Office).

for higher education largely victoriously. In those heady days as graduate schools one by one opened their doors to women, anything might have seemed possible, even a career as a woman economist."[58]

But after receiving a Ph.D., a woman had yet another hurdle to jump to be considered a professional economist—she needed an academic appointment. The founders of the AEA not only had reform on their minds, they also had their place in it firmly imagined. As Haskell argues, "[T]he economists wanted not only to reform society, but also to give institutional structure to a developing community of inquiry that was rooted deeply in the academic world."[59] Professionalization of economics not only meant training in institutions of higher education but getting jobs there, too. Employment in the same institutions that trained economists became (and continues to be) the hallmark of credibility. Unfortunately, women found it very hard to get academic jobs with one exception—women's colleges employed women scholars.

Women's colleges had already been proven extremely important as a baccalaureate institution for the newly trained female economists.[60] So, too, they were to become the primary employers of female economists. Economic historian Barbara Libby found that only 25 percent of Ph.D.-trained female economists ended up with academic jobs, and almost one-third of them were employed at one of the women's colleges. In a study of all academics, Helen Sard Hughes found that 9.7 percent of all assistant and associate professors and 3.7 percent of all full professors in coeducational institutions were female compared with 70.7 percent among assistant and associate professors and 59.4 percent of full professors in women's colleges.[61] But the women's colleges held a lower status than their elite male counterparts or large public and private coed universities. Further, due to weak finances, women's colleges rarely offered graduate studies—the one exception was Bryn Mawr.

Without much access to university positions, women were excluded from the club that was defining the profession. Of the almost 900 AEA members in 1905, about 25 members were female, but only 5 listed university affiliations.[62] Seven members listed only a private address while the rest listed themselves as writers, artists, and activists in reform movements.

Bibliographic materials on women with Ph.D.s in economics suggest that many wanted academic positions but could not get them. Only a few are described here. Helen Francis Page Bates, the first woman Ph.D. in economics in the United States, was never able to find a permanent academic job. Instead, like many other women with postgraduate degrees, she worked with settlement houses all over the country. Her last job, one that she held for 19 years, was the position of librarian in the Department of Economics at the University of California in Berkeley.[63] Helen Laura Sumner Woodbury, also a University of Wisconsin graduate and protégé of Richard T. Ely and J. R. Commons, could "not readily find permanent employment commensurate with her professional training and her outstanding record as investigator and scholar"[64] —this despite helping write *History of Labor in the United States* and authoring numerous important studies on women and child labor in the first two decades of the 1900s.

Many fewer African-Americans than white women got Ph.D.s in economics, and those who did also faced similar discrimination. W. E. B. DuBois completed his Ph.D. in history and political economy at Harvard University in 1896. But despite his enormous contribution to understanding the economic, political, and social conditions of African-Americans, "he was never offered an appointment at a predominately white institution."[65] The first African-American woman to receive her Ph.D. in economics (from the University of Pennsylvania in 1921) was Sadie Tanner Mossell Alexander. She was unable to find academic employment in or around Philadelphia and by 1923 had virtually abandoned economics. She later became the first African-American women to receive a law degree from the University of Pennsylvania and became among other things a civil rights activist.[66] Her daughter told economist Julianne Malveaux that her mother quit economics because "there was no way for her to make a living in the profession."[67]

Some women economists were able to find work in government employment, but their work was often typecast. For example, the Children's Bureau, established in 1913, employed mostly women—including the director Julia Lathrop. As in academia, women were paid less than their male counterparts, and prior to 1918 not all fields were open to women.[68] Ironically, just as the newly formed Women's Bureau was able to make sure all civil service employment was open to women, the establishment of veterans' hiring preferences meant that women's employment opportunities did not increase.[69]

Although discrimination kept many women from becoming employed economists, it was the ideological battles that kept feminists and other dissidents at bay. The academic freedom cases at the turn of the century and the repudiation of radical causes had important implications for feminists (and socialists) in the Progressive Era and beyond.[70] Beyond limiting the number of women in the profession, the ascendancy of moderate views limited who could participate in the debate. Although the censoring process first was begun by academic administrators and trustees, it soon was carried on by the professionals themselves. By 1905 anyone or any groups challenging the perceived progress of the capitalist order were by definition not playing by the rules of the game. And even though liberal progressive reformers remained in their academic positions over the Progressive Era, their views were tempered (Thorstein Veblen is a notable exception). Aligning with popular groups like feminists or workers was beyond the pale. "Thus, the economic expert was an objective scientist and custodian of the common good, standing above class and special interests as well as partisan politics."[71] While the Progressive Era rewarded empirical, applied scholarship, marginal analysis (the precursor of neoclassical economics) was emerging as the preferred method. Ahistorical and deductive reasoning fostered the belief that economics was (and remains) a positive, value-free science that would work to winnow feminism (and socialists) from its ranks.

Specialization served both to marginalize the women who were already in economics and to redirect women newly interested in social and economic questions. The proliferation of social science disciplines at the turn of the century as well as specialization within economics seemed to be one important means of making economics a "masculine" field. Whether by choice or by design, women economists were clustered in a handful of fields, and increasingly those fields were being displaced or marginalized. For example, in Libby's study of the 520 known dissertation topics of the 621 women Ph.D.s in economics between 1900 and 1940, she found 32 percent were written in the topic area referred to as social problems, 23 percent were on economic history, and 14 percent were on labor topics. In a study of all doctoral students between 1904 and 1940, Lewis Froman found that 9.4 percent of dissertations were on social problems; 10 percent, on topics in economic history; and 11 percent, on labor. Historical analysis, though popular in the 1910s, was in decline by the 1920s, and economics had minimized the attention it paid to social problems, no doubt arguing that they were more in the purview of social work, psychology, and sociology.

The effects of specialization are more clearly seen after the Progressive Era. In the late 1920s and 1930s, fewer women (as a percentage of all doctorates) got Ph.D.s in economics, whereas there was a corresponding rise in the percentage of female doctorates in sociology and anthropology (see figure 2.2). By the mid-1910s, women economists had begun to be referred to as social economists, regardless of whether that was the actual work women

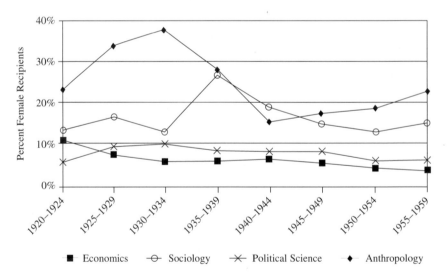

FIGURE 2.2. *Percentage of social science doctorates awarded to women by five-year periods, 1920–1959.*

Source: National Academy of Science, *Doctoral Production in U.S. Universities, 1920–1962* Publication 1142 (Washington, D.C.: National Research Council, 1963), 50–53.

were performing. In describing the rise in the demand for statisticians in several government agencies in the 1910s and 1920s, Rossiter writes, "All these [agencies] hired women statisticians, though often under the rubric of 'social economist,' a designation so clearly sex typed to contemporaries that most of the persons taking Civil Service tests for it in the 1920s were women."[72] Journals also shifted their emphasis. In 1925 the University of Chicago– based *Journal of Political Economy* stopped publishing articles in social economics at the same time the University began publishing a journal on social work.

A Case in Point: Edith Abbott

The way in which economics both attracted and repelled women is best exemplified by the story of one woman—Edith Abbott.[73] Abbott entered the University of Chicago in 1903 and studied with two of the most famous economists at Chicago: Thorstein Veblen and J. Laurence Laughlin. Laughlin considered Abbott among his most brilliant students and clearly encouraged her work. But unlike Laughlin's bright male students (like Wesley Clair Mitchell), Abbott was unable to find an academic job upon completion of her degree. Although Edith Abbott was affiliated with reform movements and women's groups, she was not radical in her approach to economics. Like her mentor Laughlin, she firmly believed in the need for objective, scientific studies and in the notion that knowledge would and could advance social reform. Her graduate work was a study on wages in the United States from 1850 to 1900, in which she attempted to show that real wages for most workers had not fallen. In many ways she fit the professional economist's mold of the first two decades in the twentieth century to a tee, except on one account: she was a women.

Upon graduation, unable to find an academic job, Abbott traveled in Europe. When she returned, Laughlin helped secure a job for her at Wellesley College working with Katharine Coman. Finding the students not serious enough, she quit and returned to the University of Chicago to work in a social research institute alongside her friend and fellow Chicago graduate Sophonisba Breckinridge. Edith Abbott published books and articles regularly, often in the *Journal of Political Economy*. Along with Breckinridge, she convinced the Census Bureau to include data on women workers in its 19-volume comprehensive study *The Report on the Conditions of Women and Child Wage Earners in the United States* in 1910. In 1913 the University of Chicago gave Abbott a part-time job as a lecturer in sociology, where she taught for seven years. Abbott found permanent, full-time employment at an academic institution only when the University of Chicago reluctantly (after years of negotiations) agreed to establish a school of social work (the School of Social Service Administration) in 1920. Throughout her years in Chicago, Abbott did find a welcome home among the community of women activists and reformers—notably Jane Addams and those affiliated with Hull House. Although Abbott and Breckinridge succeeded in establishing a research-oriented, social science wing of social work, it seems to have come at an unintended cost—a great justification for the economics profession to exclude social problems from its purview. Once Breckinridge and Abbott founded the *Social Service Review*, a journal dedicated to publishing investigative findings, there was little need to publish such articles in economics journals. Edith Abbott was clearly one of the profession's star pupils, yet she was marginalized and finally displaced entirely from the economics profession.

BEYOND THE PROGRESSIVE ERA: WOMEN ECONOMISTS FROM THE 1920s TO THE 1960s

Despite a vocal feminist movement fresh from a suffrage victory, by and large, women academics fared poorly in the 1920s. An extensive study by the American Association of University Professors (AAUP) in 1921 and again in 1929 found that women were relegated to the lowest-paid and least-prestigious positions in academia. Of the 13,000 faculty members at 145 institutions belonging to the AAUP in 1921, women were 4 percent of full professors and 23.5 percent of instructors. Close to two-thirds of all women in faculty positions held the title of lecturer or instructor. Little had changed by 1929.[74]

The depression of the 1930s brought little hope for women academics, as scarce jobs were reserved for men. Further, with the beginning of the institution of tenure in university jobs, women who had been forever kept on as instructors or assistant professors were more likely to be let go than promoted. In economics, the percentage of women doctoral recipients began its decline in the 1930s. Rossiter speaks only of the natural and physical sciences, but her observations seem to pertain equally to economics: "The essential structure of women's place in American science had been set by 1910; thereafter sexual segregation not only persisted but even spread into other newly emerging areas of science. Protest movements were unable to change this pattern in any significant way, and war and depression only strengthened it."[75]

Outside of the women's colleges, only one coeducational institution engaged in training economists seemed to have hired women permanently at the professorial level—University of California-Berkeley. By the 1930s, 3 of its 23 members were tenured women.[76] Berkeley was also the first economics department to have a woman chair, however briefly—Jessica Blanche Peixotto.[77] Peixotto became a full professor at Berkeley in 1918, after earning her doctorate from the same institution in 1900 (the second woman to receive any doctorate from Berkeley). Peixotto was elected vice president of the American Economic Association in 1928—the association's first female officer. But the main reason for the presence of so many women is attributable to the decision to keep social economics as a subfield within Berkeley's economics department, rather than allocating it to social work, sociology, or home economics.

The late 1940s witnessed an enormous expansion in the ranks of students in higher education, but women were often pushed aside in favor of veterans paying tuition with the G.I. Bill. Women's place was clearly not as professional economists. As figure 2.2 depicts, the percentages of women doctorates awarded in several fields in social sciences fell to their historic lows in the 1950s. By the 1960s, while the other fields see a rapid rise in the percentage of female doctorates, economics' pace is much more tempered, with an average of 8.2 percent in the 1960s.

No systematic studies of women in economics in the 1950s and 1960s exist to my knowledge, although studies of women in academia indicate that this was a period of further retrenchment for women. Research took on a new and higher value in institutes of higher education after World War II. But the research-oriented universities and colleges historically did not hire women. Even the women's colleges, once bastions for women scholars, aggressively pursued male professors in order to boost their prestige and ability to attract top-notch students. As the data in table 2.1 reveal, in a relatively short period of time women *lost* ground in their once strong foothold in women's colleges.[78] Indeed, in the 1950s it appeared as if the way for a college or university to be more prestigious was to have fewer women faculty. In an extensive 1958 study on academic hiring and firing in the liberal arts departments in 10 top-ranked U.S. universities, sociologists Theodore Caplow and Reece McGee note: "Women scholars are not taken seriously and cannot look forward to normal professional careers. This bias is part of the much larger pattern which determines the utilization of women in our economy. It is not peculiar to the academic world, but it does blight the prospects of female scholars."[79]

TABLE 2.1   *Percentage of Female Faculty in Selected Women's Colleges, 1940–41 and 1956*

	1940–41 (%)	1956 (%)
Smith	58	37
Wellesley	90	67
Bryn Mawr	52	50
Vassar	70	62
Goucher	72	60

Source: Jessie Bernard, *Academic Women* (University Park, Pa.: Pennsylvania State University Press, 1964): 55, Table 3/4.

Anecdotal evidence about the economics profession is consistent with the preceding accounts of women in academia. Women were at best ignored (rather than mentored or groomed) when in graduate school and found it very difficult to find academic jobs once they finished. Irma Adelman, a development economist and the most frequently cited female economist, recently wrote about her experiences as an economist in the 1950s and 1960s. Adelman was born in Romania and emigrated to (then) Palestine in 1939. From there she went to Berkeley to study economics, intending to return, but instead married and stayed in the United States. She writes:

> I hit discrimination against women for the first time when I got my Ph.D. in 1955. I was totally unprepared for this. . . . In the fifties, discrimination against women in U.S. academia was incredible. I had graduated from a top institution, at the top of my class, in a period of high demand for college teachers. Nevertheless, when it came to entering the job market, no one would waste a recommendation on a low probability hire. At the time, openings were not advertised, and were publicized only through a network of personal contacts. When I applied for a teaching job at San Francisco State, the chairman suggested that I might look for a position in a local private high school![80]

In an article reflecting on hiring practices in the 1960s, Daniel Orr recalls that "women often did find themselves set apart as graduate students, perhaps not *de jure* different, but nonetheless objects of curiosity, subjects of speculative conversation, and while officially in the group, sometimes not fully welcome at the center where informal learning occurs through social interaction. Nor did women at that time have much of a support network on most campuses."[81] This situation was echoed by one of the recipients of my mail survey to a random sample of the AEA. Two days after I mailed out the survey on the impact of feminism on economics (discussed in chapters 4–6), I received a phone call from a now-retired economist. He wanted to tell me how much things had changed since his graduate school days at a top-ranked university he attended in the late 1950s. He told me about the three women who had entered graduate school with him. One woman dropped out after the first year without so much as a call from any faculty—something he claimed would never have happened to a male graduate student. A second woman, from India, was treated respectfully, if not deferentially. My caller attributed this to the university's considerable emphasis on economic development at the time and fear of casting aspersions on a person from a developing country. The third woman, he recalled, was most often referred to disparagingly by other male graduate students ("battle ax" was the term he remembered) and was rarely taken seriously by her peers.

In the 1950s and 1960s few conditions in economics (or in academia in general) were conducive to women scholars or feminist ideas. The profession emphasized and rewarded mathematical and deductive theoretical work—from within the more liberal Keynesian framework to the more conservative and developing general equilibrium models. Societal attitudes toward women were especially retrograde. Youthfulness, beauty, and fertility were among women's most valued attributes. Although never at parity with their male peers, women as participants and as subjects were almost completely invisible in the economics profession on the eve of the modern-day women's movement.

CONCLUSION

For two brief decades at the turn of the century in the United States, the economics discipline provided a place for women. It wasn't the best seat in the house, but the profession's mission and its emphasis on historical research made room for women economists and for looking at issues of concern to women and feminists. Economics then was a discipline struggling to define itself on a variety of levels: what it was, who could become economists, and what economists should do. It emerged from the social science movement in the United States, which was first and foremost about reform during a time of remarkable economic, social, and political upheaval caused by the insurgence of capitalism. Understanding the economic underpinnings of legal, social, and political life was of vital interest and concern. This study was also consistent with feminine pursuits. By the 1930s that opportunity was gone. That women were so effectively removed from practicing economics and as subjects of economics by the onset of the modern-day women's movement is exceptional and worth economists' attention.

Discrimination by university administrators, trustees, and academics that precluded women from being offered jobs in graduate departments, the narrowing of the scope of economics to place "social" issues in other disciplines, and the turn toward deductive formalism all served to make and keep economics a male field and profession. Despite women's relatively high participation and research contributions, especially in labor economics and economic history, during the Progressive Era, women with doctorates in economics were not in the prestigious positions in the profession. Many women made it to the door of professionalization in economics—getting a doctorate. But few were allowed to come in—secure employment in an academic institution. The topics women studied (whether tracked or chosen makes little difference) were increasingly being pushed out of the economics discipline, and economics methodology discouraged anything but moderate political views. Once the parameters of who could be economists and how economic analysis was going to take place were established, specialization served the dual purpose of attracting women to other fields and isolating those who were already in the profession. It would not be until the 1970s and the modern-day women's movement that women regained the foothold they once had a half century earlier.

3

FINDING THE WOMEN: WOMEN'S REPRESENTATION IN THE ECONOMICS PROFESSION, 1970–1990

In the late 1960s and early 1970s, the modern-day women's movement exploded. Women began demanding equal opportunities and access to all aspects of public life. Feminists argued that important political, economic, and social institutions were dominated by men, which served to keep women excluded from participating in much of civil society as equal partners. Further, women's relegation to separate spheres assigned them a status subordinate to men. Feminists argued that women's unequal position was not the result of their intellectual or physical inferiority but, rather, caused by individual and systemwide discrimination. More importantly, feminists not only interpreted the world, they organized to change it by demanding women be treated as equals, forming political organizations, and working to enact legislation.[1]

Access to the academy was crucial to the women's movement for economic, intellectual, and political reasons. Individual economic advancement was one of the major goals of the 1970s women's movement. Clearly, the credentials and knowledge obtained by higher education were seen as a proven means to achieving that goal. The university was (and still is) where ideas about the world were formed, debated, and disseminated. For disenfranchised groups, battles over ideas, knowledge, and representation have been a crucial component to breaking down ideological and knowledge-based barriers to advancement. Academic scholarship and intellectuals also informed policy decisions, especially in the first several decades of the post–World War II United States. Feminist scholarship was seen as one important and systematic way to participate in policy debates.

Unlike other areas of public life—notably the political and economic arena—change in the gender composition in certain areas of academia came relatively quickly. In the 1970s, women and people of color were able to expand their ranks in elite and professional schools and make an impact on the curriculum. Most elite male undergraduate schools opened their doors to women for the first time. Graduate programs, especially the professional schools, reexamined their admission procedures in an attempt to be less exclusionary. By popular demand (literally), many campuses established women's studies (and black studies) departments throughout the 1970s and 1980s. By the 1980s all academic disciplines had increased the percentage of female faculty and administrators, and campuses increased the number of courses offering more systematic studies of women and gender roles. In the 1990s feminist scholarship has become an established and accepted scholarly framework. In some cases—particularly in history, anthropology, philosophy, and literature—feminism has transformed the discipline's methodology. Many academic disciplines in the humanities and social sciences have thriving feminist journals and feminist organizations.[2] Testimony to feminism's foothold is the backlash it is experiencing. Regardless of how one feels about the so-called PC (politically correct) debates in many colleges and universities, they can be seen as an attack on the success of feminists and feminism in academia.

Despite the relatively rapid rise of women in academic professions and increasingly wider acceptance of feminist scholarship, the economics profession and discipline has remained nearly immune to feminist influences. Although calculating the impact of a political and social movement on a discipline is difficult, there are some measuring posts. A first, but important, indication of the marginal impact of feminism on economics is the small percentage of women economists and new female entrants into the profession relative to other disciplines. Without women scholars, feminist scholarship is unlikely. Men can be feminists and employ feminist techniques, but the main impetus for feminist scholarship has come from women. So, at a very fundamental level, the small percentage of women in the profession is one reason that the discipline has been relatively unaffected by feminist thought and scholarship.

Other measuring posts include the existence of feminist organizations and publications; the degree to which practitioners in the profession see feminist analysis as a valid methodology; and the ability of feminists to reconstruct theory to address gender questions. The later two measures will be examined in chapters 7 and 8. This chapter is a "head count"; that is, it examines women's representation in the economics profession, organizations, and the curriculum.

WOMEN ECONOMISTS

Table 3.1 depicts the percentage of employed female Ph.D.s in a variety of disciplines in 1979 and 1989. In 1989, 12 percent of employed Ph.D. economists were female. Compared with 21 percent in social sciences, 36 percent in psychology, and 23 percent in the life sciences, women's representation in economics is strikingly low. The percentage of women Ph.D. economists is only slightly higher than the percentages in mathematics, computer science, and chemistry. In 1979 just over 7 percent of all Ph.D. economists were women. And although there was a steady increase over the decade, overall representation of women in the profession remains slim.

Table 3.2 depicts the number of male and female doctoral recipients and the percentage of female recipients in various fields in 1970, 1981, and 1992. Although it could be argued that math and quantitative analysis, which are heavily emphasized in economics, could be serving as a screening device, other quantitatively based fields seem to be attracting a higher percentage of women than economics. In fact, the percentage of new female doctorates in economics in 1992 is considerably lower than the percentages in the other social sciences, psychology, education, mathematics, biology, chemistry, and business. Further, economics has seen less improvement than these fields over the last two decades. Of the fields listed, the percentage of women receiving Ph.D.s in economics surpassed those in business, computer science, physics and astronomy, and agricultural sciences in 1970; by 1992 only physics and computer science awarded a smaller percentage of female doctorates than did economics. The relatively low percentages of women in eco-

TABLE 3.1   *Percentage of Employed Female Ph.D. Scientists in the United States, 1979 and 1989*

	Percent Female (%) 1979	Percent Female (%) 1989	Percent Change (%) 1979–89
Psychologists	24.20	36.05	48.97
Life Sciences	14.37	22.68	57.83
Agricultural Scientists	2.27	7.40	226.00
Biological Scientists	17.26	23.36	35.34
Medical Scientists	15.47	29.13	88.30
Social Scientists	14.13	21.20	50.04
Economists	**7.15**	**12.34**	**72.59**
Sociologists and Anthropologists	25.00	30.50	22.00
Other Social Scientists	13.62	22.22	63.14
Computer Specialists	5.48	11.64	112.41
Mathematical Sciences	7.51	10.47	39.41
Mathematicians	7.62	10.26	34.65
Statisticians	6.98	11.66	67.05
Physical Scientists	5.21	8.65	66.03
Physicists and Astronomers	2.80	4.74	69.29
Chemists	6.46	10.74	66.56
Environmental Scientists	4.16	8.41	102.16
Earth Scientists	3.70	8.42	127.57
Oceanographers	9.15	10.93	19.45
Atmospheric Scientists	1.83	5.48	199.45
Engineers	1.04	3.10	198.08
Total	10.63	17.20	61.81

Source: National Science Foundation, *Women and Minorities in Science and Engineering: An Update,* prepared by Patricia E. White (Washington, D.C., January 1992), 80–81.

nomics, then, does not seem to be merely a vestige of sexism from the 1950s and 1960s. Almost one-quarter of a century has passed since the beginning of the modern-day women's movement, but the economics profession is not attracting women to the same degree as other social sciences are or other male-dominated fields seem to be.

TABLE 3.2 Doctorates Awarded by Field and Gender, 1970, 1981, and 1992

	1970		1981		1992		Percent Female (%)			Change in Percentage Representation, 1970–92 (%)
	Male	Female	Male	Female	Male	Female	1970	1981	1992	
Social Sciences	2,387	353	2,305	843	7,707	887	12.9	26.7	34.2	21.3
Economics	**742**	**52**	**723**	**101**	**680**	**173**	**6.6**	**12.3**	**20.3**	**13.7**
Sociology & Anthropology	587	162	478	394	428	397	21.6	40.5	48.1	26.5
Political Science	469	56	316	118	385	150	10.7	27.1	28.0	17.4
Psychology	1,296	372	1,885	1,472	1,359	2,014	22.3	43.8	59.7	37.4
Education	4,698	1,196	3,955	3,534	2,783	4,801	20.3	47.6	59.5	39.2
Language & Literature	832	373	691	766	537	736	31.0	52.6	57.8	26.8
History	901	137	497	194	419	225	13.2	28.1	34.9	21.7
Business & Management	593	10	872	292	952	286	1.7	25.1	23.1	21.4
Mathematics	896	78	616	112	851	231	8.0	15.4	21.4	13.4
Computer Science	105	2	206	26	669	103	1.9	11.2	13.3	11.4
Physical and Life Sciences										
Physics & Astronomy	1,479	44	942	73	1,251	188	2.9	7.2	12.0	9.1
Agricultural Sciences	698	28	1,003	147	963	251	3.9	12.8	20.7	16.8
Chemistry	1,834	166	1,376	235	1,525	632	8.3	14.6	29.3	21.0
Biological Sciences	2,820	469	2,411	986	2,620	1,623	14.3	29.0	38.3	24.0
Health Sciences	299	58	379	670	689	963	16.3	63.9	58.0	42.7

Source: U.S. Department of Education, Digest of Educational Statistics (Washington, D.C.: Government Printing Office, 1971), 90–92; National Research Council, Summary Report, 1981 Doctoral Recipients from U.S. Universities (Washington, D.C.: Government Printing Office, 1982), 34–37; and U.S. Department of Education, National Center for Educational Statistics, Digest of Educational Statistics (Lantham, Md.: National Center for Educatioral Statistics, 1994), 250–57.

Nonetheless, the gains are unmistakable. There are still far more women—both relative to the number of men and in actual numbers—in economics now than there were in the 1960s. National Science Foundation (NSF) data indicate that since 1973 the percentage of all women Ph.D.s in economics has tripled.[3] Table 3.3 depicts the numbers and percentages of women receiving bachelor's, master's, and doctor's degrees in economics for various years between 1965 and 1992. Women undergraduate economics majors currently represent almost 30 percent of all economics undergraduate students, tripling in relative size since the mid-1960s. The percentage of female doctorates increased by fivefold.

Table 3.3 picks up a somewhat distressing trend, however. The percentage of women undergraduates in economics is currently falling, and the percentage of female doctorates is no longer increasing. The number of economics undergraduate majors has been falling nationally since the late 1980s; however, the data here indicate women's numbers are falling faster than men's. In 1989–90, the percentage of women receiving undergraduate degrees in economics fell to 31.2 percent from a record high in 1984–85 of 34.5 percent. The percentage fell again in 1991–92 to 29.9 percent. In a separate study using survey data obtained from 127 economics departments, John J. Siegfried and Charles E. Scott found an even larger decline in economics enrollments than reported by the National Center for Educational Statistics and that over 25 percent of the decline in economics majors was due to the reduction of female majors.[4] If undergraduate economics majors are the feeders to graduate work, the decline in the proportion of female

TABLE 3.3 *Bachelor's, Master's, and Doctor's Degrees Conferred in Economics, Selected Years, 1964–1992*

	Total Number Receiving Degree			Percent Women Receiving Degree (%)		
	Bachelor's	*Master's*	*Doctor's*	*Bachelor's*	*Master's*	*Doctor's*
1964–65	10,875	1,268	410	9.6	27.7	4.2
1969–70	17,197	1,988	794	10.8	12.4	6.5
1974–75	14,046	2,127	815	17.2	18.0	9.0
1979–80	17,863	1,822	677	30.2	21.0	15.1
1984–85	20,711	1,922	749	34.5	24.3	16.3
1989–90	23,899	1,965	822	31.2	25.4	20.4
1991–92	23,423	2,106	866	29.9	27.8	20.3

Source: U.S. Department of Education, National Center for Education Statistics, *Digest of Educational Statistics* (various years).

undergraduates could signal that the percentage of females receiving economics doctorates will also begin to fall.

Although professional organizations in the physical and life sciences, women's organizations, and higher education have been concerned about the representation of women in math and the sciences, there has been little interest within or outside of the profession over the relative lack of women in economics. The lack of concern for the percentage of female graduate students in economics was most evident in a recent study of economics graduate training sponsored by the AEA in which the dearth of female students received only a passing mention.[5] One exception to the lack of concern is at the National Science Foundation (NSF). In recent years, it has funded several studies on women in the economics profession and a project to train economists on integrating race and gender into the economics curriculum. However, recent Congressional budget actions have moved to substantially reduce NSF funding in the future.

WOMEN ECONOMISTS IN ACADEMIA

Rank

The majority of economists with Ph.D.s enter and work in academia (see table 3.4). In unpublished data from the NSF, the Committee on the Status of Women in the Economics Profession (CSWEP) reported that in 1985 two-thirds of all Ph.D. economists were employed in educational institutions (67 percent of men and 58 percent of women).[6] In my own 1992 survey of 400 randomly selected members of the American Economic Association based in the United States, 66 percent were in educational institutions (see next chapter). Over half of new Ph.D.s in 1981 and 1991 indicated they planned to be employed in an educational institution.[7] Debra Barbezat found, in a survey of all graduate students about to graduate in the top 46 graduate programs, that 76 percent of those responding and who had gotten a job were going to educational institutions.[8] A CSWEP survey of 81 U.S.-based degree-granting institutions found that 47 percent of all women doctorate students who were looking for jobs in 1993–94 took an academic job.[9]

Since CSWEP's inception in the early 1970s it has presented information on the number of women faculty in educational institutions and the percentage of women receiving doctorates in economics departments; its reports are based on data gathered in an annual American Economic Association

TABLE 3.4   *Distribution of Employment for Ph.D. Recipients in Economics, 1975 and 1989*

	1975 Percent		1989 Percent	
	(%) Male	*(%) Female*	*(%) Male*	*(%) Female*
Educational Institutions	57	65	49	53
Government	13	10	8	20
Private Sector	8	10	10	8
Other*	22	15	34	18

*Other includes those getting employment outside the United States, those in postdoctoral programs and those unemployed.

Note: Numbers in columns may not add to 100 percent due to rounding.

Data for 1975 are for the "Chairman's Group" of 47 institutions that grant graduate degrees as reported by Barbara Reagan, "Report on the Committee on the Status of Women in the Economics Profession," *American Economic Review* 66(2) (May 1976): 494. Data for 1989 are for students attending 45 institutions that award Ph.D.s and reported by Nancy Gordon, "Committee on the Status of Women in the Economics Profession Annual Report," *CSWEP Newsletter* (Winter 1990): 6.

(AEA)–sponsored survey of 2,000 economic departments across the United States, called the Universal Academic Questionnaire (the origins and purpose of CSWEP are discussed later in this chapter).[10] Although data from the Universal Academic Questionnaire are always presented in CSWEP's annual report, the data have not been presented in a consistent form over the years. In addition, the survey conducted by the AEA has long been considered relatively inaccurate (somewhat ironic for a profession that relishes quantification). Surveys are sent by mail to all department chairs but the responses are not checked for accuracy. Further, the response rate over the years has typically been between 50 percent and 60 percent—but the *same* schools do not necessarily respond each year.

From 1973 to 1985, CSWEP reported the data collected from surveys sent to 60 or so graduate programs called the "chairman's group," which included some but not all Ph.D.-granting institutions.[11] After that time, the raw data from the survey are either not presented, presented as a matched-sample over two years (i.e., comparing the results from the same set of departments), or presented and referred to only as graduate degree–granting institutions. Even though the data are not consistent or a controlled sample, the percentages of female faculty in the graduate degree–granting economics departments are the best indicators of the progress (or lack thereof) that women have made in the profession. That data are presented in table 3.5.

Progress has been slow but steady. Over the 20-year period shown in table 3.5, the percentage of women faculty in all ranks in graduate departments has grown, from 3.5 percent in 1974 to 9.7 percent in 1993. But women are still concentrated in the lower and less secure ranks of the profession. Indeed, only 4 percent of all full professors are women, despite representing close to 10 percent of all faculty at graduate departments.

Frustrated with the unreliability of the results from the Universal Academic Questionnaire, CSWEP has twice generated its own data. The first time, CSWEP used information provided from its own AEA-generated roster of women economists in 1980. The CSWEP roster reported twice as many women economists in tenure track positions than did the AEA survey of economics departments, largely due to nonresponses from some departments as well as the large number of women economists not in economics departments. Following up on the discrepancy, CSWEP conducted a phone survey in the spring of 1980. It found about 40 percent more women economists

TABLE 3.5   *Percentage of Female Faculty in Economics Graduate Departments, by Rank, 1974–1993*

Year	Assistant Professor	Associate Professor	Full Professor	All Ranks
1974	7.6	2.6	1.6	3.5
1975	8.6	3.5	2.1	4.2
1976	9.6	3.1	2.7	4.7
1977	10.9	3.7	1.8	4.7
1978	12.3	3.8	1.7	5.0
1979	13.6	4.0	1.9	5.4
1980	13.2	4.8	2.0	5.6
1981	13.7	5.8	2.0	6.1
1982	13.8	6.5	2.7	6.6
1983	11.9	6.0	2.7	6.1
1984	14.3	6.5	2.8	6.9
1985	14.4	5.9	2.6	6.5
1986	14.6	8.1	3.1	7.2
1987	19.6	7.4	2.9	8.3
1988	21.2	9.0	3.6	9.4
1989	20.4	9.4	2.8	8.6
1990	16.7	10.5	3.1	6.2
1991	19.6	8.1	3.8	8.9
1992	19.2	10.0	4.0	9.2
1993	22.0	10.3	4.0	9.7

Source: CSWEP Newsletter (Winter 1993): 8, and *CSWEP Newsletter* (Winter 1995): 8.

than reported to the AEA in its annual survey. Many women economists were not in economics departments or on main campuses. Further, CSWEP found considerable slippage between 1972 and 1980. In 1972, 26 percent of all women were full professors compared with 56 percent of men. In 1980, 18 percent of all women professors were full professors versus 57 percent of men. The phone survey also revealed some disappointing information about the most prestigious economics departments. Of the top six schools, only one had a tenured woman.[12]

In 1993–94 CSWEP identified contact persons in most of the degree-granting institutions. Contacts were asked to fill out a one-page questionnaire on the number of female faculty and students in their department. Of the 88 departments contacted, CSWEP received information on 81. CSWEP found that the percentages of female faculty at all levels reported by their contacts were slightly higher than those reported using the Universal Academic Questionnaire. CSWEP contacts reported that 24 percent of assistant professors, 14.5 percent of associate professors, and 6.7 percent of full professors were female.[13]

The slow progress of women at the top of the profession suggests a rather thick "glass ceiling"—that invisible barrier to advancement in the profession. Not many women are finding their way to a tenured position in one of the top graduate departments, widely considered to be the most prestigious positions in the profession because economic theory is most often shaped and defined in these departments. Jobs in graduate degree–granting institutions typically pay more than other academic jobs and require less classroom time, which allows more time to devote to research. Since the profession values published journal research most highly, being in a graduate department often is rewarding professionally.

Close to 150 colleges and universities confer graduate degrees in economics. In 1982 the National Research Council assessed these programs and ranked 91 one of them into five quality tiers.[14] In 1993 American University economist Ivy Broder conducted a phone survey of the gender composition of the faculty in the top three tiers of economics graduate schools. Among the first-tier schools (University of Chicago, Harvard University, MIT, Princeton University, Stanford University, and Yale University), 2 of the 153 (1.3 percent) full professors were women (one at Harvard and another at Chicago), 1 of the 19 (5.3 percent) associate professors was a woman (Harvard), and 11 of 59 (18.6 percent) assistant professors were women. Typically, only associate and full professors have tenure. Hence, it is likely that four of the top six economics departments in the United States had no tenured women in their faculty in 1993. This is only slightly better than survey results reported in 1980. In second-tier schools, four of the nine had no female full professors (the other five had a total of 9 women out of 185 full professors), and a different four had no female associate professors (the other five schools had a total of 5 women among 45 associate professors). In the third tier, 10 of the 15 schools had no women full professors, and 9 of the 15 had no women associate professors. In total, 3.3 percent of the full professors in this tier were women and 11 percent were associate professors.[15]

Of the top 30 economics graduate departments, then, only 12 had even one woman who was a full professor and even fewer (11) had women as associate professors. Four departments did not have any female assistant professors. Overall women's representation in the top third of all ranked economic departments is 3.9 percent of all full professors, 10.3 percent of all associate professors, and 20.1 percent of all assistant professors.[16]

Fields

Within economics, women seem to specialize in all areas of economic study, although a few fields tend to attract larger numbers of women than others. Analyzing the AEA membership in 1974, Myra Strober found that among the 10 broad fields in economics, men's and women's distribution differed rather significantly, with the highest percentage of women being in labor; welfare programs, consumer economics, and urban and regional economics; and general economics, theory, and history.[17] Debra Barbezat's survey of new doctorates in 1992 shows similar results: a large percentage of women relative to men specialize in labor—but she also found a disproportionately high percentage of women in monetary and fiscal policy and public finance, as well as in international trade theory.[18] Marianne Ferber looked at the number of male and female economists listed in the 1993 AEA directory in 12 different areas of specialization. A summary of the results can be found in table 3.6. Ferber also finds a disproportionate number of women in labor, general economics, international, industrial organization, development, and public economics.[19]

Retention and Promotion

Several studies on Ph.D. economists and the retention and promotion of women in the profession have been published recently. Shulamit Kahn found that the median time it takes women to receive tenure is three years longer than for men.[20] Using a data set containing information on economists who applied for NSF grants in 1989, Ivy Broder found women's academic rank

TABLE 3.6   *Number of Male and Female AEA Members of Subfield of Economic Study, 1993*

Subfields of Economics	Male AEA Members	Female AEA Members	Percent Female (%)
Labor Economics	1,158	298	20.5
General Economics and Teaching	411	67	14.0
International Economics	1,791	280	13.5
Industrial Organization	1,641	256	13.5
Development Economics	1,365	207	13.2
Public Economics	1,349	206	13.2
Microeconomics	1,386	203	12.8
Mathematical and Quantitative Methods	1,348	184	12.0
Urban Economics	557	69	11.0
Methodology and History of Economic Thought	339	39	10.3
Macroeconomics	2,067	210	9.2
Financial Economics	1,419	134	8.6
Total in fields listed above	14,831	2,153	12.7

Source: Marianne Ferber, reported in *IAFFE Newsletter* 5(2) (1995): 14.

and prestige of department are lower than men's after adjusting for the quality of publications.[21] Using data from AEA membership in 1989, Larry Singell Jr. and Joe Stone find significant gender differences in first placement of male and female Ph.D.s in economics.[22] In a review article on women in the economics profession, Kahn reports that women are more likely to drop out of graduate school than men and make less than men, after adjusting for experience, race, and publication record.[23]

Together these studies suggest that despite the entrance of women into the economics profession, success in finding prestigious jobs, achieving job security, and moving up the ranks is more likely for men than women.

WOMEN'S ORGANIZATIONS IN ECONOMICS

Two separate (although overlapping in membership) women's organizations in the economics profession are devoted primarily to feminist economics or the concerns of women in economics: CSWEP and the International Association for Feminist Economics (IAFFE).

The professional organization of the economics profession—the American Economic Association (AEA)—officially established the Committee on the Status of Women in the Economics Profession in 1971 in response to demands of female (and several feminist) economists.[24] The committee's mandate was to "a) support and facilitate equality of opportunity for women economists in all aspects of economists' professional activities, and b) help eradicate any institutional or personal discrimination against women economists."[25] To that end CSWEP has consistently published newsletters, provided a roster of women economists, and organized panels for major economics conferences.

CSWEP does not officially refer to itself as a feminist organization. In the first decade of its operation, based on a review of its annual reports to the AEA, the organization devoted a large portion of its research and publishing activities to analyzing women's economic status not only in the economics profession, but in the economy generally. Further, the organization, or at least leaders in the organization, pushed the committee to actively pursue women's participation in a variety of economics journal editorial boards and organizations. In its 1976 report to the AEA, CSWEP Chairperson Barbara Reagan summarized CSWEP's activities:

> We have encouraged research on the broader issues of the role of women in the economy and sex discrimination with respect to wages and occupational segregation, which affect women economists along with all others. CSWEP feels it is vital that such research provide the basis for its policy recommendations. It is CSWEP's acceptance of the responsibility to collect and analyze data relevant to the status of women economists and to further the theoretical and applied research related to the status of women in general that most sets the work of the Committee apart from that of caucuses in some other professional associations.[26]

In the first six years of the organization, CSWEP sponsored several studies on the status of women in the profession.[27] It cosponsored, along with the Wellesley College Center on Research on Women in Higher Education and the Professions, a workshop conference on occupational segregation in May 1975, which resulted in a widely used book, *Women in the Workplace: An Analysis of Occupational Segregation*. In 1979 CSWEP sponsored a study of acceptance rates of male and female authors in economics journals.

CSWEP has also organized panels for regional and national AEA meetings on women in the economy. This has two important outcomes. First, it ensures that panels on gender will be offered, providing a guaranteed outlet for research on women. Second, some subset of the papers on the panels have typically been included in the association's proceedings papers, which ensures that women's work and work on women are published by the profession's oldest journal. In 1977 CSWEP also took an active role in protesting the AEA board's decision to hold its 1979 annual convention in a state (Georgia) that had not ratified the Equal Rights Amendment.

Even with CSWEP's active participation in the association, however, progress has been slow. In a 10-year assessment, Chairperson Elizabeth Bailey noted in her 1981 report to the AEA, "The decade has not been successful in terms of improvement in the status of women in the academic labor market. Accumulating evidence continues to indicate that there is an overwhelming under-representation of women in the top ranks of the profession of economics. . . . Our hope that a substantial number of the new generation of women assistant professors would be given tenure at the major Ph.D. granting universities is not being realized."[28]

Through 1985, CSWEP continued to provide information and attempts to improve women's status in the economics profession and to promote research on women in the economy. The CSWEP newsletter also refers to official CSWEP letters of admonishment to several established and newly established economic journals and think tanks for their lack of female representation. For example, the CSWEP chair sent a letter to the *Journal of Labor Economics* (begun in 1982) remarking that its first editorial board contained no women—despite the disproportionate representation of women in labor economics. Another letter was sent to Martin Feldstein, the head of the National Bureau of Economic Research, admonishing him for having so few women affiliated with the Bureau. In addition, CSWEP sponsored a conference on gender issues in the workplace with the Brookings Institute.

In 1986 CSWEP leadership made a concerted change in the primary focus of the committee as it moved away from more feminist concerns of women's economic status and gender-related analysis. Instead CSWEP would place more emphasis on activities that would enhance the professional status of women economists and explore employment concerns of women in economics. The shift is clearly stated in the 1985 CSWEP annual report submitted by then president Isabel Sawhill. "The Committee spent a considerable time this year discussing the purposes of the newsletter (and implicitly, the purposes of the Committee). A major issue is the extent to which the newsletter should contain items of professional interest to women economists, whatever their field, and the extent to which it should feature material on gender-related research and the status of women generally. While we believe that both are important, the prevailing view on the Committee was that more emphasis should be put on the former than the later, and that any new editor should feel comfortable with this set of priorities."[29]

Despite CSWEP's status as a standing committee of the AEA since 1974, the Association has taken few steps to encourage women's participation beyond supporting CSWEP's activities (compiling a roster, organizing panels at AEA meetings, publishing a newsletter) and maintaining its committee status in the AEA. The economics profession was among the last of the professions to ensure formal arrangements for child care at its national meetings (in 1993). There are no scholarships to promote female graduate students or distinguished awards for women in the profession nor have there been any formal statements from the AEA concerning the position of women in the profession or in the curriculum.

Looking for a more explicitly feminist organization in the economics profession, several women, including many CSWEP members, formed the International Association for Feminist Economics (IAFFE) in 1991. IAFFE's brochure describes the organization as "a non-profit organization advancing feminist inquiry of economic issues and educating economists and others on feminist points of view on the economy."[30] Unlike (although not in opposition to) CSWEP, the organization is explicitly feminist and dedicated to research on economic-related topics from a feminist perspective. It holds annual summer conferences, organizes panels at national and regional economics meetings, maintains a computer Internet listserver (FEMECON-L), publishes a newsletter, compiles syllabi on gender-related courses, and compiles bibliographies on feminist economics and pedagogy. In 1995 IAFFE launched a new academic journal called *Feminist Economics*. As of 1995 the organization had more than 600 members.

WOMEN IN LEADERSHIP, JOURNALS, AND CURRICULUM IN ECONOMICS

In the 110 years of its existence, the AEA has had only two female presidents, Isabel Sawhill serving in 1986 and Anne Krueger in 1996.[31] Representation in other elected positions is somewhat higher: 6.2 percent of the 226 vice presidents elected have been women and since the AEA started electing executive committee members in 1903, 19 of the 339 (5.6 percent) have been filled by women. There has been at least one women elected to AEA leadership in 40 of the last 93 years of AEA's existence. In 21 of those years, there have been multiple women officeholders. The AEA's record since the modern-day women's movement has improved: since 1968 there has been at least one female officer in the AEA in every year but two (1972 and 1994).[32] The profession has been sorely lacking on the level of appointed leadership in AEA's journals. There has never been a female editor of any of the three publications of the AEA, the *American Economic Review* (published since 1885), the *Journal of Economic Literature* (started in 1969), and the *Journal of Economic Perspectives* (published since 1987).

This raises a related issue on ability to publish in economic journals. Women economists are published less frequently than men. A recent study of the publication records of 30 male and 30 female Ph.D. economists with doctorates from similar institutions on similar dissertation topics found: "The percentage of women with publications was lower than the corresponding percentage of men in each dissertation field, with a 7.1 percent difference overall."[33] But are women producing less (or lesser quality) research than men, or do they face discrimination when they send their research to journals? To answer precisely that question, economist Rebecca Blank conducted a carefully controlled experiment of submissions in the early 1990s to the *American Economic Review*. Half of the submissions received by the journal were passed on to reviewers with the authors' names while half were not. If reviewers actively discriminated against women, presumably fewer articles would be accepted by the group that knew the authors' names (and presumably the gender) than the group that did not. Blank found that although the difference in men's and women's rejection rates was higher in the case when article referees knew the author(s) than they were when the author was unknown, the differences were not statistically significant. However, there was significant difference in rejection rates depending on the rank of the university the author(s) was from.[34] Given that women are much less likely to find employment in high-prestige institutions, women's low acceptance rates into the *American Economic Review* may be the result of discrimination that takes place somewhere other than at the referees' desks. Recent research by Van Kolpin and Larry Singell Jr. suggests this is the case. They found that economics departments with the highest rankings for publications per faculty member were also the ones least likely to have women. But they also found that the research output of women in the 1970s outpaced that of men at similarly ranked institutions, implying that women's low representation in the top-ranked schools explains their lower publication rates in top-ranked journals.[35]

Quality of academic scholarship is very difficult to measure and quite arguably is a socially defined and rather subjective determination. In eco-

nomics, however, quality is almost uniformly defined by the number of cita
tions and/or the number of articles published in prestigious journals. Of
economists ranked by their citations in 1989, Marshall Medoff's list of the
150 most often cited authors included two women: Irma Adelman ranked
50th with 1,059 citations and Karen Davis ranked 142nd with 471 citations.[36] Only examining authors who were 40 or younger in 1985, Medoff's
list of the 50 most cited economists included only one women: Francine Blau
with 227 citations.[37]

The issue of citations as a measure of quality is a very sticky one. First,
of those economists most cited, 94 percent were employed at the top 16 economics departments in the country. As previously discussed, women have
very low representation in these universities. Second, as Marianne Ferber
argues, the "old-boys' network" has resulted in women's scholarship not
being adequately recognized by the most prestigious authors in the profession, which leads to women's work not being cited and by definition, then,
not considered as high quality as men's work. She found that in five distinct
fields (labor economics, financial economics, sociology, developmental psychology, and mathematics) women authors cited other women authors at
rates considerably and significantly higher than did male authors.[38]

Women's underrepresentation in the top economics graduate programs
creates problems for several reasons. There is a network among those in top
universities—seminar series, papers exchanged on panels, and mentoring of
new scholars—that excludes women. Economists at the top universities are
much more likely to have lower teaching loads than at other institutions,
affording them considerably more time to do research. Further, women and
men who do not employ mainstream methodology and/or approach topics
often considered outside the narrow range of economics will be less likely to
be published in prestigious journals or cited by many published authors.

A final place where women are underrepresented in economics is in the
graduate and the undergraduate curriculum. In a survey of 21 major introductory economics textbooks published in the 1980s, Susan Feiner and Barbara
Morgan found an average of 10 pages per text, or 1.3 percent, devoted to
specifically addressing women and/or people of color. Further, when women
are referred to as actors in the text (in examples of economic principles), the
authors found they were uniformly stereotyped; men were depicted in a wide
range of occupations, women were only depicted in a few low-wage and low-
status jobs.[39] Feiner updated her study and found that in 1990 the percentage
of space devoted to discussions of race and gender in introductory economics
textbooks had indeed risen—but only to an average of 1.7 percent![40]

In a world in which the economic activities of men and women are so distinct, it is difficult to imagine how one could avoid these discussions in economics classrooms and textbooks. Yet, even in labor economics textbooks, economists have managed to avoid much explicit discussion of the differential labor market outcomes of men and women. Tara Gray, in a survey of nine labor economics textbooks published in the late 1980s and early 1990s, found an average of 14 pages (2.5 percent) explicitly devoted to material on women. Additionally, Gray found that when women were discussed, in about half the cases the treatment of women's differential outcomes are attributed to women's choices rather than to discrimination or institutional constraints, and only the costs—not the benefits—of remedies like comparable worth (equal pay for similarly skilled work) or affirmative action are discussed.[41]

Increasingly, however, economics departments are offering courses focused on women. In a survey of course offerings in the 132 top-ranked liberal arts regional and national colleges in the early 1990s, Nancy Burnett found that 31 offered economics courses that focused on gender. However, these courses are almost exclusively taught in the national liberal arts colleges. Of the top 35 nationally based liberal arts colleges, 25 of them offered a gender-based economics course.[42] In the survey I conducted of randomly selected members of the American Economic Association in 1992 (see chapter 4 for discussion of survey results), I found that 20 percent of the respondents who taught said that their department offered a course primarily about women in the economy.

The economics profession seems not very concerned about the underrepresentation of women (or people of color) in the economics curriculum. A committee for Race and Gender Balance in the Economics Curriculum originally was established under the auspices of CSWEP, but it is currently not affiliated with any organization. The committee published a document entitled *Guidelines for Recognizing and Avoiding Racist and Sexist Bias in Economics*, but the guidelines have not been endorsed by the AEA. Further, an AEA–appointed blue-ribbon commission to study economics graduate education did not even consider gender or race underrepresentation in its curricular analysis. The sole mention of gender in its main report implied the increase in the number of women economics graduate students does not appear to have adversely affected the quality of graduate students.[43]

The commission did, however, raise an issue that might help explain the lack of women's representation in economics. The report laments the lack of creativity and linkages between theory and practice in economics graduate education, "We fear that the way graduate education is currently structured may be excluding some potentially creative and insightful economists from economic Ph.D.s. Likewise, we are concerned that some graduate students who come to economics from other fields can obtain Ph.D.s with little or no knowledge of economic problems or institutions."[44] This concern was never discussed in the context of the narrowness of economics methodology, but it might well have been. Indeed, the lack of concern for gender and race under-representation in the field is consistent with mainstream interpretations and understanding of economic issues—especially as they concern women and people of color. The main actor in economic models is *homo economicus*—economic MAN—a genderless, raceless self-actualizing individual who maximizes his or her utility (or profit) in a world devoid of institutions, historical time, and all power except that of market purchasing power. To gain real insight into the lack of women and feminism in economics, one must look at the ways in which mainstream economic theory understands economic phenomena, the subject of chapter 7.

II

RESPONSES TO AMERICAN ECONOMIC ASSOCIATION SURVEY

4

WHAT'S A NICE GIRL
LIKE YOU . . . ? PROFILE
OF THE PROFESSION

Economics is the oldest of the social sciences, the most established, the most quantitative—and has been the most dominated by men.

—Marianne Ferber and Michelle L. Teiman[1]

The small representation of women and of feminist analysis in economics is a curious outcome for two reasons. First, other male-dominated professions have managed to attract a much larger percentage of women than economics over the last 25 years. Second, economic analysis is a crucial component of understanding women's oppression today. This latter reason alone would suggest that economics would be a "natural" field for feminists to enter. It is not.

Who, then, becomes an economist? What do they think about the role of gender and feminism in economics? To answer these questions, I designed and distributed a survey on this topic to a random sample of economists. Survey research, although an important quantitative and qualitative methodology in the social sciences, is underutilized in economics. It is not, however, a com-

pletely foreign method of data collection and analysis in the profession, especially for research on the composition of the profession. Several economists
have sent surveys to economists and economic graduate students to solicit
their opinions on economic phenomena and the economics profession. For
example, David Colander and Arjo Klamer surveyed and interviewed graduate students about their interest and views on graduate work in economics.
The results of that survey seem to have been part of the impetus to launch a
panel to study economics graduate education.[2] Debra Barbezat surveyed graduate students and discovered interesting gender differences in fields.[3] Marsha
Shelburn and Patsy Lewellyn's survey of graduate students discovered gender-
based differences in peer relationships, concern for safety, and collaborative
publications.[4] Richard M. Alston, J. R. Kearl, and Michael Vaughan used a
survey to measure the dispersion of views among economists.[5] Myra Strober
conducted a survey of CSWEP members in the late 1970s.[6]

This and the following two chapters discuss findings from my survey on
the impact of feminism on economics, which was distributed to a randomly
chosen sample of American Economic Association (AEA) members in the
spring of 1992. The survey covered a wide range of topics, most of them per-
taining to AEA members' views on the impact of feminism on economics.
Those receiving the survey were told the results would be used for research
on the impact of feminism on economics and that their responses would be
confidential. A copy of the cover letter and questionnaire sent are included in
the appendix.

In addition to questions about economics and feminism, the survey
included questions about the respondent's age, gender, sexual orientation,
family size and composition, and personal and family income. It also asked
questions about work, including type of employment and title, teaching
responsibilities, the number of women economists at the respondent's workplace, and women recently hired or interviewed for a job at the respondent's
workplace. The survey results provide new data on the profile of the economics profession. No one to date has accumulated more information on the
personal characteristics of economists who join the AEA, the main and rather
large organization of economists. A tabulation and discussion of those results
are presented in this chapter. Views on feminist approaches to economics, the
quantity of journal articles on topics about women and feminist approaches
to economics, whether certain economic policies affecting families and
women's earnings improve or harm women's economic status, and whether
there has been a positive or negative impact of feminism on economics are
discussed in chapter 5. Written responses concerning advice to a hypothetical

feminist undergraduate student considering a graduate degree in economics are discussed in chapter 6.

The survey results indicate that the profession is overrepresented by white, high-income, married men. Since many professions in the United States have a similar demographic profile, the portrait of a profession painted here may be of little consequence in understanding the impact of feminism on economics. However, at least one important feminist contribution to the study of knowledge suggests that the researcher's "standpoint"—that is, one's social and economic location in the world and the status one confers from it—influences his or her understanding of the world.[7] If these situation-based knowledge arguments are true, then the preponderance of people in economics who historically have been afforded relative privilege (in terms of their race, sex, and income) suggests that the understanding of the world projected by them may not be as complete as it might otherwise be if the profession had a broader and more diverse population. So, if standpoint theory is in fact correct, the demographics of the profession matter greatly.

THE SURVEY SAMPLE

In April 1992 I sent a seven-page survey to 400 U.S.-based members of the AEA, randomly selected from the 1991 AEA telephone directory list of more than 14,000 members. Thirteen questionnaires were returned unanswered, leaving a potential sample response of 387.[8] In total, I received 223 responses; however, ten respondents did not fill out the survey.[9] This left 213 usable surveys, yielding a response rate of 55 percent. This compares favorably with other mail surveys of economists.[10] Ninety-four percent of the AEA members responding had at least a master's degree in economics.

Although the response rate was rather high, it is possible that those returning the sample were unrepresentative of the entire sample of 400. Using the 1989 annotated directory of AEA members, I was able to obtain limited information (age and/or employment) on 158 of the 174 people who either did not return a survey or returned the survey but did not complete it. Women were more likely to respond to the survey than men (8.5% of the nonrespondents versus 13% of respondents were female), and those not responding were on average older than those responding. Barbezat (1992) also had a higher rate of women respondents in her survey of graduate students. Of the 16 people not listed in the 1989 directory, it is quite probable that many of them were graduate students at the time of survey and therefore not AEA members in 1989. Since graduate students are younger (on average) than other AEA members, this might account for the larger percentage of older persons found in the known nonrespondents. The distribution of men's employment was very similar in the sample for those completing the survey and for those who did not. Of the characteristics I was able to trace, those who did not respond to the survey did not differ much from those who did, suggesting that the survey response can be considered a random sample of AEA members.

The gender composition of the sample corresponds to that of the economics profession as a whole. The distribution by gender of those in the private and academic sector is very similar to distributions of economists in 1989 compiled by Shulamit Kahn using the National Science Foundation Survey of Earned Doctorates (reported by Hoffman 1992) and those reported in table 3.4.[11] Despite the relatively small numbers, the gender distribution of respondents to my survey corresponds closely to the one tabulated by the AEA and reported by CSWEP on the percentage of female professors and graduate students (see table 4.1). The respondents in my sample, however, included a higher percentage of female full professors and somewhat fewer assistant and associate professors than in CSWEP's 1994 annual report. This is consistent with what we know about the CSWEP data. It is based on the responses received from an AEA survey sent to the chairs of institutions that award graduate degrees (in the Universal Academic Questionnaire), and those departments have fewer women, especially at the full professor level than other economics departments.[12] Further, the Universal Academic Questionnaire sample primarily includes economics departments; respondents in my sample could be situated in any department. It is quite likely that the dis-

TABLE 4.1 *Percentage of Females by Rank in Survey Sample of AEA Members 1992 and CSWEP 1992*

Title	AEA Sample		CSWEP Sample*	
	(%) Female	*(%) Male*	*(%) Female*	*(%) Male*
Full Professor	9.6	90.4	4.0	96.0
Associate Professor	7.0	93.0	10.0	90.0
Assistant Professor	16.7	83.3	19.2	80.8
Graduate Student	12.5	87.5	11.2**	89.8

*CSWEP data come from the AEA survey of graduate departments.
**Data are for 1989 and have not been reported since that date.
Source: Author's survey results 1992; CSWEP data from *CSWEP Newsletter* (Winter 1994).

TABLE 4.2   *Characteristics of the AEA Sample*

	All		Male		Female	
	Average	*N**	*Average*	*N*	*Average*	*N*
Average age	44.6	210	45.0	183	41.3	27
Average number of years in current job	9.5	200	9.7	174	9.4	26
Average number of years since highest degree	14.7	201	15.2	175	11.7	26
Average family size	2.8	210	2.8	184	2.9	26
	Percent	*N*	*Percent*	*N*	*Percent*	*N*
Total of Sample	100.0	213	86.9	185	13.1	28
Type of Employment:						
Academic	66.0	209	67.4	181	57.1	28
Government	12.0	209	10.5	181	21.4	28
White	88.0	209	87.4	182	92.6	27
Married (living with spouse)	80.3	213	82.7	185	64.3	28
Heterosexual	99.0	203	98.9	177	100.0	26
With Personal Income:						
Less than $20,000	4.5	201	4.0	174	7.4	27
Between $20,000 & $29,999	2.5	201	1.7	174	7.4	27
Between $30,000 & $39,999	7.5	201	6.3	174	14.8	27
Between $40,000 & $49,999	17.4	201	17.8	174	14.8	27
Between $50,000 & $59,999	20.4	201	21.3	174	14.8	27
Between $60,000 & $74,999	15.4	201	15.5	174	14.8	27
Between $75,000 & $100,000	15.9	201	14.4	174	25.9	27
Over $100,000	16.4	201	19.0	174	0.0	27
With Family Income:						
Less than $20,000	2.5	200	2.3	174	3.8	26
Between $20,000 & $29,999	1.5	200	1.2	174	3.8	26
Between $30,000 & $39,999	5.0	200	5.2	174	3.8	26
Between $40,000 & $49,999	8.0	200	8.0	174	7.7	26
Between $50,000 & $59,999	8.5	200	9.2	174	3.8	26
Between $60,000 & $74,999	16.0	200	17.2	174	7.7	26
Between $75,000 & $100,000	22.0	200	23.0	174	15.4	26
Over $100,000	36.5	200	33.9	174	53.9	26
With children (any age)	71.3	209	72.2	184	57.7	26

*N = Number responding
Source: Survey results, computed by author.

tribution reported by CSWEP probably underestimates the percentages of female faculty at the full professor levels.

Table 4.2 contains a summary of the characteristics of the respondents. The most striking observation is the homogeneity of the profession. Eighty-seven percent of the sample were male and 88 percent were white. The largest nonwhite group was Asians (6%), followed by African-Americans (1.5%) and Latino (1%). The profession is also very "straight": only two respondents indicated they were not heterosexual.

Women in the sample were much less likely to be married than men.[13] In this case, the AEA sample differs little from the U.S. population with doctoral degrees. Table 4.3 compares marital status of the U.S. population of men and women at all educational levels, men and women with Ph.D.s, and men and women in the AEA sample. Highly educated men are much more likely to be married than less-educated men, whereas precisely the opposite is true for women.

More than two-thirds of the sample earned over $50,000 a year (see table 4.2). The distribution of men's income was significantly different (and higher) than women's in this sample, but once adjusted for other variables like age, race, and type of employment, income levels do not differ significantly.[14] Whereas none of the women reported making over $100,000 per year, 19 percent of the men did. Further, 15 percent of the women in the sample reported incomes of less than $30,000, but only 6 percent of the men reported incomes that low. Family income, however, had the opposite pattern: female members of the AEA were much more likely to live in families

TABLE 4.3   *Marital Status of Men and Women Ages 25–65 for AEA Sample, Total U.S. Population, and U.S. Population with Ph.D.s*

	All Women 1991 U.S. (%)	All Women w/Ph.D.s (%)	Women in AEA Sample (%)	All Men 1991 U.S. (%)	All Men w/Ph.D.s (%)	Men in AEA Sample (%)
Married	70.4	59.9	66.8	70.6	81.5	83.1
Single	13.1	23.2	20.8	19.1	12.3	12.1
Widowed	4.3	4.2	0.0	0.0	1.4	1.2
Divorced	12.2	12.7	12.5	9.4	4.8	3.6

Note: Numbers in columns may not add to 100 percent due to rounding.

Source: Survey results, computed by author; U.S. Commerce Department, Bureau of the Census, *Marital Status and Living Arrangements, 1991* (Washington, D.C.: Government Printing Office, 1992): 15; and U.S. Commerce Department, Bureau of the Census, Current Population Survey, March 1992, computed by author.

with higher income levels than their male counterparts; 54 percent of the women in the sample claimed over $100,000 of annual family income compared with 34 percent of the men.

About half the sample indicated they were white, married men with personal incomes over $50,000. And although it is not surprising to find that professionals in the United States are disproportionately comprised of white men earning considerable salaries, even when compared with others with Ph.D.s, the economics profession seems especially homogeneous. Among the entire U.S. population of people over 25 years of age and holding a doctorate, 35 percent were white men with incomes over $50,000 in 1991.[15]

Four out of five respondents indicated that they lived with at least one other adult, and 48 percent of the men and 38 percent of the women indicated that they lived with at least one child under the age of 17. There was one single (male) parent in the sample.

Women in the sample were on average only slightly younger than men. Almost two out of every three respondents had academic employment. As table 4.4 indicates, male economists are more likely to be in senior positions than are females. Among those with Ph.D.s, the average number of years since receiving their degree for men was 15.6 years and for women was 13.1 years, but the difference is not statistically significant. Further, among Ph.D. economists, women, on average, had spent more time at their

TABLE 4.4 *Presence of Full-Time, Senior, and Part-Time Men and Women Economists at Respondents' Workplaces*

	Mean Number	Median Number	Average Percent	Percentage with Zero (%)
Full-Time				
Men	18.9	12	83.1	1.6
Women	3.6	2	16.9	19.7
(n = 188)				
Senior*				
Men	14.5	8	87.6	3.0
Women	1.9	1	12.4	37.7
(n = 167)				
Part-time				
Men	2.0	0	34.4	54.1
Women	0.9	0	65.6	64.0
(n = 172)				

*In the case of academic employment, senior means having tenure.
Source: Survey results, computed by author, 1992.

jobs, with an average of 11.6 years at current jobs versus 10.0 years for men. Again, the difference is not statistically significant.

Table 4.4 presents the mean, median, and average percentage of full-time, senior, and part-time men and women economists present in respondents' workplaces. It also includes the percentage reporting no male and female full-time, senior, and part-time economists at their workplaces. The number of full-time economists in workplaces ranged from 0 to 500 with the median being 13 full-time economists. Overall, respondents' replies suggested that 17 percent of all full-time economists were female—16 percent in academia, 17 percent in government employment, and 21 percent in the private sector—slightly larger than the average of the number of women in this sample and the national average of women in academic workplaces. Forty-five percent of the respondents indicated no more than one full-time female economist in their workplace and 20 percent of the respondents said there were *none*. The more full-time economists present in a workplace, the more likely one of them would be a women. Among workplaces with more than five full-time economists, only 8 percent of respondents indicated there were no women.

Fifty percent of the sample indicated that there were eight or more senior economists in their workplace (in the case of academic work settings, a tenured professor was considered senior). Just over 37 percent of the respondents indicated there were no senior women economists in their department or agency, and an additional 30 percent reported one senior woman. Respondents indicated that their workplaces hired few part-time economists; however they were disproportionately women. Almost two-thirds responded that there were no female part-time economists in their workplace, but among those that did hire part-timers, one out of every three was female—twice their reported representation among full-time economists and about three times their representation among senior economists.

Three out of every five persons returning the survey indicated that their department or agency had hired a full-time, permanent economist in the last year. However, only about two-thirds of those had specific information concerning the number and gender of those interviewed and/or hired. Respondents were given space to answer questions about four separate hirings. With several respondents reporting multiple hirings, there were a total of 184 people hired, with four out of every five positions in academia.

Of all the applicants interviewed for jobs, respondents reported that 26.2 percent were female. This is higher than the total percentage of new female doctorates (20.3%) in economics that year.[16] Further, the respondents indicated a relatively high rate of females hired. Of those who indicated that they knew the results of their workplace's job search(es), 35.1 percent of all the initial offers went to women, whereas 30.1 percent of the jobs were filled by a woman. This is similar to the 31.8 percent of new female doctorates hired reported in 1992 by CSWEP using the AEA's Universal Academic Questionnaire.[17] Regression analysis indicates that having a higher percentage of full-time female economists in the workplace did significantly improve the likelihood of that workplace having a higher percentage of female candidates and new hires, but it did not matter if currently employed women were in senior positions.[18]

The results reported in the survey indicate a higher percentage of women were hired than their representation among new doctorates and than among their numbers in the hiring pool. This is positive news, but it should be interpreted cautiously. Respondents not active in a job search are less likely to know how many and what gender persons interviewed for a job were, so the responses to this question may not be as accurate as other responses (e.g., they are likely to know the outcome of a job search—i.e., the gender of person ultimately hired). But even if the responses were accurate, there is another reason why the percentage of women hired is high. The pool of new doctorates includes a very large and growing number of non-U.S. citizens with temporary visas—disproportionately male. United States–based employers are likely to prefer hiring economists who are U.S. citizens or non-U.S. citizens with permanent visas (because of discrimination against non-English speakers for teaching jobs and unwieldy immigration laws). Further, many of those with temporary visas are likely to remove themselves from the hiring pool for U.S.-based jobs, seeking (or returning to) jobs in their countries of origin. Women represent 35 percent of all 1991 doctorates who are U.S. citizens or non-U.S. citizens with a permanent visa.[19] In this case, then, women seeking U.S. jobs may not be overrepresented among new hires.

Three of every five respondents said that they usually teach economics courses, with the average number being four courses per year. Of those who did teach economics, 61 percent said they taught graduate students, with 18 percent only teaching graduate students in the last year. Over half of the total respondents in the sample taught courses in economics departments. Those teaching economics courses were asked to approximate the percentage of females in their classes in the last year they had taught. Table 4.5 summarizes the results. Respondents report relatively high numbers of women in their undergraduate economics courses, especially in introductory classes, with 86 percent indicating that at least one-third of their students were female. Fur-

TABLE 4.5   *Reported Percentages of Female Students in Economics Classes*

	Undergraduate Classes		Graduate Classes
	Intro	Other	
Less than 10 percent	4.8%	5.8%	11.9%
Between 10 percent and one-third	9.5%	32.6%	47.8%
Between one-third and 50 percent	77.9%	54.6%	40.3%
Over 50 percent	7.9%	7.0%	0.0%
Number responding	63	87	67

Note: Excludes one respondent who taught only women.
Source: Survey results, computed by author, 1992.

ther, 62 percent claimed that their other economics undergraduate courses had more than one-third female students, and 40 percent of those who taught graduate school said their classes were more than one-third female. These perceptions are consistent with percentages contained in the U.S. Department of Education's annual report on education statistics reported in table 3.3. Respondents indicate a sharp decline in the percentage of female students from their introductory to nonintroductory undergraduate level courses and then again from undergraduate to graduate level courses. This suggests that women, more so than men, find economics a less attractive field of study as they take more courses in it.

Finally, respondents were asked if their department had any course offerings that were primarily about women in the economy. Of the 125 respondents who teach, 25 indicated there is at least one such course in their department, 83 indicated there is not a course like this, and the rest did not know. Of those whose departments had such an offering, it was most often taught once a year. Six people indicated that more than one such course is offered in their department.

THE ECONOMIST'S STANDPOINT

The data collected from the survey present a profile of a profession blessed (or cursed?) with a very privileged set of characteristics in today's society. Almost 9 out of every 10 economists are male, the same proportion are white, and almost 60 percent are in family income brackets that put them among the richest 15 percent of the entire population.

Recent feminist literature on the development of science and knowledge suggests that one's location—or standpoint—in the realm of knowledge seeking matters greatly in the development of that knowledge. Feminists Nancy Hartsock and Sandra Harding have argued for almost a decade that the way science is conducted and knowledge is acquired is influenced by the knower's standpoint because the way one lives and acts in the world shapes the way one understands that world.[20] The social conditions of the profession and the social organization and atmosphere in which the development of knowledge in the profession takes place will be cast and directed by those professionals in it. In Sandra Harding's words:

> The starting point of standpoint theory—and its claim that is most often misread—is that in societies stratified by race, ethnicity, class, gender, sexuality, or some other such politics shaping the very structure of a society, the *activities* of those at the top both organize and set limits on what persons who perform such activities can understand about themselves and the world around them. . . . In contrast, the activities of those at the bottom of such social hierarchies can provide starting points for thought—for *everyone's* research and scholarship—from which humans' relations with each other and the natural world can become visible. This is because the experience and lives of marginalized peoples, as they understand them, provide particularly significant *problems to be explained* or research agendas.[21]

If dominant groups in society are the ones that mold theory and discourse about research, and the questions asked and answers given, then that knowledge will be predicated on that group's understanding and vision of the world.

When people who are not in the dominant group come in, they are afforded a peculiar, if not uneasy and contradictory status—what Patricia Hill Collins calls the "outsider within."[22] The outsider within has the potential to view the questions differently and present anomalies. Not unlike Thomas Kuhn's understanding of changes in sciences, the outsider can push the parameters of the paradigm or bring about a new set of ways to do what he calls "normal science."

If few outsiders are let in, then there is less likelihood that the prevailing institutions and knowledge will be questioned. Further, the lack of participation from a diverse group of people might serve to continually discourage others from entering, creating a feedback loop of continual underrepresentation. This implies that if people from nondominate groups entered and successfully raised different questions and employed alternative methods, the discipline would likely attract a more diverse group.

An example may be instructive. The main paradigm in economics, neoclassical economics, takes as its basic unit of analysis the individual and considers individual's interactions in markets where goods and services are purchased and produced as the primary economic activity that economists analyze. Many economists (some who call themselves feminists and some who do not) have long criticized this understanding of economic activity as being unnecessarily narrow. They argue that work in the home is also important economic activity and should be included in models of economic behavior. Further, feminists have directly questioned the primacy of the individual economic actor. They note that all people, at least at some point in their lives (especially the formative part), live in families and depend on some adult(s) for their livelihood. Acting individually and selfishly is *not* an appropriate assumption much of the time. If one takes instead the family as the unit of analysis, the methodology and outcomes change considerably.

One way to think about the impact a disproportionately white, male perspective on economics has would be to pose the following questions: What would the field of economics look like if it had been a female-dominated profession? Would it focus on the same questions, using the same methods, and arrive at the same conclusions? Hypothetical questions like these are impossible to answer. However, the gendered differences in some of the responses to the survey on the treatment of women in economics do suggest that women think about economic problems and solutions differently than do men. It is that part of the survey we turn to in the next chapter.

5

MARGINAL, AT BEST: ECONOMISTS' VIEWS ON FEMINISM AND WOMEN IN THE PROFESSION

This chapter and the one that follows present and discuss the findings from the survey concerning what "rank and file" economists think about women's participation and status in economics, the impact of feminism on economics, and the current and future status of feminism in economics. Those findings are:

- Almost universal agreement exists that feminism has had little or no impact on most aspects of economics. The exceptions include a perceived impact on the total number of women economists and in a few fields in economics.

- Economists have little desire to see more feminist economic analysis.

- Large and consistent gender gaps emerged in responses to survey questions regarding the treatment of women in the economics profession and the way gender is discussed in economic analyses.

69

- Despite the view that feminist economic analysis is not warmly welcomed, the vast majority of economists identify themselves as being sympathetic to the women's movement—much higher than the public in general. The majority agree that policies which promote child care, employment and training, and pay equity strategies would improve women's economic status.

- The majority of economists recognize a conflict in feminists studying economics at the graduate level, although they are split on how they think this conflict should be reconciled.

GREAT EXPECTATIONS?

I conducted a survey of a random sample of AEA members on their perceptions of the impact of feminism on economics because it would allow me to empirically test several hypotheses. Most fundamentally, I would be able to test my own perceptions that feminism's impact on economics was minimal. Beyond that, I was curious to see whether women economists perceived things differently than men did, and whether age, race, or type of employment (in the academic, government, private, or nonacademic sector) mattered in views on women, gender, and feminism in economics as standpoint theory (discussed in the previous chapter) would predict.

I expected a random sample of economists to agree that feminism's impact on most areas of economic study has been marginal. Given that the economics profession has not attracted or rewarded feminist analysis or even feminist-leaning men or women, there was little reason to believe a random sample of AEA members would openly welcome feminists or feminist analysis. Therefore, I also anticipated some hostility to suggestions about integrating feminists and feminist thought into economics.

However, I was much less certain of what the range of reactions to feminism in economics would be. The type of training economists receive, the recent challenges in the profession, and the personal changes this generation of economists has experienced make it hard to predict how rank and file economists might view feminism. Certainly the women's movement in the United States (and around the world) has affected many people's personal lives. Women's representation in the political, economic, and social realms has certainly improved over the last 40 years. Society's expectations of women have changed dramatically as well, even though the sexual division of unpaid labor has not. The women's movement in the United States has made an indelible mark on people's lives, their language about inclusion, and their views about women's capabilities—especially among professionals.

Neoclassically trained economists are the majority and dominate in graduate programs and economic journals, but there are a cadre of non-neoclassical economists, especially in liberal arts colleges. A small resurgence of less orthodox economic thinking in the profession—most notably Marxian, institutional, and post-Keynesian economics—has occurred since the 1970s. There are pockets of people, lodged mostly in liberal arts colleges but also clustered in specific graduate departments, interested in dissenting schools of thought. In addition, several journals are devoted primarily to developing nonorthodox economic thought.[1] Although certainly not powerful, the group of dissenters may indeed be larger than one might believe from reading articles published in the American Economic Association's three journals.[2] Even though these nonorthodox schools of thought are not necessarily feminist, they have taken feminist scholarship more seriously than those in the neoclassical mainstream (chapter 8 discusses the relationship between feminism and Marxism).

Even beyond those who use more heterodox methods, mainstream economics is in a period of theoretical fluctuation and doubt. The last 20 years of economic policy in the United States—both traditional neoclassical *and* Keynesian prescriptions—have seemingly failed to reinvigorate a stalled economy. Not surprisingly, this has led some economists to rethink their models. One indication of change in economics is the use of bargaining models to predict market outcomes instead of traditional neoclassical deductive models. Further, a rather substantial internal critique of neoclassical methodology and economics education is being waged by noted economists more aligned with the mainstream of the profession than with its alternative fringe.[3] It is possible, then, that the continued critiques offered by a growing number of disaffected, nonmainstream economists, including feminists, might resound with AEA members in the survey—those not, by and large, publishing in the top-ranked journals and teaching in graduate programs.

I expected women economists would be more interested in issues concerning women than men, but I was not sure if women would be more receptive to applying feminist approaches to economic analysis than their male counterparts. If most feminists or feminist-leaning women are effectively screened from economics because it offers so little to them or discourages them from studying it at higher levels, then women economists might be as hostile to feminism as are men. At the same time, women's experiences in the profession might have made them more aware of gender bias than when they first entered the profession and, as a result, more open to feminist approaches than men. Economics is hardly immune from the institutional and personal forms of discrimination that exist in many workplaces, notably sexual harassment and barriers to promotions. The more male-dominated the profession, the less likely it is to pay much attention to discrimination and have avenues of redress available. The personal can become political quickly, shaping one's view of the profession and perhaps even the approaches used in the field.

Finally, since feminism focuses on understanding differential treatment by gender, I expected that those men who were not in the dominant race or ethnicity might also be more sympathetic to feminism than white respondents. I did not have any preconceived hypothesis about whether type of employment (e.g. academic, government, or private sector) mattered in views toward feminism.

To test for potential differences in responses, I used ordered probit regressions on each response using the respondents' sex, age, type of employment, and race as explanatory variables (see table 5.1 for description of variables). Regression analysis is a standard empirical technique used by economists. For regression analysis, the researcher hypothesizes a relationship between a particular (dependent) variable and other (independent) variables that may help explain that outcome. A regression estimates whether or not the postulated independent variables actually provide a plausible explanation for the variation in the dependent variable. An ordered probit regression does the same thing as an ordinary regression and is used when the dependent variable has a small set of discrete, ordered values. The chi-square statistic indicates whether the variables taken together have explanatory power, and the t-statistic indicates whether each individual variable has significant explanatory power (i.e., if one can be 90%, 95%, or 99% sure that the coefficient of the variable is different from zero). As always, the usual precautions on interpreting regression results from survey data apply: some important variable(s) may be excluded and some survey answers may be influenced by how questions are posed.

Before proceeding with results of the survey, I should note that no definitions of the terms *feminism* and *economics* were included in the survey. Since there are many types of feminisms, just as there are many different types of economists and economic approaches, I chose not to impose my definitions of either on respondents. Although several respondents requested a definition of feminism or gave one themselves, I imagine that if I had provided a definition of feminism, an equal (if not greater) number of respondents would have disagreed with, corrected, or amended that definition.

TABLE 5.1 *Variable Description*

Independent Variable	Variable Definition
Male	Dummy variable; 1 = male, 0 = female
Age	Reported age of respondent
Private employment	Dummy variable for type of employer; 1 = nonacademic private employment, 0 for nonacademic government employer and academic employer
Government employment	Dummy variable for type of employer; 1 = nonacademic government employment, 0 for nonacademic private employer and academic employer
White	Dummy variable for race; 1 = white, not of Latino origin; 0 = Asian or Pacific Islander, Black, Latino, or Native American

About 40 percent of the survey questions referred explicitly to feminism or the women's movement; the other 60 percent included questions about the respondent's workplace, personal characteristics, or the degree to which the respondent agreed or disagreed with the ways economists explain certain economic phenomena.

What follows is a summary of the responses to five distinct parts of the survey: (1) the impact of feminism on specific areas of economics research and teaching; (2) the desire to see more published research on women and feminist concerns; (3) the treatment of women, gender, and feminism in economics; (4) the ability of certain policies to improve women's economic position; and (5) the role of feminism and the women's movement in the respondent's own life. In each case I present the distribution of answers, and, with the exception of the first set of summaries, I present the results from the ordered probit regressions.[4]

THE IMPACT OF FEMINISM ON ECONOMICS

Respondents were asked directly about their views on the impact of feminism on economics. The distribution of answers from those who responded can be found in table 5.2. The topic areas covered included economics (in general), neoclassical and non-neoclassical methodology, teaching and the economics curriculum, numbers and promotion of women in the profession, and a list of 15 fields of specialization chosen from the classifications for books and articles used in the *Journal of Economic Literature*, one of the three journals published by the AEA.

TABLE 5.2 *Percent Distribution of Responses to Survey Request:*
"Please check what kind of impact you think feminism has made on these areas of economics."

	Substantial Positive Impact (%)	Some Positive Impact (%)	Little or No Impact (%)	Some Negative Impact (%)	Substantial Negative Impact (%)	Don't Know (%)	Sample (N)
Economics, in general	1.0	24.9	51.7	2.4	0.0	20.1	209
Economics methodology							
Neoclassical economics methodology	1.0	4.8	69.7	1.9	0.0	22.6	208
Non-neoclassical methodology	1.4	17.8	45.7	3.9	0.5	30.8	208
Teaching and the curriculum							
Teaching of economics	3.3	24.9	45.0	2.9	1.0	23.0	209
Undergraduate economics curriculum	1.9	19.6	59.8	3.4	0.0	15.3	209
Graduate economics curriculum	0.5	15.4	64.4	1.5	0.5	17.9	208
Women in the economics profession							
Number of women undergraduates	14.4	52.2	20.1	1.0	0.0	12.4	209
Number of women graduate students	21.0	51.4	13.3	0.5	0.0	13.8	210
Number of women economists	14.3	55.2	18.1	0.5	0.0	11.9	210
Promotion and retention of women	11.0	55.0	19.1	1.5	0.0	13.4	209

TABLE 5.2 *continued*

Specific fields	Substantial Positive Impact (%)	Some Positive Impact (%)	Little or No Impact (%)	Some Negative Impact (%)	Substantial Negative Impact (%)	Don't Know (%)	Sample (N)
Labor market analysis	12.3	52.2	12.1	3.4	0.5	19.3	207
Household behavior & family economics	11.1	51.7	14.5	1.0	0.0	21.7	207
Health, welfare & education	7.2	48.8	19.1	2.4	0.0	22.5	209
Economic development	7.6	21.0	42.9	1.9	0.0	26.7	210
Data collection	3.4	25.0	46.2	1.0	0.0	24.5	208
Urban & regional economics	2.9	21.1	47.9	2.4	0.5	25.4	209
Economic history	1.4	21.5	48.3	2.4	0.0	26.3	209
Industrial relations	1.4	24.5	42.8	1.0	0.0	30.3	208
Game theory	1.9	1.4	69.9	0.5	0.0	26.3	209
International trade & finance	1.4	2.9	70.8	0.5	0.0	24.4	209
Economic growth	0.5	9.2	63.1	2.4	0.0	24.8	206
History of economic thought	1.0	8.1	61.7	1.0	1.5	26.8	209
Theory of the firm	0.5	5.3	72.3	0.5	0.5	21.0	209
Analysis of collective decision making	0.0	17.8	52.9	0.5	0.0	28.9	208
Fiscal theory & policy	0.0	10.1	64.6	1.0	0.0	24.4	209

N = Number responding

Respondents indicated the largest positive impact of feminism has been on the number of women in the economics discipline and in three specific fields within economics (labor market analysis; household behavior and family economics; and health, welfare and education), with anywhere from 56 to 69 percent indicating a positive impact. The perceived impact of feminism on these three fields of specialization should come as no surprise, since they are where women are most visible as economic agents. Further, these are the areas in which women economists are more likely to specialize. There were no other topics in which a majority of the sample felt feminism had a positive impact.

Between 25 and 30 percent of the sample indicated there has been a positive impact on economics in general, the teaching of economics, the undergraduate curriculum, and in five specific fields (economic development, data collection, urban and regional planning, economic history, and industrial relations). In all other cases, less than 20 percent of the sample indicated any positive impact, a smaller percentage than those who indicated they did not know what the impact was. Few saw much positive impact on the graduate curriculum, economics methodology (especially neoclassical economics), or half of the fields listed.

There seems to be considerable agreement among respondents concerning feminism's impact. For each of the 25 topics listed in table 5.2, not one of ordered probit regressions had significant explanatory power (as measured by the chi-square on the regression at or below the 10% level), indicating that the responses of women were generally not statistically different from men's, nor were whites' responses different from those who were not white. Age and type of employment did not seem to influence the distribution of answers either.[5] The coefficient on the male dummy had a significant t-statistic (at the 10% level) in only two equations: men were more likely to reply there was a positive impact on neoclassical economics than women and less likely to think there was a positive impact on the number of graduate students than were women.[6] The t-statistic on the coefficient of the age variable was significant in three responses in this section—the impact of feminism on neoclassical economics, theory of the firm, and international trade and finance. With a positive coefficient, the older the respondent the more likely he or she was to think there was a positive impact in these areas.[7] Only two other variables had significant coefficients: those in private employment, compared with those in academia or government, thought there was less of an impact of feminism in non-neoclassical methods, and those in government employment were more likely to see a positive impact in the graduate economics curriculum than were those in academia or the private sector.

WOMEN'S ISSUES IN ECONOMIC JOURNALS

In an attempt to explore the importance of research on topics concerning women, children, and families and of feminist perspectives in economics research, respondents were given a list of 11 topics and asked whether they thought each should receive more, less, or the same amount of attention as they currently do in the major economic journals. Further, the question specified no new journal space would be forthcoming; therefore, an answer indicating more attention would imply a decrease in other topics covered.

To gauge the current allocation of journal space devoted to the areas listed in the survey, the titles of the journal articles listed in English in the March 1991 issue of the *Journal of Economic Literature* were examined. This examination indicated that about 100 (or 4.4%) of the approximately 2,250 journal articles addressed any of the 11 topics.[8] To get a more accurate account of the contents of the articles, a careful reading of the abstracts found that 3.7 percent (22 of 590) of the abstracted articles focused on gender or gender differences, fertility, or dependent care. At least by this measure, currently very little attention is paid to these 11 topics. Nor did these articles appear to be particularly feminist; very few articles on the 11 topics were in economics journals that explicitly welcome feminist contributions.[9]

Yana van der Meulen Rodgers found similar results in her search for articles on gender in the major economics journals between 1984 and 1994. Of the two most widely read journals plus the five top-ranked journals, she found that 1.3 percent of the articles pertained to gender topics. Labor and development journals had considerably more, 16.2 percent and 4.7 percent, respectively.[10]

Table 5.3 depicts the distribution of all responses and the results of ordered probit regressions for each of the article topic areas. With the exception of two topics (the economic well-being and care of children, and changes in family structure and poverty), the majority of respondents *do not* want more attention paid to the list of 11 areas. In most areas, the majority preferred the same attention. In two topic areas, more than 20 percent of the sample indicated they thought less attention should be paid in journals. Those two areas are women's economic history and feminist contributions to economics. Over one-third (36%) of respondents indicated less time should be allocated to feminist contributions. Since there is almost no attention paid to feminist perspectives on economic issues in the major economic journals currently (as one respondent penned in next to her response "How could

TABLE 5.3   *Percentage Distribution and Ordered Probit Regression Results for Responses to Survey Request: "For each area listed below and assuming no new journal space, indicate if you believe it should receive more attention (implying a decrease in research published in other topics), the same attention, or less attention than currently received in the major economics journals."*

	Distribution of responses		
	More Attention (%)	*Same Attention (%)*	*Less Attention (%)*
1. The economic well-being and care of children	60.4	36.0	3.6
2. Changes in family structure & poverty	56.0	40.5	3.5
3. Women's labor force participation and occupational structure	34.9	58.5	6.7
4. The impact of fiscal and monetary policies on women and family structure	32.6	49.2	18.1
5. The allocation of time in the household	21.1	53.9	14.0
6. The measurement of women's contribution to economic output	30.8	53.5	15.7
7. The economic status of minority women	30.5	54.5	15.0
8. Wage discrimination by gender	27.9	59.9	12.2
9. Women's contribution to the development of economic thought	25.0	56.1	18.9
10. Women's economic history	21.6	49.0	29.4
11. Feminist perspectives on economic analysis	18.6	45.3	15.9

Notes: Percentage may not add up to 100 percent because of rounding. For ordered probit regressions, the responses were given values as follows: 1 for less attention, 2 for same attention, and 3 for more attention.

there be less than zero attention?"), this response suggests substantial resistance to publishing feminist perspectives on economic analysis.

Unlike the perceptions of feminism's impact on economics, ordered probit regressions on each of the 11 equations concerning attention in journals indicated some significant differences in responses—particularly by gender. The explanatory power of the entire regression equation was significant (at

TABLE 5.3   *continued*

			Ordered Probit Results				
			Independent Variables				
Sample N	Male	Age	Private Employer	Government Employer	White	Chi-2	Regression N
197	−.2299 (.2781)	−.0116 (.0082)	−.1088 (.2261)	.3486 (.2884)	−.3971 (2.993)	7.37	191
200	.0270 (.2636)	−.0014 (.0008)	.1081 (.2273)	.6288** (.2986)	−.0079 (.2713)	4.81	193
197	−.7715*** (.2714)	.0103 (.0080)	−.1954 (.2234)	.2574 (.2791)	−.2422 (.2643)	13.08**	189
193	−.7246*** (.2586)	.0007 (.0076)	−.2350 (.2145)	−.1475 (.2660)	−.5496** (.2739)	13.64**	186
193	−.0462 (.2474)	.0005 (.0078)	−.3710* (.2136)	−.1814 (.2637)	.1255 (.2691)	3.25	187
198	−.5016** (.2530)	.0032 (.0077)	−.3561 (.2155)	.1476 (.2561)	−.6263** (.2647)	14.51**	191
200	−.5129** (.2518)	.0054 (.0076)	−.2616 (.2138)	.1569 (.2512)	−.4706* (.2604)	10.73*	193
197	−.5185** (.2554)	.0050 (.0077)	−.2172 (.2179)	.0918 (.2635)	−.3749 (.2611)	8.18	191
196	−.4061 (.2538)	.0142* (.0077)	−.3363 (.2170)	.1075 (.2555)	−.5331** (.2592)	13.09**	189
197	−.5327** (.2481)	.0045 (.0078)	−.4755** (.2176)	−.1852 (.2501)	−.1613 (.2563)	10.21*	190
192	−.2399 (.2503)	.0053 (.0078)	−.3727 (.2233)	−.0150 (.2499)	.0473 (.2555)	4.03	182

Notes: *Significant at 10 percent level
           **Significant at 5 percent level
           ***Significant at 1 percent level for a two-tailed test. Standard errors are given in parenthesis.
           N = Number of responses.

or below the 10% level) in 6 of the 11 responses. In 6 of the 11 regressions, the coefficient on the male dummy was significantly negative. Men are much less interested than women in having more attention paid to the following topics: women's labor force participation and occupational structure, the impact of fiscal and monetary policies on women and family structure, the measurement of women's contribution to economic output, the economic status of minority women, wage discrimination, and women's economic history. In four of the ordered probit regressions, the coefficient on the race dummy was also significant, indicating that white respondents are less likely than nonwhite respondents to want to see more attention paid to the impact of fiscal and monetary policies on women and family structure, the economic status of minority women, and women's contribution to economic thought.

There is much less consistency in explaining variations in responses by age or type of employment. The older the respondent, the more he or she wanted to see more attention paid to women's contribution to economic thought. Those in government employment were more likely, compared with those in academic and private workplaces, to want to see more journal attention to articles on changes in family structure and poverty. Respondents in private employment (compared with their academic counterparts) were more likely to indicate they wanted less attention in journals paid to the allocation of time in the household and women's economic history.

ECONOMISTS ON WOMEN IN THE ECONOMY, ECONOMIC THEORY, THE PROFESSION, AND FEMINISM

The survey included a set of 14 positions about women and the economy, gender in economic theory, women in the economics profession, and feminism in economics. Respondents were asked to indicate whether they agreed with (strongly or somewhat), disagreed with (strongly or somewhat), or had no opinion on each of the positions. A numbered list of the positions with the total distribution of responses and the results of ordered probit regressions for each can be found in table 5.4. The regression model was able to explain the variation in responses to a significant degree (at or below the 10% level as measured by the chi-square statistic) in five cases. However, the coefficient on men's responses was significantly different (at or below the 10% level) from that of women's in 9 of the 14 statements.

Positions 1 to 4 relate to economic outcomes of women in the labor market. Despite the rather mainstream interpretation that discrimination is eroded by markets over time, the majority of economists agreed that women face wage discrimination. Further, 40 percent did not think that over time the market would eliminate discrimination. In the ordered probit regressions, the coefficient on the sex dummy was significant in positions 1, 2, and 4—with women disagreeing more than men that business and government policies have accommodated women's entry into the labor force and that the market will eventually eliminate the gender wage gap. Women were much more likely than men to agree with the statement that women face wage discrimination.

Positions 5, 6, and 7 address some of the ways in which economists have modeled gender differences. Although a large percentage of the AEA sample seemingly adheres to the mainstream neoclassical interpretations of women's wages and household work, once again men and women have different distributions of responses with the coefficient on the sex dummy being significant (at the 10% level and below) in all three cases. Many in the sample recognized the importance of gender distinctions in economic analysis, with close to 60 percent disagreeing with the statement that gender distinctions are usually unnecessary in economic analysis. As indicated by responses elsewhere in this survey (position 14 below, notably), however, most do not look to feminist perspectives to shed light on those distinctions.

As to the economics profession and women's place in it, men and women again differ sharply in their perceptions. Statements 8, 9, and 10 pertain to men's and women's attraction to and success in the economics profession. Almost one-third of the male respondents agreed with the statement that it is easier for women to get tenure and promotions than it is for men, but less than 4 percent of the female respondents did. Similarly, 26 percent of the men in the sample agreed that relative to the number of women in the economics profession, women are proportionately represented in the prestigious positions in the field, whereas less than 4 percent of the women agreed they are. Although the distribution of the responses of men and women did not differ significantly, just under half of the women and 35 percent of the men agreed with the statement that economics was a more attractive profession for men to enter than it is for women.

The results on positions 11, 12, and 13 are consistent with earlier ones on the impact of feminism on economics. Very few surveyed indicated there is a distinct feminist approach to economics, that feminism has had much impact on economics when compared with other social sciences, or that feminist analysis has been incorporated into mainstream economic theory over the last 20 years. And as before, very few significant differences emerged in the distribution of those surveyed by sex, age, type of employment, or race. White respondents were more likely than nonwhite respondents to think that there is a distinctly feminist approach in economics. Those in government employment, compared with their academic counterparts, were more likely to disagree with the statement that feminist analysis has been incorporated into mainstream economic theory.

Responses to position 14 indicate the reluctance of economists to accept feminist economics. Less than one-third of the respondents agreed with the

TABLE 5.4 *Percentage Distribution and Ordered Probit Regression Results for Responses to Survey Request: "Please indicate if you agree or disagree with the position stated below."*

	Distribution of responses				
	Strongly Agree (%)	*Somewhat Agree (%)*	*Somewhat Disagree (%)*	*Strongly Disagree (%)*	*No Opinion (%)*
1. Businesses & government policies changed as a result of women's increased labor force participation over the last forty years	30.1	57.3	8.0	1.4	3.3
2. Women face substantial wage discrimination	22.2	44.8	21.2	9.4	2.4
3. Occupational segregation explains much of women's wage gap	21.4	48.1	18.1	6.2	6.2
4. Over time, the market will eliminate women's wage gap with men	15.0	39.0	26.8	16.9	2.3
5. To the degree that the rational economic behavior assumption of utility maximization applies to men, it equally applies to women	60.4	25.9	6.1	3.3	4.3
6. "New household economics," developed by the Chicago school, provides a useful framework for analyzing economic relationships between men and women	12.4	35.2	9.5	9.1	33.8
7. Gender distinctions are usually unnecessary in economic analysis	11.9	25.2	35.2	23.3	4.3
8. The economics profession is more attractive for men to enter than it is for women	12.8	24.2	24.2	14.7	24.2
9. In economics, it is easier for women to get tenure and promotions than it is for men	8.5	20.9	25.1	24.6	20.9
10. Relative to the number of women in the economics profession, women are proportionately represented in prestigious positions in the field	5.2	17.5	32.6	31.6	13.2
11. There is a distinct feminist approach to economic problems	2.8	10.4	26.5	30.8	29.4
12. Feminism has had a larger impact on economics than on other social sciences	1.0	4.8	22.5	47.4	24.4
13. Over the last 20 years, feminist analysis has been incorporated into mainstream economic theory	0.0	4.8	28.2	44.5	22.5
14. Mainstream economics would be enriched if it incorporated more feminist analysis	6.2	25.2	22.9	25.7	20.0

Notes: Percentage may not add up to 100 percent because of rounding. For ordered probit regressions, the responses were given values as follows: 1 for strongly disagree, 2 for somewhat disagree, 3 for somewhat agree and 4 for strongly agree.

TABLE 5.4   *continued*

| | | | *Ordered Probit Results* | | | | |
| | | | *Independent Variables* | | | | |

Sample N	Male	Age	Private Employer	Government Employer	White	Chi-2	Regression N
213	.5794** (.2428)	−.0002 (.0075)	.1290 (.2104)	.1514 (.2599)	.0250 (.2590)	6.32	199
212	−.4067* (.2294)	−.0024 (.0072)	−.0991 (.1981)	−.0859 (.2357)	−.1293 (.2491)	4.05	199
210	−.1971 (.2299)	−.0062 (.0073)	−.2930 (.2067)	−.2178 (.2579)	.5544** (.2509)	7.74	190
213	.8201*** (.2325)	−.0012 (.0070)	.1644 (.1970)	.2070 (.2473)	.1473 (.2414)	13.87**	200
212	.4535* (.2496)	−.0050 (.0081)	.3517 (.2343)	.0962 (.2789)	−.1038 (.2843)	5.60	195
210	.6136** (.2972)	.0247** (.0092)	.1507 (.2499)	.2214 (.3690)	−.0963 (.2748)	11.15**	136
210	.4356* (.2348)	.0083 (.0072)	.2270 (.1997)	.0914 (.2489)	−.0066 (.2469)	7.03	193
211	−.1808 (.2619)	−.0123 (.0080)	−.3728 (.2343)	.0918 (.2707)	−.1154 (.2573)	7.40	155
211	1.5133*** (.3012)	−.0144* (.0083)	.3854 (.2439)	−.0518 (.2825)	−.0051 (.2624)	33.20***	160
212	.6350** (.2535)	−.0053 (.0074)	.1295 (.2181)	−.5168* (.2915)	−.2352 (.2572)	12.96**	177
211	−.0906 (.2865)	−.0059 (.0082)	.0225 (.2378)	−.1429 (.3118)	.6683** (.3137)	5.57	144
209	.1686 (.3210)	.0137 (.0088)	.0409 (.2432)	−.1809 (.3261)	.4673 (.3261)	5.51	155
209	.2969 (.2966)	.0123 (.0088)	.2092 (.2458)	−.6826** (.3394)	.0517 (.3058)	9.84*	158
209	−.5416** (.2602)	.0131 (.0078)	−.1971 (.2150)	.0325 (.3031)	−.3375 (.2837)	9.03	162

Notes: *Significant at 10 percent level
**Significant at 5 percent level
***Significant at 1 percent level for a two-tailed test. Standard errors are given in parentheses.
N = Number of responses

TABLE 5.5 *Percentage Distribution of Responses to Survey Request: "Please indicate if you agree or disagree that the policies below improve women's economic position."*

	Distribution of responses				
	Strongly Agree (%)	Somewhat Agree (%)	Somewhat Disagree (%)	Strongly Disagree (%)	No Opinion (%)
Employment and training programs	37.6	45.2	9.1	1.9	6.2
Universal health coverage	36.0	34.1	14.1	8.1	7.6
Paid parental leave	30.3	40.9	13.9	8.7	6.3
Equal pay for comparable work	29.8	16.1	13.0	17.3	3.9
Subsidized child care	29.7	47.2	12.3	7.1	3.8
Child-care tax credits	29.2	54.0	8.1	2.9	5.7
Affirmative action	25.7	47.1	11.4	11.0	4.8
Child allowance	20.4	35.6	19.0	10.9	14.2
Higher AFDC benefit levels	14.5	30.4	22.7	19.8	12.6

Notes: Percentage may not add up to 100 percent because of rounding. For ordered probit regressions, the responses were given values as follows: 1 for strongly disagree, 2 for somewhat disagree, 3 for somewhat agree and 4 for strongly agree.

Source: Survey results, by author, 1992.

statement that mainstream economics would be enriched if it were to incorporate more feminist analysis. Women were more likely to agree with that statement than men (46% versus 29%), which is reflected in the significant coefficient on the sex dummy in the ordered probit regression.

POLICIES TO IMPROVE WOMEN'S ECONOMIC STATUS

Respondents were given a list of nine policies that have been part of a feminist economic agenda over the last 20 years and asked whether they agreed

TABLE 5.5 *continued*

Sample N	Male	Age	Private Employer	Government Employer	White	Chi-2	Regression N
			Ordered Probit Results				
			Independent Variables				
210	−.4116	.0064	.0142	.3217	−.4602*	7.60	190
	(.2562)	(.0075)	(.2137)	(.2721)	(.2658)		
211	−.5330**	.0081	−.4046*	−.2615	−.0993	9.69*	187
	(.2475)	(.0075)	(.2087)	(.2509)	(.2547)		
208	−.0557	−.0131***	−.7111***	−.3192	−.1111	17.29***	188
	(.2470)	(.0073)	(.2074)	(.2540)	(.2559)		
208	−.3954	.0056	.0711	.0207	−.3468	4.81	192
	(.2523)	(.0072)	(.2031)	(.2470)	(.2507)		
212	−.2341	−.0062	−.4708**	−.4037*	.0728	8.79	191
	(.2346)	(.0072)	(.2038)	(.2428)	(.2565)		
209	−.2808	−.0054	−.0772	−.1075	−.1828	2.71	190
	(.2507)	(.0076)	(.2107)	(.2574)	(.2657)		
210	−.1969	.0056	−.2281	.3559	−.5993**	10.76*	192
	(.2381)	(.0072)	(.2092)	(.2600)	(.2605)		
211	−.0653	−.0027	−.5317**	−.2796	.1431	7.06	174
	(.2435)	(.0075)	(.2122)	(.2592)	(.2577)		
207	−.1518	.0021	−.6358**	−.3919	.3249	10.82*	174
	(.2506)	(.0075)	(.2156)	(.2602)	(.2650)		

Notes: *Significant at 10 percent level

**Significant at 5 percent level

***Significant at 1 percent level for a two-tailed test. Standard errors are given in parentheses.

N = Number of responses

(strongly or somewhat) or disagreed (strongly or somewhat) that each policy would improve women's economic position. The distribution and ordered probit regression on these responses are found in table 5.5. A majority of respondents agreed that all but one of these policies would improve women's economic status. The one exception was the policy of increasing AFDC (Aid to Families with Dependent Children) benefit levels.

The largest percentage of respondents indicated agreement with a policy of improving women's economic status via training and education, a view consistent with human capital theory. However, high percentages of AEA members also agreed that women's economic standing would be improved with a variety of policies that economists have often characterized as ineffective because of their blatant interference with market mechanisms. For example, close to two out of every three persons agreed that comparable worth is a policy that would help women's economic status, a surprising finding since there is a strong neoclassical critique against this policy. Similarly, 73 percent of those responding agreed that affirmative action policies improve women's economic position. The sample clearly ties women's economic fortunes to policies directed toward children. Close to 30 percent of the sample strongly agreed that paid parental leave, subsidized child care, and child-care tax credits would improve the economic position of women, and less than 23 percent disagreed.

Although women were more likely than men to agree that each policy listed improved women's economic status, the coefficient on the sex variable in the ordered probit regression was significant in only one case—universal health coverage. Once adjusting for race, type of employment, and age, men's and women's views are not significantly different from each other. In this set of responses only one variable consistently turns up as being significant. Those in private, nonacademic employment are significantly less likely to agree that universal health coverage, paid parental leave, subsidized child care, child allowances, or increases in AFDC benefits will improve women's economic status than those in government or academic employment—holding constant the age, race, and sex of those respondents. These results possibly suggest that those who think that government policies are not very effective in promoting gender equality are less likely to be in government or academic jobs.

Race shows up as a significant explanatory variable in the distribution of answers in the case of questions concerning affirmative action and employment and training programs. In both cases, whites are less likely to think these policies help women's economic status than are people of color. Age is only a significant factor in one policy prescription—paid parental leave, with older respondents being less likely to find it improves women's economic status than younger respondents. Finally, government employment explains very little in terms of variation among responses except in the case of subsidized child care; those in government employment indicated they were less likely than those in private or academic employment to think subsidized child care was an effective policy in improving women's economic status.

PERCEPTIONS OF THE WOMEN'S MOVEMENT

The last set of quantitative responses focused on a set of nine statements; seven taken from national surveys about the role of the women's movement in people's lives and two questions gauging the degree to which the respondent considered himself or herself a feminist or sympathetic to the goals of the women's movement. Respondents were asked whether they agreed with (strongly or somewhat), disagreed with (strongly or somewhat), or had no opinion on each statement. The percentage distribution and results from ordered probit regressions are included in table 5.6.

What is most striking about the responses to this set of questions is the degree to which respondents claim to support the goals of the women's movement and agree with its claims of improving women's and men's lives. For a profession that clearly is uneasy with feminist analysis, the separation of the personal from the professional is remarkable. Three-fourths of the sample said they agree with the statement that they were sympathetic to the goals of the feminist movement and that the women's movement has made women's lives better now than they were 20 years ago. Close to two-thirds agreed that the United States continues to need a strong women's movement. Over half agreed that the women's movement had made men's lives better. A full third of the sample agreed with the statement "I consider myself a feminist." Three out of four respondents disagreed with the statement that women and minorities have the same opportunities to advance in American business as white males.

In six of the nine statements, the coefficient on the gender variable was significant in the ordered probit regressions. Men were more likely than women to agree that women and minorities have the same opportunities for advancement as do white males. But women were more likely than men to agree that the women's movement had bettered both men's and women's lives generally, bettered their own life, was still a necessary component for achieving changes to benefit women, and to personally identify as a feminist. Women in the sample were much more likely to recognize the benefits of feminism to themselves and to women than were men. Men's and women's responses did not differ significantly from each other, however, on the two questions concerning the toll of success for men and women or in their degree of sympathy with the goals of the women's movement.

Age made very little difference in the responses. In only two instances were older respondents less likely to agree with statements. Fewer older recipients felt that men's lives had benefited from the women's movement, and older respondents were less likely to agree with the statement "I consider myself a feminist." Racial differences in responses were significant in three of the statements, with whites less likely than nonwhites to agree with the statements concerning sacrificing personal and family life for the sake of

TABLE 5.6   *Mean Responses by Gender and Age to Survey Request: "Please indicate whether you agree or disagree with the following statements."*

	Distribution of responses				
	Strongly Agree (%)	Somewhat Agree (%)	Somewhat Disagree (%)	Strongly Disagree (%)	No Opinion (%)
1. Women and minorities have the same opportunities to advance in American business as white males.	6.2	18.1	37.4	36.0	2.4
2. Women who have successful careers end up sacrificing too much of their family and personal life.	8.5	39.2	24.5	13.7	14.2
3. Men who have successful careers end up sacrificing too much of their family and personal life.	9.0	38.2	27.8	12.7	12.3
4. Changes brought about by the women's movement have made *women's* lives better than they were 20 years ago.	14.8	60.5	11.9	3.3	9.5
5. Changes brought about by the women's movement have made *men's* lives better than they were 20 years ago.	8.5	47.4	23.2	3.8	17.1
6. Women's organizations have done something that has made my life better.	10.1	34.5	19.1	11.0	25.4
7. The United States continues to need a strong women's movement to push for change that will benefit women.	19.4	46.5	13.7	12.3	8.1
8. I am sympathetic to the goals of the women's movement.	22.8	53.1	10.9	5.2	8.6
9. I consider myself a feminist.	11.4	25.6	18.5	21.8	22.8

Notes: Percentage may not add up to 100 percent because of rounding. For ordered probit regressions, the responses were given values as follows: 1 for strongly disagree, 2 for somewhat disagree, 3 for somewhat agree and 4 for strongly agree.

Source: Survey results 1992, by author.

successful careers. White respondents were also less likely to agree with the statement about being sympathetic to the women's movement than were people of color.

How do the responses of the random sample of AEA members stack up to the rest of the population? Table 5.7 compares responses to seven of those positions in this sample to responses (from three separate surveys), to the

TABLE 5.6 *continued*

| | | | *Ordered Probit Results* | | | | |
| | | | *Independent Variables* | | | | |
Sample *N*	*Male*	*Age*	*Private* *Employer*	*Government* *Employer*	*White*	*Chi-2*	*Regression* *N*
211	.4068* (.2377)	−.0019 (.0073)	.1667 (.2018)	−.1942 (.2479)	.2253 (.2551)	6.02	199
212	.0583 (.2409)	−.0040 (.0075)	.3269 (.2153)	.0117 (.2425)	−.5734** (.2575)	6.66	178
212	.3402 (.2410)	−.0064 (.0073)	.2127 (.2097)	−.0325 (.2474)	−.4707* (.2552)	6.84	182
210	−.5968** (.2580)	−.0118 (.0080)	.0353 (.2164)	−.1861 (.2676)	−.0422 (.2761)	8.31	185
211	−.5940** (.2694)	−.0145* (.0083)	−.0313 (.2181)	.2068 (.2719)	−.2154 (.2965)	11.19**	170
209	−.8527*** (.2641)	.0107 (.0082)	−.1183 (.2307)	.1631 (.2825)	−.2360 (.2849)	15.21***	151
211	−.7890*** (.2562)	−.0064 (.0074)	−.1543 (.2051)	.2116 (.2538)	−.3483 (.2650)	15.22***	187
211	.1467 (.2484)	.0078 (.0074)	.0459 (.2094)	.0387 (.2468)	−.4735* (.2749)	4.43	186
211	−.6321** (.2471)	−.0143* (.0082)	−.4332* (.2280)	−.0567 (.2704)	.2276 (.2197)	14.42**	155

Notes: *Significant at 10 percent level

**Significant at 5 percent level

***Significant at 1 percent level for a two-tailed test. Standard errors are given in parentheses.

N = Number of responses

same—or very closely worded—questions. The sample of AEA members appears to be much more sympathetic to the women's movement and more optimistic about mixing career and family than the population at large. Much larger percentages in the AEA sample than the *New York Times* and Gallup poll samples think that changes resulting from the women's movement have benefited men and women and think the United States needs a strong

TABLE 5.7   *Responses in the AEA Sample, 1992 Versus Recent Surveys Concerning the Women's Movement*

	AEA Sample Percentage Who Agree (%)		Other Surveys Percentage Who Agree (%)	
	Women	Men	Women	Men
1. Women and minorities have the same opportunities to advance in American business as white males.	10.7	26.2	44*	
2. Women who have successful careers end up sacrificing too much of their family and personal life.	46.4	47.8	69	69**
3. Men who have successful careers end up sacrificing too much of their family and personal life.	35.7	48.9	68	64**
4. Changes brought about by the women's movement have made *women's* lives better than they were 20 years ago.	88.9	73.2	53	55**
5. Changes brought about by the women's movement have made *men's* lives better than they were 20 years ago.	71.4	53.6	36	36**
6. Women's organizations have done something that has made my life better.	81.5	39.0	25	15***
7. The United States continues to need a strong women's movement to push for change that will benefit women.	82.5	63.4	67	51***

Notes: *This is the percentage of executives who agreed with this statement, from a Harris poll survey of 502 executives from the *Business Week* top 1000 corporations. *Index to International Public Opinion, 1989–90,* (Westport, Conn.: Greenwood Press, 1990):529.

**A national Gallup poll: *The Gallup Poll, 1990,* Wilmington, Del., Scholarly Resources, 1991 (Interview date 12/89):12–13. For questions 2 and 3 above, the Gallop poll question was phrased "Do you think the changes brought about by the women's movement have made women's/men's lives easier or harder than they were twenty years ago?" The percentages above are for those who responded "easier."

***A national *New York Times* survey, E. J. Dionne, "Struggle for Work and Family Fueling Women's Movement." *New York Times,* 22 August 1989, 1, A18.

women's movement; a smaller percentage agreed that men and women have to sacrifice too much of their personal and family lives to pursue successful careers, and that women and minorities have the same opportunities in business as white men.

CONCLUSION

In many ways the survey points to considerable resistance to feminist analysis in economics while at the same time points to a group of people largely committed to women's equality generally. Most in the survey thought that feminism has made little impact—positive or negative—on economics generally, and in neoclassical economics (the prevailing methodology) in particular, yet respondents consistently responded that they did not necessarily think this was a problem. Only 5 percent agreed with the statement that feminism has been incorporated into mainstream economic theory, but less than one-third agreed that mainstream economics would be enriched by incorporating more feminist analysis. Seven out of ten respondents indicated that feminism had made no or little impact on neoclassical economics, yet 80 percent wanted to see the same or less attention to feminist perspectives on economic analysis. Curiously, only 37 percent thought that gender distinctions were usually unnecessary in economics, suggesting some understanding that gender matters, but only 12 percent indicated they thought there was a distinctly feminist approach to economic problems.

At the same time, the sample indicated immense receptivity to the women's movement and women's equality generally. Three out of every four persons responding to the survey agreed that they were sympathetic to the goals of the women's movement, and over half agreed that the United States continues to need a strong women's movement. Further, the majority of respondents agreed that policies like comparable worth, affirmative action, and paid parental leave would improve women's economic status. This is notable in a profession in which policy prescriptions often warn against direct government intervention in markets.

Even though economists generally appear to have little desire to see more feminist analysis, there are indications of some sharp divides. Large and consistent gender gaps emerged in responses to survey questions regarding the treatment of women in the economics profession and the way gender is discussed in economic analysis. Although men's and women's answers were similarly distributed on their opinions on feminism's impact in economics, the similarity stops there. Responses to statements concerning women's successes in the labor market, women's ability to succeed in the economics profession, the theoretical building blocks of gender analysis in the neoclassical framework, the importance of gender distinctions in economic analysis, and the potential for feminist economic analysis, indicate significant gender differences in the distribution of responses. Other differences did appear but not as often or consistently as gender differences.

Together these results point to a tension between economists' liberal views toward one of feminism's goals—women's equality—and the reluctance to see feminism brought into economics itself. That tension was revealed even more strongly in the qualitative responses—the subject of the next chapter.

6

"CHECK FEMINIST BELIEFS AT THE DOOR": THE INCOMPATIBILITY OF FEMINISM AND ECONOMICS?

Several of the responses to the AEA survey questions indicated substantial resistance to feminist analysis in economics. But it was the written responses to the only open-ended question in the survey that provided a nuanced and deeper sense of the uneasy relationship between feminism and economics.[1] This chapter is devoted to a discussion of those responses.

Respondents were presented with the following hypothetical situation and question: "Assume for a moment that you teach economics and one of your best undergraduate students is an ardent feminist who wants to pursue economics at the graduate level. What advice would you give her or him?" The question was phrased to allow all respondents to answer regardless of where he or she worked or what rank he or she held in the profession. Unlike other questions in the survey, this one asked respondents to attach a real face to a feminist and posed the polemic of feminist as economist. This fictional person was not just any feminist, but one who wants to study economics in graduate school—the training ground for the discipline. Eighty-three percent of the 213 respondents wrote something in response to the question about advice to a young feminist. Those not responding to this question were spread evenly across age, gender, race, and type of employment.[2]

I grouped the advice given into five distinct categories with only a few responses left over that did not fit into any category. The categories and groupings along with the percentage of responses broken down by sex are contained in table 6.1. The five groupings can be aggregated into just two broad types of responses: one in which the student's feminism seem to make no difference in the type of advice offered and one in which the respondent recognized that the student's feminism would present some problems, conflicts, or incompatibilities in studying graduate-level economics.

The categories were culled from repeated reading of the responses but, as is the case with survey coding, some responses just simply did not clearly

TABLE 6.1   *Categorical Answers to Question: "Assume for a moment that you teach economics and one of your best undergraduate students is an ardent feminist who wants to pursue economics at the graduate level. What advice would you give her or him?"*

Response category	Total (%) (N)	Female (%) (N)	Male (%) (N)
I. No reference to student's feminism, advise to continue			
1. Go for it	40.1 (71)	21.7 (5)	43.4 (66)
2. Take more math	9.0 (16)	13.0 (3)	8.4 (13)
Subtotal	49.1	34.7	51.2
II. Student's feminism will present some problem in studying graduate economics			
3. Hard, but do it anyway	18.6 (33)	39.1 (9)	15.6 (24)
4. Do it, but be selective	8.5 (15)	13.0 (3)	7.8 (12)
5. Feminists won't make good economists	15.8 (28)	13.0 (3)	16.2 (25)
Subtotal	42.9	65.1	39.6
III. 6. Miscellaneous, nec	8.1 (14)	0.0 (0)	8.9 (14)
Total	100 (177)	100 (23)	100 (154)

Note: Totals do not add up to 100.0% due to rounding.
Source: AEA Survey, by author.
N = Number responding.

fit together with any other subset of responses (hence the miscellaneous category), and some longer responses fit into several categories (I placed each of these into what seemed to be the most important advice given). In addition, a few comments were difficult to interpret and hence difficult to categorize. For example, was the person who simply wrote "Good luck" being sarcastic or sincere? If the tone was sarcastic, did this remark imply graduate school would be hard or that the student shouldn't bother at all? In cases that required more interpretation, I looked for some guidance from the respondent's comments at the end of the survey (if present). But clearly, categorization and interpretation of the results are subjective and some other researcher might find different patterns or emphasis. Nonetheless, I found a distinct pattern of responses emerge that provides insights into how "rank and file" members of the profession view feminists as economists.

FEMINISM DOESN'T MATTER

By far, the most popular response was to tell the student to simply go ahead. Many literally told the student to "go for it," as plainly as the Nike shoe commercials do. Two out of every five persons responding at all to this question gave the green light, with very little other advice to the young feminist. Other typical comments in this category included: "work hard," "strive for excellence," "same advice as I'd give anyone," or "do good work and it will be recognized anywhere." Many suggested the student apply to the best schools (some mentioned particular schools ranked in the top six) and to pursue any goals that made him or her happy.

The "go for it" response was particularly popular among male respondents, with 43 percent of men responding in this fashion compared with 19 percent of the women. Answers in this category were typically quick and uncritical. The respondent did not pass judgment on the student's beliefs or capabilities, the profession, or the training economists receive. Although it is difficult to know what meaning to bring to the set of responses in this category, they clearly represent more than a nonresponse. If the person filling out the survey merely had wanted to move through the survey quickly, he or she would have not bothered to write anything in this space. A possible interpretation is that some respondents did not want to come across as seeming "antifeminist." A brief word of encouragement would serve that end. This interpretation is consistent with the responses such as "fine with me" and "go for it, I have no problem," almost as if the respondent were giving his or her approval.

To see if there was any pattern of those responding with a simple "go for it" and their own self-identification as a feminist, I compared the responses by category to the responses to the statement "I consider myself a feminist," which appeared later in the survey. Table 6.2 contains that cross tabulation. Almost half of those who gave the "go for it" advice disagreed with that statement (46.5%). This is a somewhat higher percentage of the entire sample that disagreed with the statement "I consider myself a feminist."

Just under 10 percent of those responding had one primary piece of advice: Take math. Graduate economics, regardless of the program, requires students to be familiar with modeling and econometrics. Therefore, a sophisticated knowledge of and comfort with math is a precursor for studying economics successfully, regardless of one's interest or orientation. As such, it is impossible to know if this response was generated by an assumption that feminists (or women) would know less math than nonfeminist women (or men), or if the respondent would actually advise *any* student going to graduate school to get the necessary math skills. The tabulations in table 6.2 suggest that this response was much more likely to be given by those who considered themselves feminist than those who did not.

The responses "go for it" and "take more math" together account for about half of the total responses, although only one-third of all the female responses. These two responses made no reference to the student's feminism. Several even explicitly stated their advice was universally applicable (one response included, "the same advice I'd give an ardent anti-feminist"). This type of written advice suggests that these respondents find no reason that a

TABLE 6.2 *Categorical Responses to Hypothetical Graduate Student Question by Response to Statement in Questionnaire: "I consider myself a feminist."* *

	Agree (%) (N)	Disagree (%) (N)	Don't Know (%) (N)
Total Sample	36.9 (78)	39.3 (85)	22.8 (48)
Go for it	29.6 (21)	46.5 (33)	23.9 (17)
Take more math	53.3 (8)	26.7 (4)	20.0 (3)
Hard, but do it	66.7 (22)	24.2 (8)	9.1 (3)
Be selective	47.7 (7)	33.3 (5)	20.0 (3)
Don't be an economist	14.3 (4)	57.1 (16)	28.6 (8)
Miscellaneous	28.6 (4)	35.7 (5)	35.7 (5)
No response	34.3 (11)	40.0 (14)	21.7 (9)

*Only includes those who responded to the statement "I consider myself a feminist."
N = Number responding.

feminist should not consider studying economics as long as she or he has the requisite skills and desire. The student should find the best school possible and get down to hard work.

FEMINISM MATTERS

The rest of the respondents, however, felt quite differently. Just under 43 percent responding referred to the student's feminism as cause for concern when studying economics. These respondents indicated that the scenario posed in the question was going to be problematic if the student didn't take certain precautions. In short, "feminist" and "graduate student in economics" in the same sentence sent out some red flags. The advice on resolving the uneasy combination varied considerably, from shoring up on mainstream theory to being the best critic one could be, from holding on to one's goals (even if it meant not doing any feminist work until after tenure) to studying sociology instead of economics, from picking schools in which nonmainstream approaches are taught and/or where there are other known feminists to "coming out" as a feminist only after finishing graduate work. Nearly two-thirds of the women respondents' advice was of this nature, versus 40 percent of the men's responses.

Among the responses that refer to the uneasy relationship of feminism and economics, three distinct patterns of advice emerged. One set of responses (categorized in table 6.1 as "Hard, but do it anyway") expressed leeriness but encouraged the student to pursue economics. In this category, the respondent usually, although not always, encouraged the student to keep his or her feminism in tact while studying economics and becoming an economist. A second category of responses ("Do it, but be selective") advised the student (usually guardedly) to go on in economics but included some advice that would help the student find a "safe harbor" for his or her feminism. Some advised the student to study particular fields (ones which women are more likely to be in), to go to particular schools (ones known for their heterodox programs), or to find a particular mentor. The third category of responses in this grouping (labeled "Feminists won't make good economists" in table 6.1) urged the student to drop her or his feminism if she or he were going to succeed as an economist, or to study something else entirely. Responses in the first two categories were often more critical of the profession, whereas those in the latter group were more critical of the feminist.

Almost one out of every five of those responding to this question fell into the "hard but do it" category. They thought the student should pursue further studies in economics but suggested she or he would likely have a difficult time in graduate school because the student's feminism would clash with how graduate school in economics was conducted. The gender gap was large for this category of responses; close to 40 percent of the female respondents' answers fell into this category versus about 16 percent of the male respondents. Further, two-thirds of those who responded in this fashion considered themselves feminists—higher than in any other category of advice.

Some of the answers that most clearly refer to the problems a feminist in economics would face include:

- To be aware that most of the economics profession is at best indifferent to, and at worst hostile to, feminism in its political and methodological dimensions.

- Go ahead but recognize that your philosophical position may often clash with the mainstream of the profession.

- She must be patient because at the top 30 schools she would have to wait until she reached her dissertation stage to fully pursue her interests.

- Get the highest quality training available and be prepared to fight for your perspective.

- Realize that most graduate school faculty are white males who are antagonistic or at least highly suspicious of feminist theory. As such, choose a school sympathetic to your concerns.

- Encouragement, with a caution that the atmosphere in most U.S. graduate programs will be hostile ideologically.

- To do what you want, be ready to expect some resistance and discrimination but stand up and resist it.

Graduate studies in economics is a difficult place for many students, not only feminists. Certainly, many students who enter their studies with a set of goals that include understanding contemporary economic policy and events or concern over the maldistribution of income and wealth in market economies would soon become disillusioned. Graduate studies in economics is much more theoretical than applied—leaving many "real world" phenomena unexplored. Certainly, responses like the following two could be given to a variety of students, not just feminists. However, they did assume that feminism has a political as well as an intellectual project that would be difficult to maintain in economics graduate studies.

- Go to a school where there are sympathetic faculty members and/or tenured women professors. Maintain a sense of your personal goals in studying economics. They are easily lost in the arduous task of graduate studies.

- Emphasize that technical expertise is almost universally valued throughout the profession, but at the expense of ideology, and often ideas. A Ph.D. in economics is hardly the best means of achieving social change.

As one respondent noted: "Go for it if you really want to be an economist, but be warned that gender issues and feminist approaches are considered 'fringe,' not 'mainstream' by many in the profession. It's more like being a pioneer than being an outcast, but it's not the same as if one simply pursues compatible general equilibrium models." In short, feminism is one of many "fringe" studies in economics—not found in economics departments without a search.

Indeed, not only was feminism considered fringe to some; another respondent suggested that just being a woman who has ideas of her own might present a problem. She offered the following advice: "Basically the same as a male: 1. If you are interested and have the background. Go ahead; 2. Be careful to select a committee with whom you are personally compatible, but the differences for a women: watch for misogynists—they are out there; be very deferential in manner, but not substance, to older males."

Several respondents wanted to encourage the student but wanted the student to know that she or he would be facing an enormously difficult task. One researcher wrote, "If she/he wants to challenge the conventional economic paradigms with a feminist paradigm, she/he must be committed and focused because it takes a special person to want to run uphill all day." One respondent even turned the tables when he commented at the end of his survey; "The profession needs to address in its basic theory, in addition to empirical work, the humanistic concerns that are associated with feminism. The economics profession needs to change. Arrogance and narrow perspectives have no place in science."

Another group of respondents had very specific advice for the student—as if to help guide the student away from the land mines that might explode in the student's face while navigating through graduate school in economics as a feminist. Several respondents steered the student to a handful of graduate programs well known for their programs in non-neoclassical approaches, such as University of Massachusetts-Amherst, Notre Dame, University of California-Riverside, and The New School. Several people suggested going to a school where there were interdisciplinary opportunities or a clear support system. A few respondents suggested particular fields to study, such as labor or development economics, because there are more women economists in these fields and the specific role that gender plays receives more attention in the literature in these fields. The advice clearly conveyed the lack of support that the hypothetical student would find.

The last group of answers in this category indicates the extreme conflict some perceive between being a feminist and studying graduate-level economics. Close to 16 percent of those who responded to this question indicated that economics has little room for feminists (category called "Feminists won't make good economists"). Several of these respondents consider economics as a "positive" science that is objective and tries to remain as value-free as possible. For them, feminism is much too biased a position to allow for rigorous, objective graduate studies in economics. This group of respondents had a variety of recommendations: forget economics altogether, stop being a feminist in order to study economics, or study economics with the understanding that objective study would dissuade the student of feminist bias. Some of the comments in this category included:

- The pursuit of scientific knowledge should be gender blind most of the time (i.e., check feminist beliefs at the door).

- Don't let your ideology cloud your academic research.

- Feminism has no place in any scientific discipline. I don't believe the economics profession is sexist.

- Think of nothing less than a Ph.D. Aim at the top 10–15 departments. Don't think of yourself as pursuing feminist economics, think of arming yourself with rigorous analytical tools, not "soft" philosophies. A feminist economist will be a bad economist. A good, well-trained economist will best serve women's interests.

- If you want to pursue feminism, specifically in academia, economics isn't the place.

- Do not let feminist concerns impede your learning—rather, let the economic analysis/tools you learn help you address the questions that interest you most, including women's/gender issues.

Also included were a set of curt and even hostile responses such as: "Be a sociologist"; "Study economics, not feminism"; "Pursue economics and cool it on your prejudices"; "Won't be able to make a career out of being a feminist"; "Don't be like this survey and identify yourself with a label. Be a thinker, not a feminist"; and "Chill out." Not surprisingly, over half of those with this type of response do not consider themselves feminists.

Finally, a small set of answers did not fit into any of the categories above ("Miscellaneous, nec" in table 6.1). The answers in this category included three responses that politely signaled total ignorance of the issues the student might be facing; one response discussed the ability of women to get hired in economics; two stated they saw no connection; one recommended the student teach in a business school; and one said he doesn't advise any student to go to graduate school in economics. Those with answers that were hard to categorize also had the highest percentage of respondents who did not know if they considered themselves feminists.

CONCLUSION

About half of those who wrote down their thoughts encouraged, usually enthusiastically, their hypothetical best student to pursue economics as long as that is what she or he wanted to do and had the right skills to do well. A generous interpretation of this response is that being an ardent feminist makes no or little difference. Getting into the best of schools and taking lots of math comes through as the most consistent advice in this group of respondents.

Regardless of the tone or specific advice, over 40 percent of responses recognized the mismatch between feminism and economics. The incompatibility surfaced in many ways, from the utter disdain of feminism in economics, to the more sympathetic suggestions of suppressing feminist beliefs until it was safe, to the older and wiser approach of "As you learn more economics, you will be challenged to reconcile economic theory and feminist positions." For 43 percent of those responding, the advice to a young feminist is not straightforward: a full 15 percent find feminism and economics to be incompatible, some arguing that feminists will lack objectivity in her (or his) studies.

As in many other parts of this survey, there were distinct gender gaps. Women tended to give much fuller advice than men did and that advice was much more likely to recognize difficulties that feminists might face.

In thinking about my own advice to feminists who ask me about studying economics, I often do exactly what those in this survey did: I warn students about the narrowness of economics and its hostility toward feminists and feminist ideas, and I tell students they need to know math and steer them toward those schools in which there are feminist and nonorthodox economists.

But what would a young feminist consider good advice? In my notes on this survey I found one answer to that question. I hired a bright undergraduate student in the summer of 1992 to help me tabulate results from the survey. She had just graduated as a double major in sociology and women's studies. Although she had never been the least bit interested in studying economics at the graduate level, she was an "ardent feminist," exceptionally bright and likely to do graduate work at some time. She helped type up and categorize the written responses in the survey and often included handwritten reactions to the comments. Next to one comment she penned: "This, I think, is the best, supportive response. Perhaps the *only* feminist response in the lot." Her sensibilities seem worth reporting here. It was the advice of a 32-year-old female assistant professor, who said:

> Learn the tools, etc., so you'll be at least as competent as everyone else. Just because not everyone agrees with your politics doesn't mean you'll have to change. And even though many of your classmates decry the word "feminist," many of them really are. And the ones who aren't? Don't let 'em get you down, they don't understand how the world works. Hook up with a professor (full, preferably) who'll support you; this helps a lot. And keep in touch!

III

FEMINISM AND ECONOMIC THEORY

7

THE INVISIBLE HAND'S
STRANGLEHOLD:
NEOCLASSICAL
ECONOMICS AND
FEMINISM

> Marital patterns have major implications for, among other things, the number of births and population growth, labor-force participation of women, inequality in income, ability, and other characteristics among families, genetical natural selection of different characteristics over time, and the allocation of leisure and other household resources. Therefore, the neglect of marriage by economists is either a major oversight or persuasive evidence of the limited scope of economic analysis.
>
> —Gary Becker[1]

The preceding quote was written in 1973 by University of Chicago economist Gary Becker—father of the modern-day neoclassical "new household economics." Becker is primarily responsible for bringing women into modern neoclassical economic analysis. His work on women and marriage is recognized throughout the profession and was part of the reason the Royal Swedish Academy of Sciences awarded him a Nobel Prize in economics in 1992. But Becker's treatment of women and marriage plagues most feminist economists because it provides a rationalization of women's unequal economic status rather than an explanation for it. Becker's work serves as the starting point in understanding the lack of progress feminism has made in mainstream economic analysis since the beginning of the modern-day feminist movement.

On the surface, Becker's declaration in the preceding quote is both brash and insightful. Although Becker refers specifically to an economic analysis of marriage, he is in effect discussing the relationship between men and women *as they interact in families*—both inside and outside the home. If we take Becker at his word, he opens the economist's door to exploring the economics of the household as an important, vital, and compulsory sphere of economic activity.[2] Becker's work on marriage and the household was developed in the early 1970s concurrent with the rise of the modern-day women's movement. Before then, most economic theories made women and their specific economic contributions invisible or subject to an entirely different set of theoretical underpinnings than those used in explaining market economic phenomena.

Although feminist claims have grown and developed in the economics discipline as a whole, neoclassical economics remains stubbornly resistant to feminist insights and critique. Feminist economic theory has not and probably will not develop very far within this framework because of two major impediments. First, most feminists argue that women's unequal status has something to do with past discrimination that continues to persist. Neoclassical economics largely denies the long-term existence of discrimination. Second, and perhaps more important, neoclassical methodology, which posits an objective truth that can be theoretically modeled and empirically substantiated, finds feminist analysis too subjective to appropriately explore economic questions.[3]

To twist one of neoclassical economics' most popular metaphors, the theory's invisible hand has kept a very tight grip—if not a stranglehold—on the credibility of feminist explanations of women's unequal status in the marketplace of economic ideas. Further, the theory's adherence to positivist methodology means feminists are unlikely to see much hand-holding—invisible or otherwise—in the future. The claim here is *not* that the majority of those who practice neoclassical (or any other) economics are particularly antifeminist (although in my experience I can say that at least some are).

Indeed, as the survey results presented in earlier chapters indicate, as a group, economists hold rather liberal positions concerning women's equality compared with the population as a whole. Rather, and consistent with survey results, there is an incompatibility of neoclassical economic theory and feminism, despite inroads and important contributions made by feminist economists and feminist analysis over the last several decades.

THE NEOCLASSICAL MODEL: A BRIEF OVERVIEW

Although many identify Adam Smith as the "father" of modern neoclassical economics, Smith (along with David Ricardo and Karl Marx) was considered a classical political economist.[4] Classical political economists dealt with a broader arena of topics than many modern-day neoclassical economists are comfortable with and were distinctly "normative" in their approach to the production and reproduction (i.e., growth) of societies. Despite being more widely interested in both the production and reproduction of people and material resources, classical political economic thinkers applied sharp distinctions to analysis of the marketplace and analysis of the home. The "private/public" split is most obvious in Smith's own writing. His magnum opus, *The Wealth of Nations*, dealt with exchange and manufacturing. But Smith had another great work, *The Theory of Moral Sentiments*, which laid out his notion of what home life should be. It was not guided by the invisible hand.

The more appropriate patriarchs of modern neoclassical economic discourse include Carl Menger from Austria, William Stanley Jevons from Britain, and the French economist Leon Walras who simultaneously in the 1870s developed general equilibrium models of price determination—the current mainstay of neoclassical economic analysis. Their work represented a sharp break with the classical political economists. History of economic thought specialist Mark Blaug depicts the change in focus as: "After two centuries of being concerned with the growth of resources and the rise of wants, economics after 1870 became largely a study of the principles that govern the efficient allocation of resources when both resources and wants are given."[5] This (then new) brand of economics used utilitarian theory and differential calculus while borrowing tools and terminology from the burgeoning field of the physics of energy. Calculus and physics made economics a real "science," not unlike the natural sciences of the times.[6] The resurrection of this so-called "marginalist revolution" some one hundred years later is what is broadly referred to today as neoclassical economics. Marginalist economics came to the United States in the 1910s and 1920s but only became the centerpiece of economics analysis in the post–World War II period—coming of age primarily in the 1970s (Keynesian economics usurped marginal analysis in the 1940s). The University of Chicago is among the most prominent theory-building neoclassical economics departments in the country.

Neoclassical economics begins with a simple, flexible model of individual behavior and ends up with the well-behaved sets of supply and demand curves well known to every introductory economics student. The importance of the supply and demand curves is that their intersection (called equilibrium) provides a unique market price and quantity for every good and service in an economy. Equilibrium, and the process by which markets get there, ultimately explains the entire allocation of limited resources through market production. The unique market equilibrium price and quantity are stable and represent the market-clearing price where individual consumers' and producers' desires (for maximizing consumption and profits) are simultaneously satisfied (see figure 7.1).

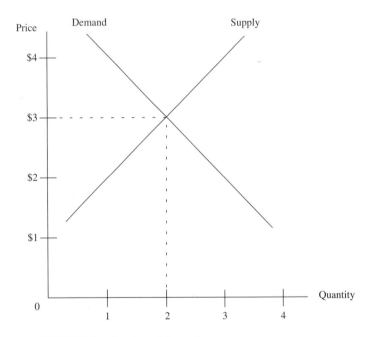

FIGURE 7.1.   *Supply and demand curves.*

Neoclassical economics takes its unit of analysis (the individual), its underlying behavior principles (rational choice), and concept of value (utility) from the utilitarians of the nineteenth century. In the neoclassical model, individuals engage in only two types of activities: consumption and production. All personal interactions are reduced to those involving exchanges and contracts mediated through the competitive marketplace. Individual behavior is based on a particular understanding of rationality within the context of a set of constraints. Those constraints—such as income, personal and inherited endowments, custom, and personal preferences—are taken as given (i.e., exogenously determined) and are usually of little interest to neoclassical economists.

What gives goods and services their value—that is, marketability—in neoclassical economics is the utility received from the consumption of each additional unit of the good or service. In the neoclassical model, then, individual consumers act to maximize both the relative and absolute utility they derive from the consumption of a variety of goods and services. Consumers make choices based on their own, predetermined tastes and preferences and are constrained by their own ability to purchase commodities (i.e., their income).

Individual consumers are assumed to act "rationally." That is, they know what they want and are consistent in their tastes and preferences. Individuals' preferences are not affected by how others maximize their utility, and having more of a good or service is better than having less. In this rational choice model, all individual consumers are self-interested. Each acts voluntarily to please himself or herself only. All are equipped with perfect (or at least equal) information about prices of goods and services so as to be able to make rational choices.

The production of goods and services for markets are understood and analyzed in the same way as consumption. Producers act in their own self-interest and have complete information about input and output prices and the level of existing technology. Instead of maximizing utility, producers maximize profits. For this model to work there must be many producers and consumers of goods and service, so that no individual can control either the market price or quantity.

The calculus of neoclassical economics emerges when solving the utility and profit maximization problems subject to income and technological constraints and in determining the changed bundle of goods and services desired and produced when prices, income, technology, or preferences shift.

Supply and demand curves are derived from the behavior ascribed to individual producers and consumers and a set of economic "laws." The first law states that any additional consumption generates more utility (i.e., more is better than less) but less *additional* (or marginal) utility than previous consumption. The second law is similar: adding more inputs to production will increase output, but after some point, as long as one of the inputs is fixed, additional output will fall. In economics textbooks the first law is referred to as the law of diminishing marginal utility, and the second is the law of diminishing marginal returns.

Economics textbooks, equipped with a depiction of rational behavior and the laws of diminishing marginal returns and marginal utility, tell the neoclassical economics "story" of supply and demand—or the allocation of goods and services through the marketplace. All points on the supply curve represent profit-maximizing output levels, just as every point on the demand curve corresponds to a range of utility-maximizing possibilities. It is only where supply meets demand that provides the best possible allocation solution. At this point—equilibrium, where the quantity demanded equals the quantity supplied—there is no reason for either individual firms or producers to change their behavior (i.e., equilibrium is a stable state).[7]

Equilibrium has other desirable qualities besides ensuring that individuals get what they are willing to pay for and individual firms make a profit. With many buyers and producers, there are benefits to the economy as a whole. Firms will make sure they employ workers in the most efficient way (in this case efficient is most output per worker), to reduce their costs relative to other producers of the same good. If they don't, someone will "invent the better mousetrap," make more profits, and either drive others out of business or make them produce more efficiently. The lure of profits keeps producers on a constant search for new and cheaper input markets, improved technology, better production processes, and new and better products. The solution is also efficient in the sense that no one person can be made better off without making someone else worse off.

Any change to equilibrium—which must be caused by some external (exogenous) force—will set the whole maximizing process in motion again. But, left unfettered, individual markets will always move toward equilibrium over time. Indeed, neoclassical economics goes further to claim *all* markets will end up in equilibrium as long as prices vary freely and consumers are rational.

Relying exclusively on the metaphor of the market,[8] neoclassical economists resolve some of the most important issues in economics: what gives things their value (their utility) and how scarce resources are allocated (through price mechanism). Goods that are in high demand will command a higher price than goods and services that are not. The remarkably simple and appealing supply and demand model can be used to explain the production and consumption of virtually all goods and services, including inputs (like land, labor, and capital) as well as a host of outputs. Even those things which we often don't think of as being allocated in markets, like religion, suicide, or fertility, can and have been modeled by neoclassical economists.[9]

To work smoothly, the neoclassical model enlists a host of assumptions. Often, those who first hear about this model have a hard time accepting the initial assumptions. Equal (although not necessarily complete) access to information, the existence of a large number of firms in a market, and the homogeneity of goods and services are assumptions that are hard to swallow. Neoclassical economics has been remarkably flexible in relaxing these assumptions, but it still ends up with similar results. Neoclassical theories of monopolistic behavior and contract theories have all taken on the challenge of making the assumptions and some of the predictions of the model more realistic. Indeed, much of the progress and development in neoclassical theory has occurred in undertaking these challenges. A good example is neoclassical economic explanations of unemployment. Since all markets tend toward equilibrium, including the labor market, the neoclassical model would predict zero unemployment. Clearly, substantial unemployment has always existed. Integrating this rather obvious "fact" with a model that also argues for equilibrium in the labor market has stimulated a large literature on search theory and employment contracts. Search theory argues that information about jobs and workers is not costless, which results in some unemployment. Efficiency wage theory argues that employers will pay a little above the market wage as a screening and retention device, which improves efficiency but also generates unemployment. In a similar vein, theories of transaction costs have developed to accommodate the lack of complete information, whereas recent work on asymmetric markets has tried to model exchanges when information is unequal between buyers and sellers.

There are still, however, a few basic assumptions of the theory that are usually not so easily relaxed. One of those is the important assumption that rational choice guides individual's behavior. Another aspect of neoclassical economics that has remained a mainstay is the method of addressing economic questions: posit rational individual behavior, apply marginal analysis to build a model, and then test the model empirically often using large data sets. Neoclassical economics claims to not attach value judgments to individual's preferences and adheres to a belief that behavior can be modeled— regardless of the realism of the assumptions—and then tested with data.

The allure of neoclassical economics is its conclusions: the human activities of self-interested utility and profit maximization result in efficient and stable levels of economic activity. Resources are used to produce the most output possible, while generating maximum welfare. Unless outside forces come to alter the situations, equilibrium will reign. There are no internal forces to push the model out of balance. All this is accomplished by the metaphorical meeting of many consumers and producers in the marketplace.

NEOCLASSICAL ECONOMICS' ANTIFEMINISM

Mainstream economic analysis is antifeminist in at least two ways. The first is its explanations of women's unequal status relative to men, accepted by many neoclassical economists. At the most basic level, neoclassical reasoning claims that women's inequality is freely and rationally chosen by women themselves. This conclusion stems from the model's focus on individuals' rational choice behavior, which largely ignores the different sets of constraints—that is, the dynamic set of historical and institutional settings—under which men and women operate. In this way neoclassical economic explanations of women's unequal status serve to justify and preserve that status. The second (and not unrelated) reason is that neoclassical economic methodology precludes much of feminist theorizing. Neoclassical epistemology is predicated on a notion of objectivity that argues to be value-free. Feminism and feminists are by definition "too political" to be objective. Neoclassical economists argue that their approach is superior to other economic approaches in large part because it does not articulate explicit values (such as feminism) and relies on testable hypotheses of observed phenomena—that is, it is science. Further, its insistence on starting with individual maximization as the building block for human nature rejects feminists' analyses that focus on the ways institutions reproduce inequality and do not use a model of individual rational behavior. Let's look more closely at both in turn.

Neoclassical Explanations of Women's Economic Status

Neoclassical economics claims to be gender (and race) blind. The basic economic actor is commonly referred to as *homo economicus* (economic man), though most using this term are quick to point out that "man" is used only in a generic sense. All consumers act rationally. All producers maximize profit.

Explanations of wages and investment in one's self apply equally to women, people of color, those with physical or mental disabilities, gays and lesbians, and those whose parents are rich or poor. Further, employers and employees are seen as having equal footing. In this sense, the neoclassical approach is very much in keeping with its liberal (nineteenth-century variety) roots and appealing to at least one strand of feminism—liberal feminism.

Although neoclassical economic theory may be gender, race, and class blind, few contest that economic outcomes are. In the case of women, there are two pronounced "gendered" economic outcomes: women's low wages compared with men's and the sexual division of labor in the household.[10] A look at how neoclassical economists have explained these two outcomes reveals their antifeminist nature. It does not really matter where the story about women's wages and the sexual division of labor begins, since the two are interrelated. I begin with wage differential theories because historically these explanations preceded the development of neoclassical explanations of the household division of labor.

Women's Lower Wages   Neoclassical economists have long been aware of wage differentials (see box 7.1 for neoclassical determination of wages). Indeed, explaining the ways in which certain people with particular physical characteristics—like race and sex—face differential labor market outcomes has become an important motivator in the development of neoclassical economic wage theory and the expansion of neoclassical economics into areas of analysis that many economists previously dared not to venture—namely, discussions of race, gender, and household labor. In the development of modern economic theory, wage differential discussions were motivated by the civil rights movement.

The best-known early attempt to model wage differentials by a modern neoclassical economist was by Gary Becker in the mid-1950s. He turned his 1955 Ph.D. dissertation ("Discrimination in the Market Place") into a book entitled *The Economics of Discrimination*.[11] As Becker explains, "It was my first attempt to apply the economic approach to a problem outside of the conventional fields of economics, and was greeted with indifference or hostility by the overwhelming majority of the economics profession."[12] Becker's book was intended to understand racial wage differentials (he does acknowledges that his approach to discrimination is equally applicable to racial, religious, ethnic, age, or gender differences).[13]

Becker's first stab at explaining wage differentials presupposes the existence of discrimination as the primary reason for wage differences. Discrim-

BOX 7.1   Wage Determination in the Neoclassical Model

Wages are determined in the labor market. Labor is an input to production, and as with all input markets, individual firms become the consumers while individuals are the suppliers; but maximizing behavior still holds. Individuals choose how much labor to supply based on their preferences for income and unpaid time. Until relatively recently, economists referred to this trade-off as the "labor-leisure" trade-off. Feminists have successfully called attention to the fact that for many women (and increasingly men), the trade-off is between income-producing and non-income-producing (unpaid) activities. Now most economists refer to people's decision for market-based goods and services (i.e., purchased with income received from wages) versus home-produced goods and services.

Individuals decide how much time they are willing to allocate to the labor market based on: (1) their own work preferences (i.e., taste for work) and (2) the wage rate (i.e., the price of labor). Workers maximize their utility subject to their income, which is determined by their total wages and access to other forms of income. The price of every hour not in the paid labor force is the wage rate (i.e., the cost of not working). When the wage rate goes up, the price of not working rises, because every hour spent at home instead of at work reduces income by the hourly wage rate.

The model argues that when the price of any good goes up, a consumer will want less of it. So too with home-based work. When wages rise, the cost of staying home goes up—reducing the demand for it and simultaneously increasing the amount of market labor supplied. Economists refer to this as the substitution effect. However, as the wage rate goes up, so does one's income for any set amount of hours worked. Depending on your preferences, it is easy to imagine working less when the wage rate goes up, because now less work buys the same amount of goods and services. Working fewer hours as wages go up is referred to as the income effect. If the income effect overrides the substitution effect (and there is no way of theoretically knowing, since it depends on tastes and preferences), the supply curve becomes what economists call "backward bending."[1]

The demand for labor is based on firms' profit-maximizing behavior, the cost of inputs, and the level of technology. At any given level of technology and fixed level of inputs other than labor, a firm's demand for workers will be derived from the demand for the firm's product. In the simplest case, the model assumes that a firm can sell all it wants at the going market price, since no one firm is big enough to influence the total supply of goods and affect the market price. A firm will always maximize profit and produce the amount where the additional (marginal) cost of producing a product is equal to the additional (marginal) revenue. The marginal revenue will be the price of the product—that is, the revenue received for selling one more unit of the product. In a competitive situation, where no firm can control the supply, marginal revenue *is* the

---

[1]If part of the supply curve looks like a demand curve, this generates the insurmountable problem of the possibility of no or more than one equilibrium. To cope, economists usually assume that the income effect is not very strong.

market price. Typically, economists assume that in the short run, labor is the only variable cost, so the marginal cost (the additional cost of producing one more unit of output) is equal to the wage rate (the price of labor) divided by the marginal product of labor. For example, if hair stylists get paid $10.00 per hour and work at a rate of two haircuts per hour, the marginal cost of a haircut to a hair salon is $5.00.

A firm will be willing to hire a worker (i.e., its demand for labor) when the wage rate is just equal to the value of the additional output that the last worker produces. If the wage rate is less than the value of the output produced, the firm will increase its profits by continuing to hire more workers (assuming the firm can sell the entire product). As it hires more workers, the law of diminishing returns sets in and the marginal product decreases. The firm will hire workers only up until the point where the wage rate divided by the price of the firm's goods is equal to the marginal product. Therefore, the demand for labor will be downward sloping; as the wage increases, firms are willing to hire fewer workers.

The wage rate will be determined by the intersection of the supply and demand curve. Workers will be offered amounts they are willing to work for while firms will be profit maximizing. Importantly, it is always true that the wage adjusted for prices (i.e., what economists call the real wage) will be equal to the marginal productivity of workers at that level of employment, regardless of the level of the actual equilibrium wage.

ination occurs when two equally qualified people are treated differently in economic transactions based solely on some individual characteristic. In the neoclassical model, discrimination expresses itself in market interactions as individual tastes and preferences. Becker posited that individual consumers, workers, and/or employers with a taste for discrimination will translate those preferences into their demand for goods as well as the supply and demand for labor. Consumers who discriminate will prefer not to buy items that are made by certain workers or sold by certain store owners. When these preferences are generalized, they result in lower profit margins for products produced or sold by the group being discriminated against. If a large number of individuals discriminate, for example, against blacks—then black workers and/or black store owners will receive lower wages or profits.

When employers have a taste for discrimination, they incur psychic costs when hiring workers they don't like. Therefore, they are willing to pay a premium for hiring other workers instead. In the case of women, when employers discriminate, women will either be crowded out of some parts of the labor market altogether or forced to accept a lower wage (to compensate the employer's psychic cost) than others doing the same job. When employees discriminate, they will only work in firms that do not hire the people they have a distaste for. In this type of discrimination, wage differentials will not result, but there should be segregated workplaces.

Becker's primary motivation was to integrate a notion of discrimination into the neoclassical model of rational behavior. However, as critics soon pointed out, if there are competitive forces in the economy, the neoclassical model predicts that wage differences due to discrimination should disappear. If just one employer without a taste for discrimination exists, he or she will be able to hire from the discriminated group at lower wages—at least in the short run—and make more profits than discriminating employers. As more employers realize there are profits to be made by not discriminating, more will enter the market and drive discriminators out of business. Discrimination by employers, in the neoclassical model, cannot exist for long if employees are truly equally qualified. In Kenneth Arrow's words, neoclassical economics "predicts the absence of the phenomena it was designed to explain."[14] In fact, the market works to *erode* discrimination, not maintain it.

Despite the rather convincing critique of Becker's theory of discrimination (so convincing Becker himself accepted it), neoclassical economists did not completely eliminate the possibility of discrimination as a cause of race and gender wage differentials. In the 1970s the notion of statistical discrimination appeared in the neoclassical economics literature on wage differentials. Statistical discrimination is when employers ascribe characteristics to an individual based on statistical averages of the group to which that individual belongs.[15] Even though two job candidates may be qualified for a job, the employer will pick the candidate who belongs to a group (men, whites) whose job-related attributes, on average, exceed other groups and pay them higher wages. Finding complete information about all prospective employees is costly, so employers use shorthand techniques but, as a result, may still end up discriminating. For example, if it is well known that women are too emotional to make important managerial decisions, employers will screen out all women from those jobs, regardless of any individual woman's capabilities.

Critics of statistical discrimination point out that over time, those facing statistical discrimination will take the time to present each employer with information about their particular qualities. Employers, too, will develop better tests to capture the higher productivity of less paid workers. As better information becomes widely available, wage differences should eventually erode if male and female workers are equally productive. Again, statistical discrimination should be a short-run phenomena. Here, too, neoclassical economists' explanations of wage differences that rely on discrimination find a dead end.

But if discrimination in markets in the long run cannot theoretically exist under the conditions imposed by the neoclassical model, what then explains persistent wage differences by gender? The answer ultimately must be that workers are in fact not equally productive.[16] That is, women do not bring as many skills to labor markets as men do and are compensated accordingly.

Wage differences in neoclassical economics are primarily explained by human capital differences. Human capital theory—developed in the 1960s by Theodore Schultz and Gary Becker—states that wage differences can be explained by productivity differences, which are largely determined by individual's decisions to invest in themselves.[17] The relationship between wages and productivity is derived from the profit-maximizing condition in the labor market that producers will hire up until the point where the wage rate equals marginal productivity (see box). Any individual, it is argued, can improve his or her productivity by forgoing income today to invest in more education and/or experience that will improve his or her productivity, which in turn will improve earnings.

Women have less human capital, it is argued, because they know they will face stretches of time outside the labor force due to childbearing and childrearing responsibilities. It is irrational (in the neoclassical sense of utility maximizing) for women to forgo current income to undertake training and/or education that will not be used. The immediate question, then, becomes, why do women—as opposed to men—leave the labor force for long stretches of time? The answer lies in theories of the sexual division of unpaid labor.

The Sexual Division of Unpaid Labor   Unlike their classical predecessors, neoclassical economists have extended their model of the economy to the home. To do so, they have ascribed individual utility-maximizing behavior that takes place in markets to work done in the household. Once again, Gary Becker is the pioneer in this field. His theories of the economics of marriage, when combined with his theories of time allocation, form the basis for neoclassical interpretations of the sexual division of labor. Work in this field is referred to as the "new household economics."

The sexual division of labor in the home is explained largely by the comparative advantage model (originally employed by David Ricardo in the early nineteenth century to promote international trade), which argues that marriage provides economic gains to both partners. Households maximize their total bundle of goods and services—those produced in markets and those produced at home. Through marriage, men and women can specialize and exchange. The partner who has a relative advantage in producing home-based goods should stay home. And the other partner should offer his or her services in the labor market, receive a wage, which will then be used to purchase market-based goods. It is the gains to be made from the complementarity of men and women that explain the existence and persistence of heterosexual, monogamous marriages.[18]

Why do women have a comparative advantage in home-based production? Over the years, neoclassical economists have offered a variety of answers. The explanation presented in textbooks for why men have a comparative advantage in market-based work is that women make less money in market production than men, therefore it makes sense for women to stay home. If any individual woman earned more than her husband, and both were equally good housekeepers with similar preferences, there would be gains if she worked while her husband stayed home. But note the circularity of the argument. Why do women earn less than men? Because they choose to stay home and as a result do not invest in their income-producing capacities. And why do women choose to stay home? Because of their lower income-producing capacities.

One way to be less circuitous would be to argue women are "naturally" better at home-based production because women's biological capacity to bear children makes them biologically more suited to raising children. And although this has indeed been a historically popular explanation in economics, feminist critiques of biologically based differences (and accusations of sexism) have led some neoclassical economists to explore other explanations. One possibility raised to explain women's finely honed unpaid labor capabilities is that even when men and women are equally suited to perform home-based production, most women place a higher utility on it. Therefore, it takes a higher wage to pull them into the labor market than men. Given equal abilities and even equal wage rates offered, women will choose to stay at home. An explanation like this rests in neoclassical economics' "comfort range," because economists do not see it as their duty to explain the origins of preferences, just the way those preferences play out in the allocation of resources. To understand why women place a higher value on childrearing than men do, one is directed to other disciplines.

Although the preceding depiction of the neoclassical model as it relates to women's paid and unpaid labor is abbreviated, it provides the reader with a basic understanding of the model's prevailing explanation of women's wages and the sexual division of unpaid labor. Women economists have consistently challenged the neoclassical explanations of women's lower wages and the sexual division of paid labor since the publication of Becker's work on marriage was published. As feminist economists Marianne Ferber and Julie Nelson note, "Carolyn Shaw Bell (1974), Marianne Ferber and Bonnie Birnbaum (1977), and Isabel Sawhill (1977) all expressed early reservations about this line of research, in part because such research often served to reinforce outdated assumptions about 'natural' male and female behavior."[19] Despite the continuing feminist critiques of new household economics and human capital theory, they continue to form the basis of how many economists understand and teach women's economic status.[20] One would be hard pressed to find a textbook dealing with labor markets or women's wages without the neoclassical explanations as the most prominent, although critiques, including feminist ones, would likely be included.

The neoclassical model ultimately argues, as its explanation of women's differential labor market status, that men and women (blacks and whites) are *not* economic equivalents. Further, the differences are the result of rational utility-maximizing behavior or tastes and preferences determined outside the model. Differential outcomes are the result of freely chosen preferences. Corrective market intervention, like all market interventions, will only make matters worse. Typically, neoclassical economists argue that policies such as affirmative action and comparable worth as remedies for women's lower wages are misplaced, because they will force employers to pay some workers wages higher than their marginal product—violating a firm's ability to maximize profit. This will result in making firms uncompetitive and inefficient.

In its pure form, the theory promotes "blame the victim" explanations of women's inferior status. The results are policy prescriptions that justify and perpetuate the status quo. *At the most fundamental level, neoclassical economics argues that women receive lower wages than men and perform more unpaid labor than men largely out of women's and men's own rational choices and desires.* Often those desires are acknowledged to be shaped by previous discrimination or premarket discrimination, but neoclassical economists usually allocate those discussions to other disciplines. Neoclassical economists have written widely in opposition to comparable worth, affirmative action, family leave policies, and subsidized health and child care. Their policy prescriptions are often antithetical to what many feminists consider the most important ways to improve women's economic status relative to men.

Neoclassical Economics' Methodology

The method one employs and the explanations that result are related—but distinct. Finding antifeminist explanations in theories that developed more than a hundred years ago, when women were assumed to be intellectually and physically inferior, is not surprising or terribly insightful. A more important question is whether or not the method allows room to move beyond the old explanations to develop feminist explanations of women's status.

Neoclassical economics uses a logical positivist (also referred to as logical empiricism) methodology, developed in the early twentieth century. Economic historian Mark Blaug describes this method as a way of conducting scientific investigations that "begin in the free and unprejudiced observation of facts, proceed by inductive inference to the formulation of universal laws about these facts, and finally arrive by further induction at statements of still wider generality known as theories: both laws and theories are ultimately checked for their truth content by comparing their empirical consequences with all the observed facts, including those with which they began."[21] This particular way of doing science has been questioned and even discarded by many of the social sciences since the 1960s; nonetheless, neoclassical economics still holds on to logical positivist methodology.

Perhaps, the best-known work of neoclassical economic methodology is Milton Friedman's 1953 *Essays in Positive Economics*.[22] In the most famous of these essays, "The Methodology of Positive Economics," Friedman identifies one of the important neoclassical dichotomies—positive and normative economics. "Positive economics is in principle independent of any particular ethical position or normative judgements. As [John Neville] Keynes said, it deals with 'what is,' not with 'what ought to be.' Its task is to provide a system of generalizations that can be used to make correct predictions about the consequences of any change in circumstances."[23] This distinction is still made in most introductory economics textbooks, identifying economics (i.e., neoclassical economics) as positive science, one that stays removed from value judgments and sticks just with the facts.

Neoclassical economics applies deductive reasoning to what are claimed to be universal laws of behavior (e.g., individuals maximize their utility rationally). Armed with mathematical modeling techniques and large data sets, neoclassical economists argue that their paradigm is more objective and closer to pure science than theories primarily based in understanding economic phenomena using historical and institutional analysis. Because of its belief in value-free science, neoclassical economics claims that an individual cannot conduct economic research in an objective fashion if she or he has a set of predetermined judgments or biases such as feminism.

And although neoclassical economics can be used to understand an enormous range of human activity, there is very little leeway in the method one uses to do that. It would not be an exaggeration to say that many economists agree with Gary Becker's following depiction of "doing" economics:

> I believe that what most distinguishes economics as a discipline from other disciplines in the social sciences is not its subject matter but its approach. Indeed, many kinds of behavior fall within the subject matter of several disciplines: for example, fertility behavior is considered part of sociology, anthropology, economics, history, and perhaps even politics. I contend that the economic approach is uniquely powerful because it can integrate a wide range of human behavior. . . . The combined assumptions of maximizing behavior, market equilibrium, and stable preferences, used relentlessly and unflinchingly, form the heart of the economic approach as I see it.[24]

Of the increasingly wide range of feminist analyses that have developed over the last several decades, most rely heavily on the role of culture, history, and institutions in their explanations of women's differential and unequal status with men. Neoclassical economists have downplayed these types of approaches.

Positivist methodology, a holdover from the early twentieth century, leads many neoclassical economists to firmly reject feminist analysis (and other approaches as well) as valid ways of doing economics. The rejection of feminism as valid economic social science came through very clearly in the survey. Although it is by no means a universally held view, a strong belief still exists among economists that "doing" neoclassical economics is a near value-free enterprise with good practitioners approaching their study of the world in as neutral fashion as possible. By this definition, a feminist can never be neutral since she or he has a worldview and set of structured beliefs that are well articulated and different from those currently doing economic analysis. As such, feminist economists will never be "real" economists or conduct valid research, because they will not be objective.[25]

The mismatch between how many feminists do economic analysis and neoclassical economics was clearly articulated in a recent article by Joseph Persky discussing critiques of *homo economicus* as the basis for economic reasoning.

> Many groups over the years, starting with the historical school and including American institutionalists, have recognized that humans were a good deal more complex than the economic man [John Stuart] Mill has suggested. Like some of today's feminists, these groups have offered a range of competing motives and behaviors. But their lists were so long and unwieldy that they virtually excluded tightly reasoned generalizations. Their method could perhaps generate history, but not economics.[26]

Persky's message is very clear. Feminist efforts to broaden the range of rational behavior to include, for example, the selflessness often expected of women, creates a theory too unwieldy for economists. It is fine for history, but not for economics.

Feminist economists join a long line of critics of neoclassical economics methodology. Discussions and justifications for neoclassical methodology peaked in the 1950s and 1960s. Since that time the problems associated with neoclassical economics methodology and assumptions have been pointed out by many Keynesians, Marxian, and institutional economists. Further, there is much disagreement among neoclassical economists themselves.[27] Two concurrently developing streams of criticisms of logical positivism are of particular importance to feminists in economics. The first is the spate of criticism in the 1980s and the 1990s from discontented, mostly traditionally trained economists. They have questioned the rhetoric of economics, its ability to model behavior without institutions, its reliance on rational behavior, and its lack of historical analysis.[28] These criticisms have not been particularly feminist nor are they coming from those who have an alternative paradigm to offer. But they have called into question the role of values in economics, and recently these authors have been intrigued by and sympathetic to the development of feminist (non-Marxist) economics.

The second development is outside economics: it comes from feminist philosophers' discussions on epistemology, especially their critiques of logical positivism.[29] These feminists have questioned the idea of nearly perfect objectivity in science—any science. Their main critique is that knowledge itself is situated historically and socially. Feminist philosophers argue that if men are dominant in a society and women's experiences and positions are often distinct from men's, then knowledge generated by men in privileged positions will be only a partial reality. The questions one finds important, the explanations that result, the ability to even be a social scientist will depend on the sum of one's own experience and social expectations.

Feminist economists have drawn on both critiques of logical positivism to argue that economists cannot dismiss feminism on objectivity grounds because neoclassical economists also bring their values (i.e., biases) to their work, and all ideas are developed in the context of a larger community.[30] Still, as long as neoclassical economists resist the notion that values inform their science, feminists existing in a world of neoclassical economics will be unwelcome and it will be an economics that is antifeminist. As feminist economist Janet Seiz notes, "Thus, feminist historians of thought seeking to demonstrate that gender bias has had serious consequences in economics can

expect to meet with double resistance: one, a resistance to feminist character-
izations of gender relations and calls for change, and two, a resistance to any
arguments about the role of external values in economic inquiry."[31]

Feminist economists have challenged neoclassical economics methodology but as of yet have not developed distinctly new theories. Still, feminists
have made several important methodological critiques of neoclassical economics that others have missed and that in some ways provide the potential
to transform economics or to develop an alternative school of thought. Here I
discuss one of these critiques: the role of rational individual agency.

Feminist economists have long noted the problems of ascribing self-
serving behavior to all economic agents. Ironically, one only needs to barely
scratch the surface of Adam Smith's compelling illustration of the role of the
invisible hand, to find the perfect feminist critique of *homo economicus*. In
the following passage, feminist political economists Nancy Folbre and Heidi
Hartmann turn the building block of neoclassical economics on its head:

> The most famous quotation from *The Wealth of Nations* reads: "It is not
> from the benevolence of the butcher, the brewer, or the baker, that we expect
> our dinner, but from their regard to their own interest." But Smith never
> pointed out that these purveyors do not in fact make dinner. Nor did he con-
> sider that wives might prepare dinner for their husbands out of regard for
> their self-interest.[32]

In short, for Adam Smith's invisible hand to work, it needs the invisible
and selfless labor of women in the home. For indeed, *no* dinner would be
served, despite the hard work and self-interest of the brewer, butcher, and
baker, without the unpaid work of someone who worked at home to do it.
This observation, which is not a terribly mysterious or deep one, poses a fundamental problem for feminists interested in using neoclassical economics
tools. As Daniel Hausman notes, "One can do economics with satiation and
with some interdependence among utilities. But agents seeking their own
material welfare is what makes economics run, and theories which dethrone
this motive cease to be economics. Economic theories may not portray
agents as exploitable fools."[33] And although feminists might not think of
women as exploitable fools, their actions (and the behavior ascribed to them
in the home) in neoclassical economics cannot be considered anything but
foolish. Adding to the work of Amartya Sen on this particular aspect of neoclassical economics, several feminist economists and feminist sociologist
Paula England have developed a forceful critique of rational "man."[34] Drop-
ping the assumption that everyone always acts in a self-serving manner from

the neoclassical model creates serious problems. Although there have been attempts to generate a neoclassical model in which the entire household's utility is maximized, these have not been terribly successful.[35]

But even if one could model individual behavior to encompass altruistic and caring behavior, one is still left with a model that starts with the actions of individuals and builds to explain all economic behavior. Many feminists, however, reject the neoclassical model based on its primary unit of analysis—the individual—and its insistent avoidance of discussing nonmarket power relations. Instead they look to other social science models that are based on the conflict of self-identified groups over material resources. Marxian economics provides exactly that type of analysis and is the subject of the next chapter.

FEMINIST IMPACT ON NEOCLASSICAL ECONOMIC THINKING

Not *all* components of neoclassical economics are explicitly antifeminist. Indeed, one of the earliest contributors to the economic philosophy of utility maximization was a famous feminist himself—John Stuart Mill. Focusing on the actions of a genderless, raceless, ageless individual as the primary actor in the model does make the theory universal and inclusive. Most certainly, the neoclassical model ascribes rationality to all its adult actors—a vast improvement over early utilitarian models, which found women, children, and "natives" to be irrational or possess innate inferior mental capacities.

The political theory that most neatly dovetails with neoclassical economics is libertarianism, which values above all else individual political equality and freedom. Women, like men, should be free to maximize their utility and exercise their political franchise. The emphasis on equality of political rights and freedom to enter markets and exchange is not only powerful and politically compelling, it is liberatory on some levels.[36] In liberal feminism (one strand of feminism), individual rights for women have been of pivotal importance in understanding and achieving women's equality.[37] On one level, then, liberal feminism (which looks primarily at individual women) is quite conducive to neoclassical thinking.

Perhaps the most important impact feminism has made on neoclassical economics is that it has expanded the scope of analysis to include an examination of women's work and so-called women's issues—such as fertility, child care, abortion, women's wages, and occupational segregation—if for no other reason than the profession needed to say something about women's status at a time when the women's movement was making political headway and when one of the most important economic and social changes of the post–World War II period was occurring—the steady increase of women's paid labor force participation.

The subfield in neoclassical economics in which gender issues are likely to surface, then, is labor economics. And, indeed, one finds a larger percentage of articles devoted to gender in labor journals than in other fields. Between 1984 and 1994 Yana van der Meulen Rodgers found 16.2 percent of gender articles in the three leading labor journals (which are primarily dominated by those using the neoclassical approach) compared with 1.3 percent in the top seven (all heavily neoclassical) economics journals. Further, men were four times as likely to be authors of the gender articles in the labor journals than women.[38]

Neoclassical economics' antifeminist explanations of women's economic status and method make feminist analysis difficult and are among the least attractive of economic and social theories to feminists. The strong critiques levied by the majority of authors against neoclassical method in two recent anthologies on feminism and economics make this abundantly clear.[39] Still, some feminist economists argue that feminists can and should operate within the neoclassical framework. They have argued that the tools of neoclassical economics as they apply to individual behavior are not at fault but rather the lack of creative thinking about making constraints more integral in economic thinking.[40] For example, several feminist social scientists, using marginal analysis of individual-maximizing behavior, have produced important research on low-income women's behavior in response to changes in AFDC rules.[41] Their work argues that poor women raising their families need supports and that recent punitive welfare reform measures which force women to work in low-wage labor markets and reduce benefits to women who give birth while receiving public assistance are largely misplaced and unlikely to have the desired effects.

One feminist economist using neoclassical economic analysis is historian Claudia Goldin, whose book on the historical account of the gender gap was very well received in the profession.[42] In it she argues that women, especially married women, faced and continue to face barriers to employment that result in lower wages. She questions the economists' reliance on the benefits of economic progress outweighing its uneven effects, because gender so clearly influences the outcome.

But perhaps the most significant contribution feminist social scientists have made in neoclassical economics has been in challenging neoclassical work on gender. Feminist economists, working within the neoclassical framework, have tested models of wage differences and occupational distribution and found the models lacking.[43] In response, neoclassical economists have worked harder to refine their models, and in some cases the critiques have led to entirely new areas of neoclassical economic analysis. For example, household bargaining theory developed out of disenchantment with neoclassical models of the household. Feminist economists, using the underlying assumptions of individual rational behavior and marginal analysis, have modeled unequal power relations, including the role of domestic violence, in marriage.[44] And to some degree feminists have been successful in both doing neoclassical economics and in pushing economists to think more clearly about gender differences.

Feminist critiques of neoclassical models have spurred neoclassical adherents to refine their empirical work as well. This has been most obvious in human capital models. For years, feminists have criticized the model and pointed to its ineffectiveness in explaining wage differences.[45] In response, human capital theorists have honed their models of educational differences and worked hard to collect better data to measure the degree to which their models can explain the wage gap.[46]

Pushing the neoclassical model to be more inclusive of women corresponds to what Sandra Harding calls the application of "feminist empiricism."[47] It is an attempt to complete the analysis by including women but keeping intact the principles and method of explanation. This strategy does not call into question neoclassical tools. Whereas this approach has the clear benefit of enabling feminist empiricists to participate by speaking the same language, it does not transform the method and as such retains the model's focus on individual self-satisfying behavior.

Feminists who work within the neoclassical economic framework maintain their convictions for promoting women's equality and a commitment to look at women and gender when appropriate, using neoclassical tools and methodology. This is perfectly consistent with liberal feminism. It is also consistent with the positive attitudes toward the women's movement as well as the aversion to feminist analysis in economics expressed by the majority of economists in my survey of them. But the survey also indicated that, for many, studying neoclassical economics is at odds with being a feminist. Not surprisingly, feminist economists have looked to other methodologies to develop their analysis. We turn to one of those now.

8

STILL TOGETHER: THE "UNHAPPY MARRIAGE" OF MARXISM AND FEMINISM REVISITED

The "marriage" of Marxism and feminism has been like the marriage of common law: Marxism and feminism are one, and that one is Marxism. Recent attempts to integrate Marxism and feminism are unsatisfactory to us as feminists because they subsume the feminist struggle into the "larger" struggle against capital. To continue our simile further, either we need a healthier marriage or we need a divorce.

—Heidi Hartmann[1]

The preceding quote is from an essay that originally circulated in socialist feminist circles in the United States in the mid-1970s—just about the same time Gary Becker was extending the neoclassical model to discuss marriage. The implied threat feminists made to Marxists was if Marxism could not better integrate gender into its analysis, the relationship was off. Feminists and feminism would have to either find other theories with which to form more lasting relationships or go it alone.

Almost two decades later the marriage seems to still be intact, but as each partner has aged, the passion is gone and the conflicts that plagued their early years no longer seem so vital or vibrant. The intensity and pressure to keep the relationship together has subsided, and each partner has changed considerably over the years. Both have entertained new avenues of thought, including the role of formal bargaining models and the potentially positive role of markets. And together, Marxists and feminists have shed new light on economic development, labor markets, and the role of reproduction in the economy. However, over the years neither party has remained strictly monogamous. Most significantly, socialist feminists[2] have directed their energies to developing postmodernist theories that reject explanations based on a single motivating factor (in this case class), which is characteristic of much Marxist work. Meanwhile, Marxists have worked with Sraffians and Keynesians, whose models hardly have women in them, let alone deal with feminist concerns.

The relationship between feminism and Marxism is far different than that of feminism and neoclassical economics. As the Hartmann quote suggests, feminists freely entered the relationship because feminists were attracted to Marxism as a way to help provide theoretical underpinnings to feminist analysis. In Marxism, feminists have found and used concepts and tools that have helped further develop analyses of women's economic position. As a model predicated on unequal power and change, Marxist economic thought has offered a needed springboard for examining women's oppression. But not unlike feminism's reception in neoclassical economics, feminists' early attempts to integrate Marxism and feminism were met with considerable personal resistance and important theoretical roadblocks.

Feminists' attraction to Marxian explanations and theories of liberation are not new. Many feminists were active socialists (and later communists) in the late nineteenth and early twentieth centuries and gravitated toward Marxist and other socialist theories of liberation.[3] For more than a century, feminists have looked to Marxian political economy for a framework that argues for transformed political, economic, and social relations that will distribute wealth and power more equally—including along gender lines. Marxist theory is appealing to feminists who are also interested in understanding and transforming nongender unequal relations—particularly class-based oppression.

Marxist political economy has profoundly affected modern-day feminism. For the last 25 years, feminist theory has developed with socialist feminism as one main frame of reference and it is an important intellectual root. Virtually any book or reader on feminism includes a discussion of socialist feminism as an integral part of the evolution of modern feminist methodology and thought.[4] Feminism's impact on Marxist economic thinking, however, is much more difficult to discern. Feminists brave enough to wade into the chilly waters of the economics discipline in the early days of the women's movement often did so to study political economy. They developed analyses of gender oppression using Marxian methods and categories in hopes of furthering both feminist and Marxian theory and practice. It is difficult to measure their success. Many Marxist economists accept gender oppression as an important component in understanding contemporary capitalist life. But as feminists found with neoclassical economics, there are difficult problems with integrating gender into Marxian analysis. Some, frustrated with the exercise, have turned to other theories—postmodernism, notably.

This chapter explores the uneasy but relatively durable "marriage" between Marxism and feminism. The first section provides a brief overview of Marxian economics. The second section looks more closely at traditional Marxian economic explanations of women's position and Marxian methodology's allure for feminist theorists. Traditional Marxian treatments of women's economic status, not unlike neoclassical economics treatment, have typically been antifeminist. The explanations of women's inequality are derivative of unequal class relations; therefore, women's liberation necessarily takes a back seat to understanding and fighting against class inequities. Feminism, then, in traditional Marxist analysis, is seen as divisive; it detracts from rather than enhances an understanding of the underlying causes of economic oppression. Marxian methodology, however, is quite conducive to feminist analysis, and hence the numerous attempts to use Marxist economic thought in feminist theory and the reluctance of feminists to let it go. The last section explores some of socialist feminists' contributions and an assessment of the impact of feminism on Marxian economic thinking.

THE MARXIAN MODEL:
A BRIEF OVERVIEW

Marxian economics, like neoclassical economics, has its roots in classical political economy. Writing in the mid and late nineteenth century, Karl Marx, and his collaborator Frederick Engels, developed a theory of capitalist production and a critique of prevailing economic thought. Marx wrote extensively on the political, social, and economic aspects of capitalist production. His most famous economic work is *Capital,* a three-volume work on the dynamics of capitalist production.

Marx analyzed capitalism as a class-based system; a relatively small portion of the population, by virtue of their ownership of the facilities and tools of production, claim all the profits of commodity production. Workers are exploited because they have nothing to sell in markets other than their ability to perform work. The origins of capitalists' bounty, according to Marx, have very little to do with individual hard work and cleverness but, rather, were created and sustained through a historical process and legal system that allowed a small group of landed aristocracy and merchants to amass large sums of wealth. Property rights, trade agreements, and inheritance laws have allowed this group and their families to keep and expand their large holdings.

Borrowing from David Ricardo, Marx used a labor theory of value to develop his theory of how workers are exploited. For Marxists, exchangeable commodities do not get their value from the utility they provide, as neo-classical economics claims. Instead, the value of exchanged goods is derived from the average amount of labor time it takes to produce those goods using the level of technology available. In a capitalist economy, commodities of equivalent value (i.e., with the same of amount of live and dead labor embodied) will exchange for the same amounts of money. Competition ensures that most things exchange for what they are worth (the labor time embodied in them). But, as Marx notes, at the end of the day capitalists make a profit in this exchange of equals. In the capitalist system, then, one needs to look beyond market exchanges to understand the source of profits.

Profits exist because of the way production is organized. Marx argued that workers, although paid their value, produce more than their value. The value of the output workers produce minus their wages (workers' value) is what Marx called surplus value, or profits. Workers' value, like the value of other commodities, is the work time it takes to reproduce the worker at the socially and historically necessary standard of living. When capitalism is working successfully, the value of workers' time is less than the value of the goods they produced for the capitalist at the end of the working day. Consider the following example. A worker in a sausage factory receives the standard wage of $50.00 a day—the socially determined amount of money that reproduces the worker's daily needs. Yet in the course of the day that worker produces $70.00 worth of sausages, once the value of the raw materials and machinery depreciated are subtracted. That worker, then, according to Marx, is exploited because she generated $20.00 worth of profit for the capitalist.

The process of extracting surplus from workers when generalized to the entire system is called the process of accumulation. And the process of accumulation—the drive for profits—is the cornerstone of understanding capitalist production and Marxian political economy. The process of accumulation can be simply represented by the following flow (or circuits) of money and goods:

$$M — C — C' — M'$$

M is the money capitalists start with at the beginning of the production process and M' is the amount they end up with once the goods and services have been produced and sold. The goal of the accumulation process is to ensure that profits are generated, that is, that M' is greater than M. C represents the inputs (commodities) purchased by capitalists such as machinery, raw materials, and labor power. C' is the final output (i.e., the transformed commodities).

Each circuit in the above flow corresponds to critical aspects of capitalist production. The $M - C$ circuit requires the presence of a wage labor force, the acquisition of the capital necessary to buy equipment, and access to raw materials. The $C - C'$ circuit is the production process itself. Capitalists do not buy labor per se (as that would be slavery). They buy workers' time and the promise to do work. The way the production process is structured is a vital component of capitalism because it ensures that workers actually do work. The final circuit, $C' - M'$, represents the actual selling of the product and with it the realization of profits. If there are no markets to sell goods and no people to buy them, there will be no profits.

Analytically, the process of accumulation is to Marxian political economy what supply and demand curves are to neoclassical economics. The process of accumulation lays the foundation for explaining why and how goods and services are produced and allocated, the level and role of technology in a society, the conflict between workers and capitalists, the necessity of struggle and change, and even the roles that governments and culture play. In short, it is the conceptual framework that explains exploitation, social dynamics, ideology, and change. Capitalist accumulation is based on the relations of commodity production, which is what makes Marxism a materially based theory.

To see how the process of accumulation necessitates a wide range of social, political, legal, and cultural rules and institutions to operate smoothly, one need only consider what is necessary for each of the circuits of the process of accumulation to operate. For example, the first circuit of capitalist accumulation (M – C) requires a stable labor force—people willing to work for a wage rather than for themselves or not at all. It also is built on a family and cultural structure that ensures the important work of social reproduction will take place so that some family members can go to work every day. Access to capital entails constructing a sophisticated banking system and legal structure that defends and promotes private property. Extracting raw materials demands international relations and trade laws that provide nondomestic corporations the rights to own or purchase those materials. Any time any of these social structures breaks down or is incomplete, it potentially jeopardizes or interferes with the process of accumulation.[5]

Marxists argue that capitalist accumulation is fraught with potential pitfalls and contradictions, which makes it a highly dynamic but contentious, unstable, and ultimately unhealthy economic system. Importantly, Marxists do not think of capitalism as an economic system full of evil people doing dastardly deeds but, rather, as a system that, when successful, creates and sustains oppressive conditions for the majority of people, regardless of the intentions of individual actors.

But ultimately, Marx argued, capitalism is a system that cannot sustain itself. There are too many potential crises at every circuit in the process of accumulation and too many contradictions for it to be long lasting. The major contradiction in capitalism is that it creates unreconcilable tensions between capitalists and workers. Goods and services are produced socially by the working class but are appropriated privately by the capitalist class. The lack of ownership in the final product functions to make workers disinterested in their work and alienated from the products they produce. Workers are kept from reaping the fruits of their own labor. Capitalists, therefore, must carefully control the work process, technology, and work time to ensure that workers actually produce more than their value. Only when the ownership of the tools of production are socialized will the conflict between workers and capitalists be ameliorated.

For any capitalist to realize and continually reproduce profits, he or she must continually expand production and at the same time seek to minimize competition. As the capitalist system expands, it absorbs more and more people into the wage-labor system; moves to more remote geographic locations to procure raw materials, cheap labor, and places to sell commodities; and creates larger and larger corporations that control more and more productive resources. The international nature of capitalism is inevitable.

In the drive to boost profits and lower wages, capitalism create enormous economic dislocations (and discontent) and unintentionally squeezes its own profit margins. There is a strong tendency, according to Marxists, to drive wages down (by eternally striving to find cheaper labor) and "immiserate" the working class everywhere. It is capital's prerogative to set up management structures and implement new technologies that facilitate extracting surplus value. These may not necessarily be the most efficient, humane, or responsible structures or technologies, but they will likely be the most profitable. For example, capitalists will be very reluctant to make expenditures to ensure safe workplaces or minimal pollution because they do not directly increase output.

Individual workers have little power in the firm because they can be easily fired. The threat of unemployment and lack of other types of self-sustaining activity are the two most powerful mechanisms capitalism and individual capitalists have to ensure that workers "behave." When there are few jobs available and few alternatives to wage labor, workers will be forced to accept whatever conditions of employment are offered. The more alternatives (e.g., self-employment, government aid, plenty of jobs), the more say individual workers have over their work lives. It is only through collective responses (e.g., a strike) that workers can effectively demand changes in the conditions of work. However, workers can resist work and demand better conditions under capitalism only up to a point. Capital mobility and the threat of firing workers keeps workers in check. What is ultimately required is a different and more equitable system of economic production. According to Marx, only when workers of the world unite will they effectively combat and transform capitalism.

Capitalists need to produce and sell goods and services around the world. That requires some degree of social, ideological, and political control on the part of the capitalist class. Particularly in countries with representative governments, a small minority (capitalists) needs to be able to influence politicians who define the legal parameters of capitalist production. This is typically done through influencing the political and cultural process. Hence, Marxist theories of production require some theorizing about national governments and ideology. Marxist theories of the state and ideology vary tremendously, but they are unified as Marxian theories by their attempts to explain how political or ideological systems reproduce capitalist relations of production.[6]

Marxist economics differs radically from neoclassical economics in its unit of analysis, theory of value, and methodology. They both agree, however, on the importance of profit making and market-based production in constructing their worldview and analysis. Marxist theory uses historical analysis to explain the ever-changing nature of class relations. Embedded in Marxian economics is the premise of unequal power relations—most fundamentally class relations—that result in political, cultural, economic, and social domination of some groups over others. Further, Marxian theory begins with a theory of collective behavior and concludes that only through collective action and struggle will institutions, economic systems, and polities change.

Marxian economics is not just a theory that explains the world, it is a call to change it. To interpret capitalism from a Marxian perspective puts one squarely in a position of either defending the capitalist class or working to be liberated from it. Marxism is an explicit political project, and much of its historical appeal has been that it is both a theory and a practice.

MARXIAN ECONOMICS' ANTIFEMINISM AND ITS FEMINIST POTENTIAL

Feminists in the 1960s and 1970s were attracted immediately to Marxism for the same reasons their New Left brethren were: its materially based theory of conflict. But although the methodology and call for action were very seductive, the actual explanations of women's oppression were sorely lacking.

The "Woman Question": Marxian Explanations of Women's Economic Status

Marxist and socialist thinkers in the late nineteenth and early twentieth centuries grappled seriously with women's status under capitalism. The debate even had its own name—the "Woman Question"—and most socialist writers and political movements of the time confronted the role of women and families in capitalism, including Marx and Engels. Socialists' and Marxists' desires to understand women's position in capitalism were not merely academic. Women's emancipation movements in the industrial world were growing. Socialists wanted a way to understand women's role and to tap women's political pressure and presence. August Bebel, author of *Women and Socialism*, one of the most widely read socialist books at the time (originally published in 1879, had gone through 50 editions by 1910 and was translated into several different languages)[7] wrote:

> Accordingly, this solution of the Woman Question coincides completely with the solution of the Social Question. It follows that he who aims at the

solution of the Women Question to its full extent, is necessarily bound to go hand and hand with those who have inscribed upon their banner the solution of the Social Question as a question of civilization for the whole human race. These are the Socialists, that is, the Social Democracy.[8]

Marxism's treatment of women's oppression is much like its treatment of other important nonclass, power relations (such as between nation states, races, etc.)—it is derivative of class relations. As feminist theorists Seyla Benhabib and Drucilla Cornell summarize, "The consciousness of a social group as well as its potential for revolutionary, social transformation is determined by its position in the production process; *social classes* are defined in terms of such positions and are the most important collective actors in history."[9] In the simplest (if not simplistic) form, the relationship of the production process to all other social phenomena is traditionally designated as the "base-superstructure" relationship. Politics, culture, and social relations outside the workplace as well as family structure are considered part of the "superstructure" (i.e., not directly involved in the production and reproduction of goods and services). The superstructure is shaped by and serves the dynamics of the "base"—the material conditions of the production of commodities. Therefore, to understand women's unequal status in capitalism, one must look to class relations.

Frederick Engels was one of the first Marxist authors to deal specifically with women's relationship to the production process. In his 1884 book, *The Origin of the Family, Private Property and the State*, Engels provided a systematic materialist analysis of women's role in economic systems.[10] In the preface to the first edition of his magnum opus, Engels claimed, "According to the materialist conception, the determining factor in history is, in the final instance, the production and reproduction of immediate life. This, again, is of a twofold character: on the one side, the production of the means of existence, of food, clothing, shelter and the tools necessary for that production; on the other hand, the production of human beings themselves, the propagation of the species. The social organization under which the people of a particular historical epoch and a particular country live is determined by both kinds of production: by the stage of development of labor on the one hand and of the family on the other."[11] But Engels only discussed one side of the duality—how women's role in reproduction was shaped by the production and reproduction of commodities—in his book. The reverse relationship is left unanalyzed. However, Engels's initial conception of placing the production and reproduction of the family on equal footing with the labor process allows for a much broader analysis of women's status than Engels himself provided, which is why modern-day feminists regularly revisit Engels's work.

Engels's focus on the way the production of commodities influenced the structure of reproduction led him to link private property with family structure and women's oppression. He argued that women's oppression evolved in stages corresponding to women's relationship to physical reproduction and the development of kinship societies. Societies where individuals have significant property holdings need inheritance rules. Men must know who their heirs are and therefore enforce a system of patrilineal and patriarchal control over women through a system of monogamous marriages. "It [the monogamous family] is based on the supremacy of the man, the express purpose being to produce children of undisputed paternity; such paternity is demanded because these children are later to come into their father's property as natural heirs."[12] Engels's theorizing about women's oppression relied very heavily on the now largely discredited anthropological work of Lewis Henry Morgan.[13] Nonetheless, Engels's premise that there is a distinct economic basis for women's oppression remains pivotal to Marxist understandings of the "Woman Question."

According to Engels, men rule the household by virtue of their ownership of private property: "In the great majority of cases today, at least in the possessing classes, the husband is obliged to earn a living and support his family, and that in itself gives him a position of supremacy without any need for special legal titles and privileges."[14] Engels saw a distinction between the oppression of the bourgeois wife and the working-class wife—with the former being more oppressed by her husband than the latter. Engels goes so far as to say: "And now that large-scale industry has taken the wife out of the home onto the labor market and into the factory, and made her often the breadwinner of the family, no basis for any kind of male supremacy is left in the proletarian household, except, perhaps, for something of the brutality toward women that has spread since the introduction of monogamy."[15]

For Engels, women's economic dependence on men—which is a direct result of private ownership of the means of production—oppresses women. Hence, the elimination of women's oppression will only occur with the abolition of private property and the monogamous family: "With the transfer of the means of production into common ownership, the single family ceases to be the economic unit of society. Private housekeeping is transformed into a social industry. The care and education of children becomes a public affair; society looks after all children alike, whether they are legitimate or not."[16] Eradicating capitalism frees both men and women to love whom they want and fulfill their personal and sexual desires; it liberates workers from alienating work and liberates men and women from alienating marriages.

Marx was much less interested in thinking about the sources of women's oppression than Engels. Like most authors of the time, he simply assumed the sexual division of labor was natural and had little to say about it. In *Capital*, he touches upon the sexual division of labor when he discusses the division of labor generally. "Within a family, and after further development within a tribe, there springs up naturally a division of labor, caused by differences of sex and age, a division that is consequently based on a pure physiological foundation."[17] Engels also assumed, rather than explained, women's role as caretaker and homemaker from "prehistory" up to the present. Although this ahistorical view of the sexual division of labor was not unusual for writers of that time, it is not particularly "Marxist," as it lacks the historical specificity (and accuracy) that is pivotal to the analysis provided for the labor process.

Marx and Engels both discussed the ways in which the processes of accumulation drive capitalists to seek out cheap labor, particularly that of women and children. Marx briefly discussed the role of women wage earners in *Capital*. Accumulation demands the use of more and more machinery to increase the intensity and control of labor. This has two important consequences. To the degree that machinery quickens the pace of workers, it increases the amount of goods each worker can produce in a working day, boosting surplus value and the demand for workers. In addition, machinery that reduces the physical requirements of workers allows capitalists to replace men with women and children. Since Marx assumed that the value of women's (and children's) labor power was less than men's, the insatiable drive for profits will set into motion a tremendous demand for lower-paid female and child labor.

> Machinery, by throwing every member of that family on to the labor-market, spreads the value of the man's labor-power over his whole family. It thus depreciates his labor-power. . . . In order that the family may live, four people must now, not only labor, but expend surplus-labor for the capitalist.[18]

Engels and Marx also realized that when women are pulled into the labor process, they are subjected to the "double day"—that is, they are exploited by capitalists and still have responsibilities at home. For them, this is another reason why socialism will make life easier for women—as household tasks will be collectivized in socialism, they are no longer individual women's responsibilities. This sentiment was echoed by Lenin when shortly after the Russian Revolution he proclaimed, "Up to the present the position of women has been such that it is called a position of slavery. Women are crushed by their domestic drudgery, and only socialism can relieve them from this drudgery."[19] With socialism, public provision of domestic duties such as child care and housecleaning would theoretically free women from their particular oppression in capitalism. Women who argue for political equality without transforming capitalism are misguided at best and divisive at worst. Autonomous women's groups in the service of the fight against class oppression are welcome. Those same groups fighting for individual economic, political, and sexual autonomy from men are not.

Despite Engels's critique of monogamous marriage as the mechanism for women's oppression in *The Origin*, other works by Marx and Engels glorify the monogamous family. Passages in their joint work *Capital* and Engels's *The Condition of the Working Class in England in 1844* clearly bemoan women's and children's entrance into the labor market because working women destroy family life. Women's paid work lowers the male wage (the value of labor power is reduced when a family has two or more wage earners) and takes women away from providing the necessary unpaid labor in the home. For example, Engels laments, "The husband works the whole day through, perhaps the wife also and the elder children, all in different places; they meet night and morning only, all under perpetual temptation to drink; what family life is possible under such conditions? Yet the working man cannot escape from the family, must live in the family, and the consequence is a perpetual succession of family troubles, domestic quarrels, most demoralizing for parents and children alike. Neglect of all domestic duties, neglect of children, especially, is only too vigorously fostered by the existing institutions of society."[20]

This concern over the sanctity of the family, and the role of women in it, points to an important fissure in Marxian understandings of the sexual division of labor in the home. Modern feminist scholars of Marx point to considerable ambivalence and inconsistencies in early Marxian and socialist understanding of the roles families play in capitalism. One major source of the confusion is that nineteenth-century writers typically conflated their discussions of the "Woman Question" with discussions of families. Joan Landes, for example, argues that Marx and Engels fluctuate between adopting the Hegelian notion of the family as "the central moral structure in society" and employing a notion of the family as patriarchal and sexually repressive.[21]

Feminist political economist Nancy Folbre argues that these two visions of the family can be delineated to two distinct socialist camps.[22] The first

camp are those promoting scientific socialism who take the Hegelian position on the family—the view Marx and Engels seem to promote, especially
in later works.[23] That position argues that women's role in the working-class
family is as homemaker. The working class has solid economic and moral
reasons to fight women's entry into the labor market as a deterioration of the
family's economic position. The other view, promoted by utopian socialists
such as Robert Owen, William Thompson, Anna Wheeler, and August Bebel,
argued that traditional families are the source of patriarchal control. In the
utopian socialist version, women's entrance into the labor market represents
more independence for women and the destruction of the family—in short,
women's labor force participation is liberatory. Under the Hegelian view,
preserving the family serves the working class. Under the utopian view, dis-
mantling the patriarchal family is highly desirable for women and men,
because it liberates both. Folbre argues that turn-of-the-century feminists and
feminism were more closely linked to the utopian rather than the scientific
socialist view.

Modern-day Marxism draws primarily on the scientific socialism of the
late nineteenth and early twentieth centuries. It has largely developed from a
reworking of classical text and in opposition to utopian socialism.[24] It is not
surprising, given neoclassical economics' ascendancy and its reliance on
mathematical models, that many Marxist economists wanted their theories to
be as scientific (as opposed to moral) as possible. Arguing there are laws of
capitalist production that can be generalized to other cultures and historical
periods presumably makes Marxism as rigorous as neoclassical economics.
But when scientific socialism was resurrected, so too were the views of
women's traditional role in families.[25]

Feminists—contemporary ones and those writing one hundred years
ago—have always challenged Marxian understandings of women's oppression. A clever example of that is Charlotte Perkins Gilman's 1910 poem "The
Socialist and the Suffragist" (see box 8.1).[26] Perhaps the most important criticism was that despite Engels's assertions otherwise, women have faced gender oppression that is independent of their class status and in different types
of class societies. Although wealthy women may have more options and
privileges than other women, they still face a set of physical, social, and ideological constraints that are different from those faced by men and that place
women in a vulnerable and unequal position with men. Men as a group dominate women and benefit from gender oppression. The sexual division of
labor typifies all societies across space and time—though the specific work
done by women and men varies. Gender oppression is not merely a function

BOX 8.1

THE SOCIALIST AND THE SUFFRAGIST
BY CHARLOTTE PERKINS GILMAN

Said the Socialist to the Suffragist:
"My Cause is greater than yours!
   You only work for a Special Class
   We for the gain of the General Mass,
Which every good ensures!"

Said the Suffragist to the Socialist:
"You underrate my Cause!
   While women remain a Subject Class,
   You never can move the General Mass,
With your economic laws!"

Said the Socialist to the Suffragist:
"You misinterpret facts,
   There is no room for doubt or schism
   In Economic Determinism—
It governs all our acts!"

Said the Suffragist to the Socialist:
"You men will always find
   That this old world will never move
   More swiftly in its ancient groove
While women stay behind!"

"A lifted world lifts women up,"
The Socialist explained.
   "You cannot lift the world at all
   While half of it is kept so small,"
The Suffragist maintained.

The world awoke and tartly spoke:
"Your work is all the same;
   Work together or work apart,
   Work, each of you, will all your heart—
Just get into the game."

The Forerunner, 1(12) (October 1910): 25.

140

of propertied societies. And, as history has shown, a socialist revolution changes women's economic position compared with the previous economic system, but it by no means secures women's liberation or does away with the need or desire for monogamous relationships.

A second set of criticism has to do with Marxism's project and focus. In Marxist economic analysis, economic processes are given prominence over any other type of human interaction.[27] Production for exchange, typically men's work, takes precedence over production for use or reproduction, typically women's work. The emphasis on exploitation, which occurs in wage labor production processes, ignores the importance of nonwaged work in economic, political, and social processes. However, nonwaged work, like waged work, entails economic, ideological, cultural, and social interactions, perceptions, and control. Not subjecting reproductive work to the same historical and dialectical analysis applied to for-profit production work makes much of Marxist analysis biased and incomplete. As Joan Landes argues, "No adequate acknowledgement is made that the sexual division of labor might generate social antagonisms of equal consequence to those occurring in the property order and even foster class divisions between men and women."[28]

Many modern-day socialist feminists have also repudiated the scientific socialist view of families, preferring to resurrect Engels's interpretation in *The Origin*. Family structures in which women are economically dependent on men form the primary material basis for women's oppression. The traditional family, in this case, is an oppressive institution. Early modern-day Marxists who argued otherwise were considered antifeminist. An article by socialist feminist economic historian Jane Humphries, which defended working-class attempts to keep women out of the labor market in the eighteenth century to preserve the family wage, prompted a heated discussion among Marxist feminists.[29]

In sum, traditional Marxist explanations of women's role and status in the economy is a mixed bag for feminists. Although the explanations recognize that the unequal power relations between men and women are not freely chosen and argue for women's yoke of oppression to be lifted, they also argue that women must lift the yoke of class oppression first, then eliminate what is left of men's domination of women. For many feminists, this is no more than a "promissory note," not necessarily payable on demand after the revolution.

Like neoclassical economics, then, Marxian economics can be considered to contain antifeminist explanations of women's unequal status. Rather than preserve the status quo, however, it argues for women to fight for another cause before their own. But as feminist philosopher Alison Jaggar argues, "Marxism's failure to provide an adequate historical account of the sexual division of labor is more than just an omission from the theory. It is an omission that works systematically to obscure women's oppression. Within the conceptual framework of traditional Marxism, some questions cannot be raised."[30] Jaggar offers the question of why women are routinely the object of violence by men, rather than the other way around, as an example. In Jaggar's words, "By obscuring women's oppression, Marxist theory provides a rationale for its perpetuation."[31]

The Feminist Attraction to Marxian Economics' Methodology

Dialectical materialism (or sometimes called historical materialism) was the method Marx used to analyze class societies. Marx began with a basic assumption about human nature—that humans will purposely transform nature for their own use—but he argued that the uses and the state of nature were both socially and historically contingent. His method of analysis reflected a belief in the importance of historical conflict and the constancy of change through collective struggle. Marx explicitly repudiated the liberal utilitarian philosophy of individual rational choice precisely because it abstracts individuals and human behavior from their social and historical context.[32] For Marx, no preference is determined exogenously. We are all social beings. Everything we want or need is the consequence of the interaction of people bound by both the tools and level of technology to produce and exchange goods, and the social relations of economic production. Marx used dialectical reasoning to uncover the contradictions of capitalist production. Marxist method explores the conflicting dualities embodied in material production, exchange, and reproduction.

Despite the inadequate, if not antifeminist, explanation of women's status offered by traditional Marxists, dialectical materialism provided a very seductive method for feminists in the 1960s and 1970s who were eager to analyze women's oppression. That allure of early feminists is best seen in anthropologist Gayle Rubin's influential 1976 article "The Traffic of Women: Notes on the 'Political Economy' of Sex." Using Marx's treatment of race and slavery as a parallel, Rubin argues that no one can understand the role of women except under the social conditions in which men and women exist. She further claims, "No other theory accounts for the oppression of women—in its endless variety and monotonous similarity, cross-culturally and throughout history—with anything like the explanatory power of Marxist theory of class oppression. Therefore, it is not surprising that there have been numerous attempts to apply Marxist analysis to the question of women."[33]

Feminists find Marx's dialectical materialism method appealing for several reasons. Here I suggest three. First, the method stresses unequal power relations based on the material conditions of the oppressed group. Beginning with an assumption of embodied conflict, dialectical reasoning provides a lens on the world from the vantage point of the oppressed as well as the motivation and tools for collective action and change. This appeals to feminists who are interested in explaining as well as changing unequal relationships between men and women. Second, dialectical materialism provides a complex examination of the dynamic role and influence of structures and institutions in the production and reproduction of power relations. Relationships among people cannot be understood outside of the structures and institutions that exist to help reproduce those relationships. This particular aspect of Marx's method has been significant for advancing feminist arguments of gender as a social, not a biological, construction. Feminists are often interested in the ways women's unequal status is reproduced beyond individuals who discriminate because institutions embody rules and regulations that leave women on unequal footing with men. Uncovering institutional forms of discrimination has been important for feminist economists. Marxist methodology provides a stark contrast to the neoclassical model's reliance on individual decision making.

Third, dialectical materialism maintains that the way one interprets and intervenes in the world is itself influenced by history and conflict. Marx rejected the notion that knowledge and ideas were fixed. The ruling class promotes ideologies and theories that are consistent with their position in the world. The work of Antonio Gramsci, an early twentieth-century Italian Marxist, has been particularly important in feminist theorizing. Gramsci's work on ideological and cultural hegemony has served as a basis for contemporary critical theories of the production of knowledge, including Marxist's theories.[34] Feminists have turned to Gramsci's work as a way to interpret the development of situated knowledge. The feminist philosophy and epistemology discussed in early chapters, in particular, have been very influenced by Marxist conceptions of knowledge.

Feminist philosophers and social scientists have been attracted to Marxist methodology since the 1960s. Feminist philosopher Jane Flax posed the question in a 1976 essay entitled "Do Feminists Need Marxism?" She answers that question by claiming, "Marxism alone cannot answer our questions. But if we retain and expand our original insights into our experience as women, we will be operating within the spirit which originally motivated Marx—that history is rooted in human needs and social relations. By confronting Marxism with feminism we require an overcoming, a retaining of the old with the new. What we will create will be neither Marxism nor psychoanalysis, but a much more adequate form of social theory."[35] Flax's hope was that feminists would be able to use Marxist tools to formulate new feminist theories that explained women's status. Socialist feminists tried in the 1970s and the 1980s, but the success of those endeavors is unclear.

FEMINISM, MARXISM, AND ECONOMICS

Of all the established theories and methodologies in the social sciences, Marxism clearly provided a set of tools to construct (and later deconstruct) a new understanding and vision for the baby boomers coming of age in the New Left during the late 1960s. However, much work needed to be done in reconstructing Marx. Leftists had been summarily purged from U.S. political, cultural, labor, and academic circles first in the 1910s and early 1920s and then again in the l950s. Despite the early post–World War II industrial success of the former USSR and most of Eastern Europe, the lack of democratic rights and the legacy of Stalin's regime made many New Lefters leery of uncritically resurrecting the turn-of-the-century "scientific socialism." Further, those most clearly associated with the New Left were not workers but students, who were most interested in developing analysis of imperialism and economic development. They came out of the cultural revolution of the 1960s and also were interested in Marxist theories of culture and praxis (the combination of theory and practice).

At the same time, the feminist movement was emerging. Historian Sara Evans traces the emergence of the modern feminist movement to the women who became dissatisfied with their inferior treatment by men in both the Civil Rights and the New Left antiwar movements.[36] These modern-day feminists initially fell into two camps: radical feminists and socialist feminists.[37] Socialist feminist social scientists sought to develop a feminist theory that paid more attention to class and imperialism than radical feminists did, but both saw women as distinctly oppressed. Most socialist feminists understood feminism's call to take the personal as political and relied heavily on their own experiences with sexism to inform their motivations and the focus of their political and theoretical work. However, when it came to writing, analyzing, and theorizing, they almost always used Marxist method and theory.

The attempts to transform Marxism are evidenced in the titles of books and articles socialist feminists wrote. Heidi Hartmann's influential essay "The Unhappy Marriage" speaks of a marriage between the two; Lise Vogel's 1983 book on Marxism and feminism is subtitled "Toward a Unitary Theory" and Michèle Barrett's book *Women's Oppression Today,* first published in 1980, took as its primary task the synthesis of Marxism and feminism.[38] Sandra Morgen provides a good description of socialist feminists' early efforts:

> Trying to be good Marxists and I would argue trying to create a theoretical language that paralleled Marxism and thus was more likely to be heard by Marxists, socialist feminists sought to analyze the issues of family, procreation, and sexuality by conceptualizing a "mode of reproduction" that was to be examined historically in relation to the mode of production. These theories highlighted a series of relationships that existed between the social organization of fertility and women's reproduction, the raising of children, women's unpaid work in the home, sex segregation in the labor force, the changing demographics of the labor force, and the organization of production and labor resistance.[39]

Despite using Marxist methodology and a commitment to the eradication of class and racial oppression, socialist feminists remained critical of prior Marxist analysis of women's oppression. From the onset of the modern-day women's movement, socialist feminists both embraced and rejected components of Marxist writings in their quest to develop a theory and practice around women's liberation.

Socialist feminism was born out of New Left criticisms of orthodox Marxism and the New Left's sexism. The uneasy relationship between socialists and feminists was apparent in economics. Marxian economics was just as disproportionately male as mainstream economics and Marxist economists seemed equally as sexist as their mainstream counterparts. But, unlike mainstream economists, Marxian economists knew that socialist feminists were their allies and that they too were marginalized within the economics profession for many of the same reasons feminists were.

In the late 1960s and 1970s, Marxian economic scholarship was simultaneously providing critiques of orthodox Marxism and neoclassical economics.[40] Socialist feminist economists were involved in these projects but were also trying to integrate the role of gender into Marxian theory. It was an uphill battle. Socialist feminist economists were engaging in scholarly and political work that the mainstream profession was not interested in. And they were trying to work within a group of mostly male Marxists, many whom seemed threatened by feminism.

Interpreting the impact of feminism in Marxian economics is complicated by the interdisciplinary nature of Marxian political economy. In the late 1960s, individual fields of study in the social sciences had been well established, if not entrenched. But New Left scholars promoted a much wider purview than traditionally offered by established disciplines or traditional Marxism. Study groups and New Left publications were an important component of this integration. Nonetheless, to get a Ph.D., one needed to be trained in a particular field, and academic newcomers had to choose one. Those interested in Marxian political economy understood the importance of the material analysis of capitalism, but the economics discipline was extremely male dominated and becoming increasingly math oriented. By the mid-1970s, no one could be trained as Ph.D. economist without taking considerable amounts of graduate-level neoclassical economics courses. Marxist feminist scholarship in sociology, urban studies, philosophy, and history seemed equally, if not more, compatible with looking at gender and class and allowed one to avoid learning linear algebra, calculus, and microeconomics. Compared with other disciplines, there were fewer socialist feminist economists than sociologists or historians, mostly because there were fewer women (and feminists) in economics.

Feminism was not readily accepted by many Marxist economists or easily incorporated into Marxist political economy organizations, academic enclaves, culture, or journals. Battles over male dominance erupted in the Union for Radical Political Economics (URPE—the organization formed in 1968 by radical political economists) in the early 1970s, resulting in the formation of a women's caucus in 1971. In 1972 the women's caucus published a special issue of URPE's journal, the *Review of Radical Political Economics* (RRPE) on women.

By 1980 the RRPE had published four special issues on the political economy of women. Articles in the special issues served as a first important outlet for socialist feminist economics scholarship. Socialist feminists wrote about a wide range of feminist economic thinking: the question of how to theorize about women and families, the role of reproductive labor and control, feminist pedagogy, critiques of Marxian and neoclassical treatment of women and families, women's economic history, women in socialist economies, and women in labor markets.

Still, there were almost no socialist feminist economists with tenure in economics departments that granted Ph.D.s by the early 1980s. Even at the

University of Massachusetts in Amherst, which had explicitly developed a Marxian economics graduate program in 1975–76, there were no tenured women on the faculty until the fall of 1982. Socialist feminist economists who made pioneering contributions to socialist feminist thought had a hard time landing permanent academic positions in economics department, even ones with significant numbers of radicals.

Although Marxism and feminism's initial matchup presented some personal, political, and theoretical problems, there were some basic agreements—primarily the commitment to interpreting class dynamics and that neoclassical economics did not do a good job in explaining much of women's or men's economic activity. Marxists have shaped and refined their critiques of the neoclassical model in ways that many feminist economists within the mainstream paradigms have also pursued in their critiques. Marxist political scientist Adam Przeworski's summary of the reasons that Marxists object to methodological individualism resound with feminist's critiques. "These objections fall into three main categories: preferences are not universal or stable but are contingent upon conditions and thus change historically; self-interest is a poor description of preferences for at least some people; and under some conditions 'rational' action is not possible even if individuals are 'rational.' "[41]

Early Contributions of Socialist Feminist Scholarship in Economics

One of the first influential pieces of early socialist feminist scholarship in the social sciences was "Women: The Longest Revolution," by British psychoanalyst Juliet Mitchell, published in 1966 in the Marxist journal *New Left Review*.[42] Mitchell's starting point was a critique of the treatment of women by Marx, Engels, Bebel, and Lenin. Mitchell's analysis heavily influenced feminist action and scholarship in the United States. This particular essay was the first of many articles appearing in left journals discussing the use of Marxian concepts to develop a theory of women's oppression that was distinct from men's.[43] Even authors associated with radical feminism were heavily influenced by Marxist categories and method—in particular Shulamith Firestone's *The Dialectic of Sex* and Kate Millet's *Sexual Politics*.[44] Mitchell set the agenda for socialist feminist research by arguing that Marx's and Engels's treatment was too economistic to successfully analyze women's oppression because they relegated women's position to "institutions of private property."[45] She called for a broader analysis of economic activity and emphasized the ideological components as well as economic. Specifically,

Mitchell called for a better Marxian understanding of production and reproduction, socialization, and culture. If not, she argued, there would be little
hope for understanding women's oppression and less hope of women's liberation. She specifically pointed to the importance of further theorizing about
and transforming of four key structures: production, reproduction, sex, and
socialization of children.

Socialist feminist economists have largely focused on the relationship of
the first two of Mitchell's list of structures: production and reproduction.
What follows is not a comprehensive survey of feminists' contribution to
Marxian economic analysis of women's oppression, but rather a look at several different and important theoretical treatments of women's oppression in
class societies (particularly, but not exclusively, capitalism) using an explicitly Marxian economic framework. Although many of the authors discussed
are economists, not all are. However, each is writing about women's material
status in a class system.

The first serious and sustained theoretical discussions of women's
oppression in capitalism were referred to as the "domestic labor debates."
The debates first appeared in print with Canadian chemist Margaret
Bentson's article "The Political Economy of Women's Liberation," published in 1969 by the U.S. Marxist journal *Monthly Review*. "There *is* a material basis for women's status; we are not merely discriminated against, we
are exploited. At present, our unpaid labor in the home is necessary if the
entire system is to function."[46] The domestic labor debate continued for over
a decade with more than 50 articles published mostly in the United States
and Britain.[47]

The debate focused on the role that domestic labor played in capitalism
and served two important purposes for socialist feminists and Marxist feminist economic analysis.[48] First, it created an important, yet unresolved and
contentious, theoretical debate on how to use Marxian political economy to
understand the role of women's unpaid work in the home by linking it
directly to production. The domestic labor debate discussions opened the
door for feminists who were also Marxists to carry on a serious discussion of
gender in Marxian economics that did not reduce women's oppression to
their class position. The second important aspect of the domestic labor
debate was that it began a discussion of the direction of political action and
political platforms socialist feminists might pursue. "Wages for housework"
campaigns coincided with the domestic labor debate in Britain and in the
United States. A focus on reproductive labor also provided a link to the
reproductive rights networks that engaged many feminists at the time. Inter-

estingly, the role of domestic labor in economic accounting has taken center stage in current feminist economic research and action.

The domestic labor debate seemed to hold large stakes for socialist feminists. Feminists wanted a better theory of the family than offered by scientific socialism. Without a way to identify and integrate the specific nature of women's oppression into a Marxist theory of exploitation, then it would be difficult to discuss the political implications of women's class position. For example, Marx refers to labor that produces surplus value as productive labor. If women weren't exploited, then under Marxian terminology they would also not be considered productive. Feminists claimed that men and capitalists benefited from women's labor and that those benefits changed over time, but they wanted the theoretical apparatus to prove it.

With so many contributors and the political direction of socialist feminism in the balance, it is not surprising that the answers to the exploitation question in the debate varied remarkably. The range went from arguing that women constitute their own class and household labor represents a separate mode of production (Delphy) to domestic labor being another form of surplus labor under the capitalist mode of production (Harrison) and everything in between (e.g., Gardiner, Himmelweit, and Mackintosh).[49] Some authors argued that domestic labor actually produced value (Mariarosa Dalla Costa).[50] Others argued that it produced surplus value, allocated to capitalists or men depending on the author.

Like many heated theoretical debates, the domestic labor debate never seemed to be definitively resolved. Feminist political economist Susan Himmelweit, one of the contributors to the debate, concluded in the mid-1980s, "The 'domestic labor debate' as it became known failed to answer the question to which it was addressed: what is the material basis of women's oppression? To do so it would have had to do more than classify domestic labor using the existing categories of Marxist analysis."[51] Further, Himmelweit argues that none of the authors ever resolved why women do the bulk of domestic labor.

Not everyone was as sanguine about the results of the domestic labor debate as Himmelweit, however. Nancy Folbre, attempting to resolve some of the dilemmas in the domestic labor debate in her article "Exploitation Comes Home: A Critique of the Marxian Theory of Family Labor," suggests that the allocation of labor within families takes place in both cooperative and antagonistic ways. Further, the reproduction of labor power is not stagnant but a historical process influenced by the production process itself. Folbre optimistically suggests, "the labor theory of value can be sensibly reinterpreted in such a way as to provide important insights into both production and distribution in the family."[52] In that sense, Folbre is quite right. The domestic labor debate brought to light the importance of understanding the role of reproductive labor in the home to the functioning of capitalism. It also raised the possibility that men could exploit women at the same time that capitalists could exploit male and female labor. The domestic labor debate discussed the side of the duality Engels ignored: the impact reproduction has on production and class relations. Through the domestic labor debate, feminists were successful in confronting a Marxist model, not unlike neoclassical models of reproductive work, that was built on the unspoken assumption that labor gets performed for free in the home and that has remained historically unchanged.

The domestic labor debates were the start of a journey in which socialist feminists attempted to theorize about the connection of women's oppression to class societies. Here I discuss only three paths taken in the 1970s and early 1980s. The first path, referred to as "dual systems theory," posited two distinct systems at work—capitalism and patriarchy. Heidi Hartmann's essay "The Unhappy Marriage between Marxism and Feminism" introduced the dual systems notion. In it she argued that the system of women's oppression—patriarchy—cannot be reduced to capitalist class relations, because it has its own dynamics. Hartmann claimed that dual systems of oppression exist: sometimes these systems operate in tandem and sometimes in opposition. "We argue that a materialist analysis demonstrates that patriarchy is not simply a psychic, but also a social and economic structure. We suggest that our society can best be understood once it is recognized that it is organized both in capitalistic and in patriarchal ways. While pointing out tensions between patriarchal and capitalist interests, we argue that the accumulation of capital both accommodates itself to patriarchal social structure and helps to perpetuate it."[53] Hartmann argues that Marxism is sex-blind. It can easily define certain places in capitalism but does not have the tools to explain why certain faces (e.g., women and people of color) fill those slots. One needs a theory of gender and race to do that.

Hartmann, in effect, turned the "Woman Question" into the "Feminist Question" by calling for a dialectical materialist analysis of how men exploit and dominate women that is distinct from a class analysis. Hartmann's argument and the dual systems approach is discussed and critiqued in 12 separate articles by socialist feminists in several disciplines in the volume *Women and Revolution*. The problem of including race and arguing for separate spheres poses difficult questions for Hartmann's specifications. Still, the dual systems approach has provided one important springboard for many socialist feminist economists in their theorizing about women's oppression and in discussions of women's work in capitalism.[54]

In the early 1980s, sociologist Michèle Barrett argued for a different approach. She claimed that the ideological expressions of women's oppression in capitalism are real and too important to be seen as a reflection of the material base (as Marxists have). Further, Barrett argued that ideology was too connected to the specific class relations of capitalism to relegate it to a separate sphere. Barrett, then, attempts to meld Marxism's materialism with feminist psychoanalytical literature by using French Marxist Louis Althussar's notion of ideology. In *Women's Oppression Today*, Michèle Barrett lays out the basis for Althussarian, post-Marxist, postmodernist treatments of gender. Barrett defines ideology as "a generic term for the processes by which meaning is produced, challenged, reproduced, transformed."[55] But ideology is not separate from the relations of production; "ideology has played an important part in the historical construction of the capitalist division of labor and in the reproduction of labour power. A sexual division of labour and accompanying ideologies of the appropriate meaning of labour for men and women, have been embedded in the capitalist division of labour from its beginnings."[56]

Barrett examines how ideology has had an important role in the social and economic production of education and the division of labor. She ultimately arrives at a discussion that focuses on the construction of the actual and ideological understanding of household structure and role of family. The emphasis on the construction of cultural definitions of gender roles in the development of capitalist relations and labor markets is echoed in the work of Julie Matthaei in her book *An Economic History of Women in America*. Althussarian extensions into gender have been elaborated by Harriet Fraad, Stephen Resnick, and Richard Wolff in their book *Bringing It All Back Home*.[57]

Feminist political economist Lourdes Benería, in an article that appeared in 1979, argued for exploring a different kind of dualism than those explored by either Hartmann or Barrett—that of production and reproduction. Benería returns directly to Engels's original dualism to discuss the relationship of the sexual division of labor in production to women's role in reproduction. But rather than resort to a rather stagnant view of the family and rely on the existence of private property, Benería argues for a closer examination of the social and material conditions of reproduction and the ways in which reproduction and production are related. She suggests three important focal points: (1) the degree to which men control women's reproductive capacities, (2) the extent to which women perform child care and domestic tasks associated with reproductive labor, and (3) "the extent to which the allocation of women as agents of production is conditioned by their role in reproduction."[58] Benería emphasizes the basic contradiction of reproduction for women: the need (and shared objective with men) to produce children versus their lack of control over their reproductive capacities because of the extent of control men have over women's lives as mothers. She argues that women's roles in the home shape their roles in nondomestic spheres.

Although other important contributions have been made to socialist feminist theorizing about women's economic oppression, these works presented original, fruitful, and distinct analysis of the most enduring conflict between feminism and Marxism—the question of the source and the dynamics of women's oppression. What unifies them is their emphasis on the relationships of reproduction to production and on the family as a primary location of women's oppression.

The theoretical issues posed by socialist feminists in the late 1970s and early 1980s have not been resolved. Some engaged in those debates have moved away from Marxism all together, grabbing their tools and moving to postmodern feminism. Others have lost interest in the immediacy of developing the single theory that can explain gender and class relations across all time and histories and have turned instead to concrete analysis of women's economic situation. Still others have used these insights and dead ends to inform current debates in feminist economic thinking (the subject of the next chapter). Still, the importance of collective action and the role of social structures and institutions in reproducing women's oppression that were initially raised in the theoretical debates over women's relationship to capitalism are the same ones feminist economists grapple with today.

Assessing Socialist Feminist Scholarship's Impact on Marxian Economics

Accounting for the tangible impact of feminism on Marxian political economy is difficult. It entails subjective, if not arbitrary, evaluation of contributions to the field. The resurgence of radical political economy, including Marxian political economy, in the late 1960s offered a critical analysis of capitalism that wanted to include critiques offered by many of those confronting the system. Imperialism, racism, and the subjugation of women were always included in the list of Marxist economists' concerns; however, these topics were rarely considered central.[59] Still, feminists and the women's movement were seen as part and parcel of what it meant to want to study radical political economics, in stark contrast to neoclassical economics.

Many Marxian economists do consider gender in their work and see the feminist movement as an important and defining political movement in the recent period. It is beyond the scope of this chapter to survey recent Marxist literature to see how gender is incorporated. However, it is worth a brief look at one school within Marxian economics—neo-Marxism and the Social Structures of Accumulation (SSA) theorists—precisely because it has attempted to be more inclusive of nonclass relations, including gender. But even this school within Marxism treats nonclass relations analytically distinct from discussions of the dynamics of capitalism. Nonclass relationships, like gender, are viewed as important to discuss and are included in treatments of modern capitalist production, but they are not considered central enough to capitalist production to be built directly into models of capitalist accumulation and growth. As a result, women's political empowerment and conflicts are seen as occurring in the social or political sphere, but rarely in the economic sphere.

One example from a group of relatively prominent Marxist economists associated with this school provides a good illustration. In *Beyond the Wasteland*, Marxist political economists Samuel Bowles, David Gordon, and Thomas Weisskopf analyze the post–World War II U.S. economy and the reasons behind the secular economic decline since the early 1970s. They argue that the "pillars" of postwar growth are no longer sustainable 20 years later. One such pillar is the "labor-capital accord"—the implicit agreement between organized, blue-collar male workers and large manufacturing firms that secured steady wage growth, uninterrupted production, increased productivity, and long-term employment relations. Bowles, Gordon, and Weisskopf argue that when productivity slowed but workers still increased wage demands, the accord broke down. The *political* demands of women and blacks are seen as important demands and part of the "story" of economic change. But seldom are women's demands seen as economic demands or the result of their own integration into waged work.[60]

Probably the least affected school of thought within Marxian economics are Marxian mathematical models and neo-Ricardian (or Sfraffian) interpretations of Marxian economics. Authors affiliated with these schools include John Roemer, Michio Morishima, and Ian Steedman.[61] Following on the heels of Piero Sfraffa's contributions and extensions of the Ricardian model in the 1960s, these Marxists have formalized Marx's theories of production, reproduction, and growth, largely through the use of input-output models.

Neo-Ricardians and mathematical Marxists are credited with solving Marx's transformation "problem" (i.e., translating labor values into prices) and conjoining Marxist's theory of production with a credible mechanism of exchange. For some, this formalization has placed Marxian economics on the academic playing field. Philosopher Robert Paul Wolff proclaims: "For virtually all of this century, the study of the structure and functioning of capitalism has been in the hands of technically gifted, formally rigorous apologists of the established order. Opponents of capitalism, lacking an alternative analytical framework within which to articulate their critique, have been reduced to that most feeble of all weapons, the moral protest. . . . Now, thanks to the works of von Neumann, Sraffa, Morishima, and the others, Marx emerges once more as a major theorist of the political economy of capitalism, a powerful and fertile alternative to Walras, Marshall, Keynes, Samuelson, et al."[62] By formalizing Marx, it has become acceptable economic theory in Wolff's mind. But this work has not incorporated feminists' work on gender dynamics in either production or reproduction.

Several anthologies and dictionaries on political economy or Marxian economics have been published since the early 1980s. One indication of feminism's impact can be found in how these volumes of economists surveying radical political economy treat feminist contributions. Perhaps the most ambitious collection of economic concepts and contributions in all areas of economics in recent years is the four-volume *The New Palgrave: A Dictionary of Economics*[63] edited by political economists John Eatwell, Murray Milgate, and Peter Newman and published in 1987. The dictionary is a grand-scale effort to update and revive the three-volume *Dictionary of Political Economy* edited by R. H. Inglis Palgrave and published between 1894 and 1899. There are more than 1,900 entries, including 715 biographical listings. Of the biographical listings, 35 (5%) are on individual women. Of the remaining 1,200 entries, 25 (2%) include entries on topics relating to gender, women's work, families, or equity.

The *Palgrave*, of course, surveys much more than radical political economy or Marxian economics. The editors, however, developed a series of paperback books with handpicked entries on specific topics, presumably to make the dictionary more accessible and directed. They published 14 separate volumes on specific areas in economics, including one on Marxian economics. That volume is 383 pages long and has 59 entries. However, the volume does not contain a single entry on anything remotely related to gender relations or women. Although the complete *New Palgrave* contains a "domestic labor" entry, it is not included in the *Marxian Economics* volume, despite the fact that the discussion on household labor in those terms almost exclusively took place in Marxian political economy circles. Yet there are 14 gender-related entries from the complete dictionary in the smaller volume entitled *Social Economics*. The placement of gender-related topics is particularly curious since social economics itself is not defined by the *Palgrave*. If one takes the *Palgrave* volume on Marxian economics as a measure of feminism's impact in modern Marxian economics, then that impact is close to zero. Not unlike women's contributions in the beginning of the twentieth century, the *Palgrave*'s editors have designated feminist contributions on gender to a field called, for lack of a better title, social economics. Similarly, a 1992 two-volumed *History of Marxian Economics* has only a single, but unreferenced, mention of feminism in the text.[64]

Not all overviews of radical political economics and Marxian economics give feminists such silent treatment, however. An early survey (1980) of Marxian economic contributions by Herbert Gintis includes a lengthy discussion of the role of feminist work.[65] A durable reader of Marxist political economy contributions now in its third edition, *The Capitalist System*, has always included a section on women.[66] A 1990 two-volume edited collection of radical political economy includes a section on the family with three articles by socialist feminist economists.[67] A 1994 edited volume entitled *The Role of Economic Theory* includes essays on economics from nine distinct perspectives; the only one that mentions gender and the women's movement, however, is Howard Sherman's essay on Marxian economic theory.[68]

The debate about feminism's impact on Marxian economics may be unresolved, but at least it is contested. Bruce Roberts and Susan Feiner included a section on Marxist feminist contributions in their edited volume *Radical Economics*. In it Julie Matthaei argues for the importance of expanding the scope of Marxian economics by researching the nature of the sexual division of labor and by forcing Marxists to acknowledge the historical and analytical importance of women's reproductive labor and establishing a Marxist analysis of patriarchy. Matthaei also makes a claim for feminism's measurable gains in radical political economy. In a piece responding to Matthaei, Jane Humphries disagrees. She notes that those most concerned with value theory in theoretical Marxism still write as if the domestic labor debates never took place.[69]

CONCLUSION

Marxism held out great promise for feminists in the 1970s. Socialist feminist economic analysis developed quickly and appeared in left journals, including ones that primarily focused on economics. The "Unhappy Marriage" metaphor has been an enduring one because, although Marxism and feminism have much to offer each other, they are not always compatible. The "fruits" of the marriage are hard to quantify and are contested even among those who are both Marxists and feminists. Nonetheless, compared with feminism's impact on neoclassical economics, the impact on Marxian economics has been large.

Still, it is hard not to notice that many socialist feminists in literary and noneconomic social science fields in the 1970s have become postmodernists in the 1990s. Perhaps postmodernism offers the ideas and method of analysis that is the space between Marxism and psychoanalysis that Flax yearned for 20 years ago. A few socialist feminist economists and socialists have turned to postmodernism, but most have not, preferring a more materialist-based theory of oppression. At the same time, however, in the 1990s few of those who were socialist feminist economists in the 1970s rely solely on Marxian methods. Recently, several books have been published, two by economists, which explicitly argue that despite the enormous insights Marxism has provided feminism, it is time to move beyond it. Those authors argue for a more eclectic approach that includes modern theories of class, gender, race, and international relations.[70] These authors are helping to shape what might be a new paradigm—feminist economics—and is the topic of the next chapter.

9

THERE'S NO PLACE LIKE HOME: PROBLEMS AND POSSIBILITIES FOR FEMINISM AND ECONOMICS

[A] small group of economists has begun to criticize the economic paradigm out of an explicitly feminist perspective. . . . So far, this literature has not produced an alternative paradigm, but it has produced a set of challenges to and criticisms of standard approaches. The evolution of this literature and its impact on the economics profession will be extremely interesting to watch. The substantial agreement within the profession around a single paradigm makes this type of challenge far riskier for those who undertake it and makes it more difficult for such criticisms to seep into the generally accepted "idea set" of economists.

—Rebecca Blank[1]

I outlined three criteria necessary for establishing feminist scholarship in a discipline in the beginning of this book: diversity of ideas, receptiveness of

methodologies to feminist theorizing, and feminist organizational representation. The three feminist-friendly criteria have not existed in economics. As
I have argued and the preceding quote suggests, the profession has been
dominated by a single approach to economic thinking. Neoclassical economic theory is universally taught in undergraduate and graduate schools.
Other approaches are often viewed as optional. Even Keynesian economics,
the prevailing economic theory in the 1950s and 1960s, has been usurped by
neoclassical economics with the study of microfoundations of macroeconomic activity. Virtually all applied fields are taught from the perspective of
neoclassical theory. Students who wish to study alternative approaches in
any systematic or cohesive fashion are often directed to a handful of particular graduate schools that specialize in post-Keynesian, Marxian, or institutional thought. Neoclassical economics authoritatively controls the training
ground of economics—graduate schools. It is replicated by the "top" journals in the profession, which almost exclusively publish articles using neoclassical assumptions and analysis. Learning neoclassical economics is
inescapable for anyone wishing to become an economist today. It is virtually
essential to embrace it if one is to be recognized in the profession.

The conduciveness of economic methodology, within the prevailing paradigm, to feminist analysis is also sorely lacking. As argued in chapter 7,
neoclassical economics is antifeminist in its explanations of women's economic position and its method of understanding economic problems. For
many feminists the prominence of neoclassical economics and its analysis of
gender present large theoretical stumbling blocks and a professional
dilemma. Janet Seiz puts this as, "aside from truth, there are practical reasons
to remain in the mainstream: to suggest that feminist economists forsake
neoclassical work is, given the profession's current structure and values, to
demand that they jeopardize their careers and abandon hope of reaching
audiences unwilling or unable to hear arguments framed in different languages."[2] Marxian political economy, on the other hand, has had an uneasy
but steady relationship methodologically with feminism. If the economics
profession took Marxian economics more seriously, feminism no doubt
would have had a larger impact on the profession than it has.

The third criteria, feminist organizational representation, has until
recently been weak and isolated. Part of the reason may be due to lack of trying. The Committee on the Status of Women in the Economics Profession
(CSWEP), which has existed since 1972, has made very few inroads in promoting feminist economic theory. In 1986 the Committee made a concerted
effort to steer its activities away from analysis of women in the economy to

focus instead on enhancing the professional careers of women in economics. The Women's Caucus of the Union for Radical Political Economics (URPE), established in 1971, was primarily engaged in bringing a feminist presence to radical political economy, not necessarily the profession as a whole. It was successful in promoting feminist analysis, publishing feminist research (via special issues of URPE's journal), organizing panels at conferences, and influencing some Marxist economists to integrate gender into their analysis. URPE served as a fertile arena for socialist feminist economic analysis in the 1970s and 1980s. However, feminists who did not identify as radicals by and large did not participate in URPE activities or submit to its publications, which limited the degree to which feminists in URPE were able to influence the profession as a whole or provide support for non-Marxist feminists.

The lack of diversity of approaches, the methodological barriers to feminist analysis presented by neoclassical economics, and the lack of an explicitly feminist organization dedicated to developing feminist economic analysis has until now successfully impeded the development of feminist economic analysis. The prominent role neoclassical economics plays in the profession probably not only stifles feminists who are currently in the profession, but likely acts as an efficient screening mechanism for yet-to-be feminist economists. Feminists eager to enter graduate school in economics must be prepared for years of studying a set of ideas that they will probably find offensive. Unless they find a network of feminist economists or a body of feminist economic literature from which to study and to engage, the field will remain uninviting.[3]

However, with the recent establishment of a feminist economics organization and a journal, feminist economics has made some rapid and important leaps in a relatively short time. Feminist economic analysis is now beginning to make important insights and contributions to understanding economic phenomena that are beginning to be noticed in the mainstream of the profession. Further, via IAFFE and its Internet list (FEMECON-L), feminist economists have set up a very effective network, which includes graduate and undergraduate students interested in feminist economics.[4]

This final chapter discusses the problems and the potential promise of feminism and economics. The main problem in economics is that it is a discipline equipped with models that were constructed to explain market-based production and assumed a fixed family type in which husbands worked and women stayed home. Although this at first appears to be a problem for feminists, it is actually a problem for all economists. Without dynamic models of home-based work and family structure, economics is at best incomplete, and at worst it is wrong. Feminist economic analysis, with its attempts to view economics with a feminist lens and using a wide variety of economic and noneconomic approaches and methodologies, has the potential to transform the discipline and help make it a more complete theory of economic activity and distribution.

THE PROBLEM WITH ECONOMICS

Every introductory economics student learns economics is the study of the allocation of scarce resources. It is supposed to provide an explanation of how societies transform their limited resources into goods and services people want. This definition of economics *potentially* allows for the exploration of a wide range of activity. Further, the word *economics* has its roots in the Greek word meaning "managing the household" (oikonomous). On the surface, then, economics appears as if it is very inclusive of nonmarket economic activity. But scratch the surface and one finds that economics has very little to do with the production and management of goods for their use—especially in the home.

The origins of economics as a discipline are directly traceable to the advent of markets (production that takes place almost exclusively outside the household) and the rise of capitalist production—production for profit with the use of wage labor—in the late eighteenth century. Adam Smith's *Wealth of Nations*, written in 1776, is often considered the first, great piece of economic analysis. Even Marx wrote almost exclusively on capitalist production. As economic historian Daniel Hausman notes, "Many economists believe that their theories apply to other kinds of economic arrangements as well, and specific studies have been made of primitive economies, feudal economies, socialist economies, and various other possibilities; but the core of economic theorizing has been devoted to understanding capitalist economies."[5]

Capitalism is a system driven by commodity production—the exchange of goods and services in markets. But, unlike other economic systems, in which exchange is one of many important means of obtaining and allocating goods and services, capitalism requires that the vast majority of goods (including necessities) be purchased through markets and that much of the population must have access to wages in order to survive. Unlike socialist economies, in which a large portion of economic activity also takes place via commodity production and wage labor, capitalist production is ruled by profitability—not use or need. That is, goods will be produced precisely because they can be sold in the market for a profit. All other economic activities that also take place and are necessary in capitalism—the production and allocation of goods and services in households, communities, the nonprofit sector, and governments—are theoretical afterthoughts. Modern-day economists use the tools they have developed to analyze markets to understand other, distinct types of economic activity but, as a rule, do not do a very good job.

At the turn of the twentieth century, U.S. economists understood economics to entail a rather broad array of topics: currency, trade, poverty, child labor, women's wages, role of government, and education. But by World War I, economics had relegated the studies of households to sociology, psychology, social work, and home economics. Economic theory and analysis developed in the United States since that time has almost exclusively focused on economic activity that takes place *outside* the home—that is, market-based activity—and has made a point of considering that work as the only work that constitutes economic activity. Economic accounting at the micro and macro levels excludes unpaid work. In the early 1900s census takers in the United States and England literally removed wives from their census of the labor force,[6] and accounts of the gross domestic product exclude unpaid domestic work, which is estimated to constitute about 50 percent of the total work done worldwide.[7] As a result, the role of women's primary economic activity—the raising of children in the home—has been severely neglected or devalued in economic accounting, theory, and policy.

The main problem, then, is that economists have no place like home—literally. For a long time, there was not much interest in thinking about economic activities in the home, making women and much of the work they did invisible and almost irrelevant to economics. When economists did decide to turn their attention to the household and the role of gender, they did so by extending the models they already had. But those models were created to explain market-based behavior and were ill equipped to explain household production, fertility, and caring.

Economic theories recognize work in the home, but home production (and reproduction) is most often assumed to take place under a relatively stagnant and stable set of family structures with a given (naturally or historically) sexual division of labor. And although economic theories recognize that allocation and production of goods and services in the home is not like market-based production and exchange, they have trouble modeling it. Consider, for example, the transportation of the neoclassical assumption of utility maximization subject to income constraints used to explain markets into the household. Neither the demand for nor the allocation of home-produced goods and services is based on one's ability (or even potential) to pay or individual utility for the goods or services. Indeed, those with the most needs and least income-producing capacity may get more resources (e.g., a child with disabilities will require and probably get more care and perhaps more medical and educational services than an able-bodied child in the same household). What gives care giving and home-produced goods their value has little to do with their marginal utility.

In separate analyses feminist economists Susan Himmelweit and Nancy Folbre have argued that the quality of care and the degree of devotion are very important but are by no means guaranteed by any competitive or market process.[8] Similarly, in the Marxian model, women do not necessarily share men's interests when it comes to how work is done in the home.[9] The production of goods and services (including people) in the home does not take place under the guise of accumulation and profit-making in the Marxian model, but there can still be an oppressive power dynamic. The motivation and the nature of work in the household—caretaking—is just not reducible to market-based production in either the neoclassical or Marxian frameworks.

It is precisely economics' inability to incorporate a decent model of the household and unpaid work that leaves so much of it incompatible with feminist treatments. Although there are many kinds of feminist analyses, all are interested in women's position relative to men. Despite the myriad of ways of organizing economic production and the lack of uniformity in the types of work men and women perform, women are primarily responsible for dependent care. This care almost always is done in some kind of household unit and it universally takes a considerable amount of one's time. One cannot begin to comprehend women's economic position relative to men's unless there is a basic understanding of how the household operates within the context of all economic production.

Not only feminists are stymied by economics' inability to understand and model the household. Without a better understanding of the household, current economic knowledge is incomplete. Not being able to integrate or dynamically model the home and household production presents a problem for the economics discipline, particularly at a time when more and more women are doing paid work and family structures are changing. Economic models of long-term economic production, economic development, wages, and income distribution must specify aspects of population growth, family formation, and the division of household labor. Typically these models view fertility and reproductive technologies as technical issues devoid of economic, cultural, and political influences and struggles. Families are almost always assumed to take the same form: heterosexual, male-headed, two-adult households with a "wife." Explanations of the division of labor in the household are considered beyond the scope of economic inquiry, and there is considerable confusion about how women behave in economic models (i.e., are they altruistic, driven by sexual passions, or rational actors in the mold of *homo economicus*?).

FAULTY FOUNDATIONS:
AN EXAMPLE

The problems that arise by not integrating a better analysis of gender can be seen by looking at a specific example—economists' models of wage determination. Wages are the major source of household income and are therefore key to models of economic well-being, growth, equality, and income distribution. That is, economists' models of wage determination form a major building block for explanation of other important economic phenomena in all the major approaches used in economics, including neoclassical, Keynesian, and Marxian theories. Yet, wage theory itself is implicitly built on an unchanging family foundation with a traditional sexual division of labor—the traditional married-couple family in which a "wife" is responsible for taking care of children.

First, consider the neoclassical model. Neoclassical wage theory argues that wages are equal to the marginal productivity of the last worker hired (see box 7.1). Marginal productivity is determined by workers' human capital and the level of technology. Workers with high levels of education and experience and/or who work in high value-added industries will receive higher wages than workers who do not. Higher wages, in the neoclassical model, translate into higher economic well-being. Who has higher levels of human capital or work in high-value industries? Individual workers who choose to invest in their own human capital. Often that is the end of the neoclassical theory of wage determination unless children (and the labor involved in taking care of them) enter the picture. Once the need for care arises, the neoclassical model immediately assumes the presence of a two-adult nuclear family who must make important decisions about labor force participation versus home-based production. The model almost always assumes a women with a child is married and that she will stay married for a long time (she may not necessarily be married to the same person, but she is married nonetheless). Married couples presumably make their labor force decisions jointly (not an easy proposition in a model predicated on individual utility maximization). And though the model promotes labor market decisions as a set of choices, the bottom line is that women's ability to work, acquire human capital, and earn a wage are very much constrained by the presence of children in ways that men's choices are not. Wages are a function of individual choices for men and joint choices for women with children.

Many individuals live and share their economic resources with other people. For them, labor market supply decisions are not individual decisions, *nor* are they the sole determinant of their access to income. Indeed, family structure probably has more to do with one's access to income, and with it their economic well-being, than does human capital acquisition.[10] The development of neoclassical wage theory was constructed with a single (i.e., unmarried) worker or a worker without child-care responsibilities in mind. It extended the theory to apply to married women, but with little success. Further, with one out of every four children living in a single-parent family, the marriage assumption is outdated at best.

Marxian wage theory does not do much better. It also rests on the assumption of a married-couple family with a wife at home. The labor theory of value argues that workers are paid wages that are sufficient to reproduce a worker and his family. Marx believed capitalism would draw women and children into the labor force and erode men's family wage, but the original wage structure was assumed to be based on some notion of a traditional family structure.

Labor market segmentation serves as an important basis for modern Marxist wage theory (it is also used by institutionalist theorists). In this model, jobs (not people) are assigned different wages depending on which labor market segment they fall into. Wages attached to jobs are based on a variety of factors, including productivity aspects but also things like custom, unionization, and market structure. All labor market segmentation theorists note that jobs are not distributed randomly among workers. Women (and people of color) disproportionately have jobs in the sectors in which pay is the lowest. The reasons given for this distribution vary, although most argue that discrimination plays a large role. It is argued that the segments develop out of the dynamics of capitalist production and class struggle. But the story is really only about the development of jobs in the leading sectors and largely apply to male workers. Labor market segmentation theory has yet to consider how segments have developed within the context of a particular family structure and women's economic role in the household. For example, women's increased access to wages over the last 40 years has probably served to ameliorate men's demands for higher wages, affecting the nature of jobs and job segments. As more and more women have entered the labor force as full-time participants, the nature of labor segments has changed tremendously.

Both neoclassical and Marxian wage theories have implicitly developed to explain the labor market in the leading sectors of capitalism. Since the people in those jobs were primarily white men, the theories are largely applicable only to white men's labor market experiences in capitalism. Wage determination models typically *assume* a worker who is an able-bodied individual with no major caretaking responsibilities. That is, the worker's experience that is being explained is one who either has no children or is in a family in which someone is providing limitless, free labor in the home that makes it possible for that adult member to enter the labor market and earn wages unfettered by other responsibilities. But family structure and market production form a dynamic relation. And when family structures change, as they surely do, the foundations of current economic theories are badly shaken.

The theories can accommodate other kind of workers, but only within the context of a fast-fading family structure. Both neoclassical and Marxian theories have a story to tell about "wives" (i.e., the potential secondary earners in the household whose primary responsibility is that of caretaking) in the labor market. They are theories, then, that describe an economy with two types of workers (husbands and wives), in the case of the neoclassical model, or two types of jobs ("jobs with wives" and "jobs for wives") in the Marxian model. Husbands are people who can offer their labor time freely to employers. They are breadwinners who can work full-time and receive enough pay to support a family. Similarly, "jobs with wives" are jobs in which employers expect workers to work full-time (and usually overtime), have benefits, and pay living wages. They are jobs that assume that the worker has no dependent care responsibilities—either the worker has no dependents or a "wife" available to take care of dependent family members. Wives looking for paid work are constrained by the necessary work of taking care of family members at home. "Jobs for wives" are ones that allow some flexibility to accommodate caretaking responsibilities. Highly skilled "wives" in corporations are actually referred to as being in the "mommy track." For the majority of working mothers, "jobs for wives" are often low paying, without job benefits (e.g., health care and pensions), and often require an immense amount of time juggling, reliance on friends and families, and expensive child care.

The problem with economic theories that are predicated on two types of workers (husbands and wives) or two kinds of jobs ("jobs with wives" and "jobs for wives" in the economy) is that fewer and fewer adults are "wives"—the person who provides limitless unpaid labor time at home and in her community while relying on her husband's income as the main source of financial support. In 1993, in the United States, 28 percent of all families with children under the age of 18 were single-parent families.[11] Further, close to 70 percent of all married mothers were in the paid labor force. In addition, and in part due to the remarkable change in women's participation in the labor force and the change in the industrial structure, there are fewer and fewer "jobs with wives" to be had. Any theory that *assumes* any one particular family type and operates using a theory of wage determination that assumes a worker either has no children or a wife at home is deeply flawed.

DISTURBANCES IN THE FIELD: FEMINIST ECONOMICS POSSIBILITIES FRONTIERS

By and large the economics profession has done a poor job understanding the economic contributions of half the world's people. Feminist economics brings the discipline new tools and foci to take that task on and has the potential to truly transform economic analysis. To date there is no separate, definable paradigm called feminist economics, although there have been some attempts to shape new models using feminist insights.

The efforts to develop a feminist approach in economics have grown exponentially over the last five years. The confluence of a strong, viable, international feminist economics organization and world events that are making women's economic contributions and responsibilities more visible has worked to attract feminists to economic research. Generally, feminist economists are creating disturbances in the field and stretching the boundaries of economic analysis by recognizing and integrating gender differences into economic models, by spanning disciplines, and by employing a variety of analytical tools and paradigmatic approaches. Much, although not all, of that work entails integrating the household and the type of labor performed there with economic behavior and production generally, which has opened up an entire vista of possibilities in economic research, theory, and practice.

Feminist economic research has grown so rapidly in the last several years that a comprehensive review of the literature is far beyond the scope of this book. Three recently published edited volumes on feminist economics contain a wide range of short articles that cover many of the areas in which feminist economists are doing research: Marianne A. Ferber and Julie A. Nelson, eds. *Beyond Economic Man: Feminist Theory and Economics* (Chicago: University of Chicago Press, 1993); Janice Peterson and Doug Brown, eds., *The Economic Status of Women Under Capitalism: Institutional Economics and Feminist Thought* (Brookfield, VT: Edward Elgar, 1994); and *Out of the Margin: Feminist Perspectives on Economics*, edited by Edith Kuiper and Jolande Sap with Susan Feiner, Notburga Ott, and Zafiris Tzannatos (London: Routledge, 1995). In addition, literature reviews of aspects of feminist economic research are beginning to appear in journals, a testimony to the growth in the field.[12] I conclude this book—whose primary focus has been on the impact of feminism on economics—with a brief description of some of the areas in which feminist economists are currently working to both critique the current literature and to develop new economic approaches.

Given the poorly formulated models of the home, it is not surprising to find that a very large number of feminist economists have turned their research agendas to thinking about and modeling the household. Work in this area spins off in many directions. One area is household bargaining theory (discussed briefly in chapter 7), which attempts to model power in the home. Within this approach, there are discussions of both cooperative and uncooperative models.[13] Another direction is an exploration of the nature of work and caring in the home, using that as a springboard for reshaping economic theory of the household and allocation of time.[14] If caring work is necessary, not typically motivated by self-satisfying behavior, and crosses class boundaries, then economists must develop new ways of thinking about households and the work they perform. Still another direction is in macroeconomic national accounting of household work. Beginning with Marilyn Waring's book *If Women Counted*, there has been considerable interest in and attempts to include the value of household work in national accounts of economic output.[15]

As suggested in chapter 7, feminist economists (and sociologists) have questioned the androcentric nature of economic theorizing and rhetoric, which overlooks the household and the particular role of women and gender. Many in the field have previously taken the neoclassical model and its behavior assumptions to task, but only feminists have really questioned its male bias. Feminists have pursued these critiques in at least three ways. One major area of criticism involves unraveling the assumptions in the construction of economic models, in particular rational, self-satisfying behavior as it pertains to women.[16] A second direction points to the male-centered nature of the rhetoric and "stories" used by economists to construct their models.[17] A third stream of criticism entails a critique of neoclassical economics notion of objective science.[18]

An area of tremendous promise and growth is the work that brings families and household production into macroeconomic economic analysis and that studies the impact of structural economic policies on women and families in developing and developed countries. A recent issue of *World Development*, edited by Nilüfer Çağatay, Diane Elson, and Caren Grown, entitled "Gender, Adjustment and Macroeconomics" contains 15 articles on all aspects of gender, macroeconomic performance, and policies (in addition to a comprehensive introduction by the editors and a review piece on gender and economics).[19] The volume contains articles on conceptual examinations, empirical investigations, macroeconomic models, and feminist initiatives. The work in this special issue builds on an already developed feminist literature on women and economic development. Four edited volumes by feminist economists (and other social scientists) on this topic have been published since 1991,[20] which complement several books by feminist economists on the impact of free trade and other development policies on women.[21]

Feminist economists continue to work in labor economics, in which there is a long tradition of feminist work in both economics and sociology.[22] In addition to ongoing work on the history of women and work,[23] there has been new research on the direction and causes of wage differentials by gender and among women.[24] Feminists are also looking more closely at the relationships between family structure, labor markets, and poverty in their analysis of women's wages and economic well-being.[25] For feminists in this area, integrating the historical role of institutions and custom into the analysis continues to be a vital component of their work.

Feminist economists are also asking new questions in economics and are researching and theorizing about previously unmentioned and undeveloped topics. These areas include gay and lesbian labor market discrimination,[26] sexuality,[27] and feminist approaches to traditional Keynesian macroeconomics[28] and econometrics.[29] They are also finding a small but rich history of women economists.[30] Feminists are uncovering the lives and writing of women economists such as Margaret Reid, Sadie Alexander, and Mabel Newcomer.[31] Michèle Pujol's pioneering work on the history of early economic considerations of women has sparked new interest in feminist interpretations of economic history of thought.[32] Work on the history of the statistical accounts of women's work has reopened a debate on interpreting labor force participation data.[33] Finally, feminist economists are crossing disciplinary lines to use a wider array of measurement instruments currently used in anthropology, political science, and sociology (such as data collected through surveys, observation, and interviews).[34]

Like all knowledge, understanding economic phenomena will be shaped by the social, political, and economic events of the times. This goes beyond the feminist standpoint claim that men see the world differently than women do. For example, the persistence of unemployment in the 1930s helped shape the prominence of Keynesian economics. It is only with the large-scale entrance of women in the paid labor market that economists have begun to take note of the importance of women's work—both in the market and at home. These changes have profoundly affected family structure and the notion of women's work in developed and developing countries. They are felt by everyone in their daily lives. These economic transformations are potentially as revolutionizing in the economics profession as the depression was in the 1930s. Feminists in the profession have crossed theoretical lines to work together to develop feminist economic analysis that simultaneously embodies and rejects traditional tools and approaches. Whether this group can develop a cohesive and distinct methodology or theory in economics remains to be seen. As late bloomers in the social sciences, feminist economists have a way to go and can no doubt learn from the struggles of feminists in other disciplines. Still, feminist economists have the potential to push the economics profession to new theoretical and analytical insights as they work to make women's economic roles more visible. It will occur not by exchanging pronouns, but by reformulating economic models to integrate what economists never measured or theorized but the world has always expected—the production, allocation, and organization of time and care in the household.

APPENDIX:
SURVEY ON THE
IMPACT OF FEMINISM
ON ECONOMICS,
SPRING 1992

The Commonwealth of Massachusetts
University of Massachusetts-Boston
Harbor Campus
Boston, Massachusetts 02125-3393

Economics Department

April 14, 1992

Dear Colleague:

I am currently writing a book on the impact of feminism on economics to be published next year by Twayne Publishers as part of a multi-volume series on the impact of feminism in the arts and sciences. To learn more about how economists perceive economic issues of primary concern to women and how they understand the impact of feminism within economics, I have developed this questionnaire.

Your name is one of the 400 I randomly selected from the membership of the American Economic Association in 1991. In order to complete this research, your participation is important. I hope that you will take the approximately 15 minutes needed to fill out the enclosed questionnaire and return it in the enclosed stamped envelope as soon as possible.

Please be assured that your answers are confidential. The information collected through this survey will not be used in any way which will identify individual persons.

Any additional comments or suggestions would be welcome. There is space at the end of the survey for your written comments or feel free to contact me at 617-287-6963.

Thank you in advance for your help in this research.

Randy Albelda
Assistant Professor
of Economics

PART I

1. How many full-time economists are in your department or agency? _____
    Of these, how many are women? _____

2. How many senior (tenured) economists are in your department or agency?_____
    Of these, how many are women? _____

3. How many part-time or temporary (non-tenure track, excluding graduate
    students) economists are in your department or agency? ____

    Of these how many are women? ____

4. Has your department or agency hired any full-time, permanent economists in the
    last two years?
    [   ] No
    [   ] Yes
    If yes, for each new hire please indicate:

	Hire #1	Hire #2	Hire #3	Hire #4
Number of candidates interviewed	_____	_____	_____	_____
Number of candidates female	_____	_____	_____	_____
Initial offer made to a female (yes or no)	_____	_____	_____	_____
Female hired (yes or no)	_____	_____	_____	_____

5. Do you usually teach economics courses?
    [   ] No
    [   ] Yes
    If yes, how many courses last year (or most recently)?_____
    How many of those were graduate-level economic courses? _____

6. Do you teach in an economics department?
    [   ] No   (GO TO QUESTION 9 ON THE FOLLOWING PAGE)
    [   ] Yes

7. Please check the box which most closely depicts the percentage of female
    students in your economic classes in the last year you taught.

	Graduate	Undergraduate Intro	Other
Less than 10%	[ ]	[ ]	[ ]
Between 10% and one-third	[ ]	[ ]	[ ]
Between one-third to one-half	[ ]	[ ]	[ ]
Over 50%	[ ]	[ ]	[ ]
Only women	[ ]	[ ]	[ ]
Didn't teach	[ ]	[ ]	[ ]

8. Is there a course (or courses) taught in your department that is primarily about
    women in the economy?
    [   ] No
    [   ] Yes
    If yes, how many? _____
    For each course taught, indicate how often it is offered.

	Course 1	Course 2	Course 3
Every semester	[ ]	[ ]	[ ]
Once a year	[ ]	[ ]	[ ]
Once every other year	[ ]	[ ]	[ ]
Other (specify)	_____	_____	_____

9. For each area listed below and assuming no new journal space, indicate if
   you believe it should receive more attention (implying a decrease in research
   published in other topics), the same attention, or less attention than currently
   received in the major economic journals.

	MORE ATTENTION	SAME ATTENTION	LESS ATTENTION
Wage discrimination by gender	[1]	[2]	[3]
Changes in family structure and poverty	[1]	[2]	[3]
Women's labor force participation and occupational structure	[1]	[2]	[3]
The allocation of time in the household	[1]	[2]	[3]
The impact of fiscal or monetary policies on women and family structure	[1]	[2]	[3]
The economic well-being and care of children	[1]	[2]	[3]
Women's economic history	[1]	[2]	[3]
The economic status of minority women	[1]	[2]	[3]
The measurement of women's contribution to economic output	[1]	[2]	[3]
Women's contributions to the development of economic thought	[1]	[2]	[3]
Feminist perspectives on economic analysis	[1]	[2]	[3]

10. Please indicate if you agree or disagree that the policies below improve women's
    economic position.

	STRONGLY AGREE	SOMEWHAT AGREE	SOMEWHAT DISAGREE	STRONGLY DISAGREE	NO OPINION
Affirmative action	[1]	[2]	[3]	[4]	[5]
Equal pay for comparable work	[1]	[2]	[3]	[4]	[5]
Paid parental leave	[1]	[2]	[3]	[4]	[5]
Child-care tax credits	[1]	[2]	[3]	[4]	[5]
Universal health coverage	[1]	[2]	[3]	[4]	[5]
Subsidized child care	[1]	[2]	[3]	[4]	[5]
Child allowances	[1]	[2]	[3]	[4]	[5]
Employment and training programs	[1]	[2]	[3]	[4]	[5]
Higher AFDC benefit levels	[1]	[2]	[3]	[4]	[5]

11. Please indicate whether you agree or disagree with the positions stated below.

	STRONGLY AGREE	SOMEWHAT AGREE	SOMEWHAT DISAGREE	STRONGLY DISAGREE	NO OPINION
Women face substantial wage discrimination.	[1]	[2]	[3]	[4]	[5]
Over time, the market will eliminate women's wage gap with men.	[1]	[2]	[3]	[4]	[5]
Businesses and government policies have changed as a result of women's increased labor force participation over the last forty years.	[1]	[2]	[3]	[4]	[5]
Occupational segregation explains much of women's wage gap with men.	[1]	[2]	[3]	[4]	[5]
"New household economics," developed by the Chicago school, provides a useful framework for analyzing economic relationships between men and women.	[1]	[2]	[3]	[4]	[5]
Gender distinctions are usually unnecessary in economic analysis.	[1]	[2]	[3]	[4]	[5]
To the degree that the rational economic behavioral assumption of utility maximization applies to to men, it equally applies to women.	[1]	[2]	[3]	[4]	[5]
Relative to the number of women in the economics profession, women are proportionately represented in prestigious positions in the field.	[1]	[2]	[3]	[4]	[5]
In economics, it is easier for women to get tenure and promotions than it is for men.	[1]	[2]	[3]	[4]	[5]
The economics profession is more attractive for men to enter than it is for women.	[1]	[2]	[3]	[4]	[5]
There is a distinct feminist approach to economic problems.	[1]	[2]	[3]	[4]	[5]
Over the last 20 years, feminist analysis has been incorporated into mainstream economic theory.	[1]	[2]	[3]	[4]	[5]
Feminism has had a larger impact on economics than other social sciences.	[1]	[2]	[3]	[4]	[5]
Mainstream economics would be enriched if it incorporated more feminist analysis.	[1]	[2]	[3]	[4]	[5]

12. Below is a subset of the new list of classifications for books and articles used in the *Journal of Economic Literature*. Please check what kind of impact you think feminism has made on these areas of economics:

	SUBSTANTIAL POSITIVE IMPACT	SOME POSITIVE IMPACT	LITTLE OR NO IMPACT	SOME NEGATIVE IMPACT	SUBSTANTIAL NEGATIVE IMPACT	DON'T KNOW
Economics, in general	[1]	[2]	[3]	[4]	[5]	[6]
Teaching of economics	[1]	[2]	[3]	[4]	[5]	[6]
History of economic thought	[1]	[2]	[3]	[4]	[5]	[6]
Neoclassical economics methodology	[1]	[2]	[3]	[4]	[5]	[6]
Non-neoclassical economics methodology	[1]	[2]	[3]	[4]	[5]	[6]
Game theory	[1]	[2]	[3]	[4]	[5]	[6]
Data collection	[1]	[2]	[3]	[4]	[5]	[6]
Household behavior and family economics	[1]	[2]	[3]	[4]	[5]	[6]
Theory of the firm	[1]	[2]	[3]	[4]	[5]	[6]
Analysis of collective decision making	[1]	[2]	[3]	[4]	[5]	[6]
Fiscal theory and policy	[1]	[2]	[3]	[4]	[5]	[6]
International trade and finance	[1]	[2]	[3]	[4]	[5]	[6]
Health, education and welfare	[1]	[2]	[3]	[4]	[5]	[6]
Labor market analysis	[1]	[2]	[3]	[4]	[5]	[6]
Industrial relations	[1]	[2]	[3]	[4]	[5]	[6]
Economic development	[1]	[2]	[3]	[4]	[5]	[6]
Economic growth	[1]	[2]	[3]	[4]	[5]	[6]
Economic history	[1]	[2]	[3]	[4]	[5]	[6]
Urban and regional economics	[1]	[2]	[3]	[4]	[5]	[6]

13. Please indicate the impact you think feminism has made on each of the areas
    listed below.

	SUBSTANTIAL POSITIVE IMPACT	SOME POSITIVE IMPACT	LITTLE OR NO IMPACT	SOME NEGATIVE IMPACT	SUBSTANTIAL NEGATIVE IMPACT	DON'T KNOW
The number of women undergraduate students	[1]	[2]	[3]	[4]	[5]	[6]
The number of women graduate students	[1]	[2]	[3]	[4]	[5]	[6]
The number of women economists	[1]	[2]	[3]	[4]	[5]	[6]
The promotion and retention of women in economics	[1]	[2]	[3]	[4]	[5]	[6]
The undergraduate economics curriculum	[1]	[2]	[3]	[4]	[5]	[6]
The graduate economics curriculum	[1]	[2]	[3]	[4]	[5]	[6]

14. Please indicate whether you agree or disagree with the following statements.

	STRONGLY AGREE	SOMEWHAT AGREE	SOMEWHAT DISAGREE	STRONGLY DISAGREE	NO OPINION
Women and minorities have the same opportunities to advance in American business as white males.	[1]	[2]	[3]	[4]	[5]
Changes brought about by the women's movement have made women's lives better than they were twenty years ago.	[1]	[2]	[3]	[4]	[5]
Changes brought about by the women's movement have made men's lives better than they were twenty years ago.	[1]	[2]	[3]	[4]	[5]
Women who have successful careers end up sacrificing too much of their family and personal life.	[1]	[2]	[3]	[4]	[5]
Men who have successful careers end up sacrificing too much of their family and personal life.	[1]	[2]	[3]	[4]	[5]
Women's organizations have done something that has made my life better.	[1]	[2]	[3]	[4]	[5]
The United States continues to need a strong women's movement to push for change that will benefit women.	[1]	[2]	[3]	[4]	[5]
I am sympathetic to the goals of the women's movement.	[1]	[2]	[3]	[4]	[5]
I consider myself a feminist.	[1]	[2]	[3]	[4]	[5]

15. Assume for a moment that you teach economics and one of your best undergraduate students is an ardent feminist who wants to pursue economics at the graduate level. What advice would you give her or him?

_____

_____

_____

PART II

1. What is your present age? _____

2. What is your sex?
    [ ] Female
    [ ] Male

3. What is your racial or ethnic background?
    [ ] Asian or Pacific Islander
    [ ] Black
    [ ] Latino
    [ ] White, not of latino origin
    [ ] Other (specify)_____

4. What is your marital status?
    [ ] Married/Living with spouse
    [ ] Married, separated
    [ ] Widowed (or partner deceased)
    [ ] Never Married (no partner)
    [ ] Never married (have a partner)
    [ ] Divorced

5. How would you define your sexual orientation?
    [ ] Heterosexual
    [ ] Bisexual
    [ ] Gay or lesbian

6. What is your gross _personal_ income?
    [ ] Less than $20,000
    [ ] Between $20,000 and $29,999
    [ ] Between $30,000 and $39,999
    [ ] Between $40,000 and $49,999
    [ ] Between $50,000 and $59,999
    [ ] Between $60,000 and $74,999
    [ ] Between $75,000 and $100,000
    [ ] Over $100,000

7. What is your gross _family_ income?
    [ ] Less than $20,000
    [ ] Between $20,000 and $29,999
    [ ] Between $30,000 and $39,999
    [ ] Between $40,000 and $49,999
    [ ] Between $50,000 and $59,999
    [ ] Between $60,000 and $74,999
    [ ] Between $75,000 and $100,000
    [ ] Over $100,000

8. How many adults do you live with (exclude yourself)? _____

9. How many children aged 17 and younger do you live with? _____

10. How many children do you have (include natural, step or adopted)? _____

11. Which of the following best describes your primary employer?

    Nonacademic
    [ ] Government
    [ ] Private, for-profit
    [ ] Private, non-profit

    Academic
    [ ] Public university or college
    [ ] Private university or college
    [ ] Other (specify) _____

       Other (specify) _____

12. How many years have you held your current job? _____

13. Which best describes your title?
    [ ] Full professor
    [ ] Associate professor
    [ ] Assistant professor
    [ ] Instructor/Lecturer
    [ ] Graduate student
    [ ] Researcher/Staff economist
    [ ] Other (specify)_____

14. What is the highest degree in economics you hold?
    [ ] Ph.D.
    [ ] Masters
    [ ] Degree in another field
          (Specify degree and field)_____

15. What year did you complete your highest degree in economics? _____

Once again, thank you for your assistance in completing this research. Please feel
free to provide any other comments here:

The Commonwealth of Massachusetts
University of Massachusetts-Boston
Harbor Campus
Boston, Massachusetts 02125-3393

Economics Department

May 26, 1992

Dear Colleague:

Last month I sent you the enclosed questionnaire concerning the impact of feminism on economics. The results of this survey will be included in a book I am writing on this topic to be published next year by Twayne Publishers as part of a multi-volume series on the impact of feminism in the arts and sciences. Your name is one of the 400 I randomly selected from the membership of the American Economic Association in 1991. I am sending it to you again because I have not yet received a response from you.

I hope you will take the approximately 10-15 minutes needed to fill out the questionnaire and return it to me in the enclosed stamped envelope as soon as possible. In order to complete this research, your participation is very important. Please be assured you that your answers are strictly confidential. The information collected through this survey will not be used in any way which will identify individual persons.

Any additional comments or suggestions would be welcome. There is space at the end of the survey for your written comments or feel free to contact me at 617-287-6963. Thank you in advance for your help in this research. If you have already completed the questionnaire and sent it to me by the time you receive this, thank you and please ignore this request.

Sincerely,

Randy Albelda
Assistant Professor
of Economics

NOTES

Chapter 1

1. Penelope Ciancanelli and Bettina Berch, "Gender and GNP," in *Analyzing Gender: A Handbook of Social Science Research,* ed. Beth B. Hess and Myra Marx Ferree (Newbury Park, Calif.: SAGE Publications, 1987), 244.

2. Articles discussing feminism's impact on economics include: Rebecca Blank, "A Female Perspective on Economic Man?" in *Revolution in Knowledge: Feminism in Social Science*, ed. Sue Rosenberg Zalk and Janice Gordon-Kelton (Boulder, Colo.: Westview Press, 1992), 111–24; Marjorie Cohen, "The Razor's Edge Invisible: Feminism's Effect on Economics," *International Journal of Women Studies*, 8, no. 3 (May/June 1985): 286–98; Marianne Ferber and Michelle L. Teiman, "The Oldest, the Most Established, the Most Quantitative of the Social Sciences—and the Most Dominated by Men: The Impact of Feminism on Economics," in *Men Studies Modified,* ed. Dale Spender (New York: Pergamon Press, 1981), 125–39; and Martha MacDonald, "Economics and Feminism: The Dismal Science?" *Studies in Political Economy*, 15 (Fall 1984): 151–78.

3. For example, in 1992 the first book examining feminism and early economic thought was published (Michèle Pujol, *Feminism and Anti-Feminism in Early Economic Thought* [Brookfield, Vt.: (Edward Elgar, 1992]) and the first book of feminist treatments of the history of women in economics was published in 1995 (Mary Ann Dimand, Robert W. Dimand, and Evelyn L. Forget, *Women of Value: Feminist Essays on the History of Women in Economics* [Brookfield, Vt.: Edward Elgar, 1995]).

4. Thomas Kuhn, *The Structure of Scientific Revolutions*, 2d. ed. (Chicago: University of Chicago Press, 1970).

5. W. Lee Hansen, "The Education and Training of Economics Doctorates," *Journal of Economic Literature* 29 (September 1991): 1061.

6. Marianne Ferber and Bonnie Birnbaum, "The 'New Home Economics': Retrospects and Prospects," *Journal of Consumer Research* 4 (1977): 19–28.

7. Nancy Folbre discusses these trends in the context of developing a new feminist approach in chapter 1 of *Who Pays for the Kids?: Gender and the Structures of Constraint* (New York: Routledge, 1994), 15–50.

8. The strongest indication is the recent appearance of an article on the subject in one of the journals published by the AEA (Julie Nelson, "Feminism and Economics," *Journal of Economic Perspectives* 9, no. 2 (Spring 1995): 131–48).

9. Elizabeth Hoffman, "Report of the Committee on the Status of Women in the Economics Profession," *American Economic Review* 82, no. 2 (May 1992): 612.

10. Many of Gary Becker's published articles on household production can be found in his comprehensive volume, *The Economic Approach to Human Behavior* (Chicago: University of Chicago Press, 1976).

11. Marilyn Waring, a New Zealand feminist economist, discusses the invisibility of women's work in national income and output accounting in her book *If Women Counted: A New Feminist Economics* (San Francisco: Harper and Row, 1988). Nancy Folbre discusses the conscious decision to exclude women's housework from the U.S. Census collection of work activity in her article "The Unproductive Housewife: Her Evolution in Nineteenth-Century Economic Thought," *Signs* 16, no. 3 (1991): 463–84.

12. This is discussed at length as it concerns welfare policy research in Sanford Schram's *Words of Welfare: The Poverty of Social Science and the Social Science of Poverty* (Minneapolis: University of Minnesota Press, 1995).

13. Two recent accounts of graduate education in economics paint this picture rather clearly: Arjo Klamer and David Colander, *The Making of An Economist* (Boulder, Colo.: Westview Press, 1990) and Anne Krueger, et al., "Report of the Commission on Graduate Education in Economics," *Journal of Economic Literature* 29, no. 3 (September 1991): 1035–53.

14. See Marsha R. Shelburn and Patsy G. Lewellyn, "Gender Bias in Doctoral Programs in Economics," *Journal of Economic Education* 26, no. 4 (Fall 1995): 373–83.

15. Ivy Broder's findings from a study of women in the top graduate programs in economics were published in Louis Uchitelle's article "In Economics, a Subtle Exclusion," *New York Times*, 11 January 1993, D-1, D-3. At that time she listed two women in the six top-ranked schools (one each at University of Chicago and Harvard, with none in Stanford, MIT, Princeton, and Yale). Since that time Stanford has hired its first tenured women in the economics department.

Chapter 2

1. Data come from the National Science Foundation Survey of Earned Doctorates reported in Elizabeth Hoffman's "Report of the Committee on the Status of Women in the Economics Profession," *American Economic Review* 82, no. 2 (May 1992): 612.

2. When I began this project I found very little research on the history of women in the economics profession in the United States between 1880 and World War I. What was available was often hard to find. One piece was a working paper available from the author: Claire H. Hammond, *Women and the Professionalization of Economics* Working Paper Series No. 90.2 (Winston-Salem, N.C.: Wake Forest University, 1990). Another three articles were by Barbara Libby, each published in a journal not available in any library in the Boston area: "Women in Economics Before 1940," *Essays in Business and Economic History* 2 (1984): 272–90; "A Statistical Analysis of Women in the Economics Profession, 1900–1940," *Essays in Business and Economics History* 5 (1987): 180–201; and "Women in the Economics Profession, 1900–1940: Factors in Their Declining Visibility," *Essays in Business and Economics History* 8 (1990): 121–29.

3. Dorothy Ross, *The Origins of American Social Science* (Cambridge: Cambridge University Press. 1991): 102.

4. For extensive histories of the emergence of economics see Ross, *The Origins of American Social Sciences*; Thomas Haskell, *The Emergence of Professional*

Social Science: The American Social Science Association and the Nineteenth Century Crisis of Authority (Urbana: University of Illinois Press, 1977); Mary O. Furner, *Advocacy and Objectivity: A Crisis in the Professionalization of American Social Science, 1865–1905* (Lexington, Ky.: The University Press of Kentucky, 1975); Robert L. Church, "Economists as Experts: The Rise of an Academic Profession in the United States, 1870–1920," in *The University in Society, Volume 2: Europe, Scotland and the United States*, ed. Lawrence Stone (Princeton: Princeton University Press, 1974), 571–609; and A. W. Coats, "The Educational Revolution and the Professionalization of American Economics," in *Breaking the Mould: Higher Learning in the Nineteenth Century*, ed. William J. Barber (Middletown, Conn.: Wesleyan University Press, 1988), 340–75.

5. Although Rossiter does discuss the rise of home economics, but as an offshoot of the natural sciences. Margaret W. Rossiter, *Women Scientists in America: Struggles and Strategies to 1940* (Baltimore: Johns Hopkins University Press, 1982).

6. Mary O. Furner "Knowing Capitalism: Public Investigation and the Labor Question in the Long Progressive Era," in *The State and Economic Knowledge: The American and British Experiences,* ed. Mary O. Furner and Barry Supple (Cambridge: Cambridge University Press, 1990), 241–86.

7. See Ross, *The Origins of American Social Science* and Haskell, *The Emergence of Professional Social Science.*

8. Furner, *Advocacy and Objectivity*, 1.

9. Furner, *Advocacy and Objectivity*, 10–11.

10. Edward T. Silva and Shelia A. Slaughter, *Serving Power: The Making of the Academic Social Science Expert* (Westport, Conn.: Greenwood Press, 1984), 42–43.

11. From *Constitution, Address and List of Members of the American Association for the Promotion of Social Science* (1866), quoted in Silva and Slaughter, *Serving Power*, 41.

12. Silva and Slaughter, *Serving Power*, 48.

13. The desire for a more dynamic set of studies and the fact that the United States had no graduate institutions until 1876 helps explain why most academic social scientists studied abroad—particularly in Germany. See Peter T. Manicas, *A History and Philosophy of the Social Sciences* (Oxford: Basil Blackwell 1987), 207–8.

14. Ross argues that the group of young economists who most vociferously argued for the professionalization of economics were the sons of evangelical families—not the sons of businessmen. One exception was E. R. A. Seligman, and although the son of a wealthy merchant, he was Jewish, which was sufficient to disqualify him from ruling circles (*The Origins of American Social Science*, 102–3).

15. A. W. Coats, "The Educational Revolution and the Professionalization of American Economics," 340–75.

16. Edward S. Mason, "The Harvard Department of Economic from the Beginning to WWII," *Quarterly Journal of Economics* 97, no. 3 (August 1982): 383–433.

17. Ross, *Origins of American Social Science*, 63.

18. Ibid., 5.

19. Furner, *Advocacy and Objectivity*, 92–94.

20. Robert L. Church, "Economists as Experts," 582–83.

21. Ross, *The Origins of American Social Science*, 110.

22. Haskell, *The Emergence of Professional Social Science*, 187–88.

23. Ibid., 178–79.

24. Richard T. Ely, *Report of the Organization of the American Economic Association* 1, no. 1 (March 1886): 40–41.

25. Ibid., 5.

26. Ibid., 7.

27. Furner, *Advocacy and Objectivity*.

28. Ibid.

29. Church, "Economists as Experts," 589.

30. The academic freedom cases are described in chapter 7 of Furner's *Advocacy and Objectivity*. Furner focuses on the power to hire and fire wielded by those endowing and running universities as the primary way to effectively force economists to temper their left-leaning political stances. Ross, on the other hand, argues that the largely middle-class group of newly established experts wanted to maintain their position so they rather easily abandoned their left proclivities in return for establishing their careers (*The Origins of American Social Science*).

31. Ross, *The Origins of American Social Sciences*, 117–18.

32. Ross, *The Origins of American Social Sciences*, 172–218.

33. Church, "Economists as Experts," 592–93.

34. Clark's approach paralleled those being developed in 1880s by Leon Walras in France, Carl Menger in Austria, and Stanley Jevons in England.

35. John Bates Clark, *The Distribution of Wealth: A Theory of Wages, Interest and Profits* (New York: Augustus M. Kelly Bookseller, 1965), 4. This work was originally published in 1898.

36. Furner, *Advocacy and Objectivity*, 258.

37. Silva and Slaughter, *Serving Power*, 26.

38. Furner, *Advocacy and Objectivity*, see especially chapter 11 (pp. 260–77).

39. Manicas, *A History and Philosophy of the Social Sciences*, 208.

40. For economic histories of women's waged and unwaged work in the United States see Alice Kessler-Harris, *Out to Work: A History of Wage-Earning Women in the United States* (New York: Oxford University Press, 1982); Julie Matthaei, *An Economic History of Women in America: Women's Work, the Sexual Division of Labor and the Development of Capitalism* (New York: Schocken Books, 1982); and Teresa Amott and Julie Matthaei, *Race, Gender and Work: A Multicultural History of Women in the United States* (Boston: South End Press, 1991).

41. The cult of domesticity is described by a variety of authors. For an excellent treatment on its applicability to women's economic roles see Matthaei, *An Economic History of Women in America*.

42. Rossiter, *Women Scientists in America*, 9–10.

43. By the eve of World War I, women earned just under 30 percent of all undergraduate degrees. U.S. Department of Commerce, Census Bureau, *Historical Statistics of the United States* (Washington, D.C.: Government Printing Offices, 1975), 386.

44. U.S. Commerce Department, *Historical Statistics*, 386.

45. Walter Crosby Eells, *American Association of University Professors Bulletin* 42 (1956): 658.

46. Katharine Coman, a lesbian (her longtime companion was Katherine Lee Bates, the author of "America the Beautiful"), worked extensively with social reform movements of the time in Boston and often attended socialist meetings with other faculty members. See Allen F. Davis, "Katharine Coman," in *Notable American Women*, ed. Edward T. James (Cambridge: Harvard University Press, 1971), 365–67.

47. Ely, *Report of the Organization of the American Economic Association*, 39.

48. Richard T. Ely, *Ground Under My Feet: An Autobiography* (New York: Macmillan, 1938), 147.

49. Ibid.

50. Clare de Graffenried, "Child Labor," *Publication of the American Economic Association, First Series* 5, no. 2 (1890): 73–149.

51. *Publication of the American Economic Association, First Series* 5, no. 2 (1890): 179.

52. Her award-winning essay was entitled "Public Assistance of the Poor in France" in *Publications of the American Economic Association* 8, no. 4–5 (July and Sept 1893): 263–45. After Wellesley refused to renew Balch's contract in 1919 because of her radical economic views (she was a socialist) and her pacifism, she turned her full-time attention to international peace work. In 1946, Balch received the Nobel Peace Prize. For bibliographic information on Balch, see Mercedes M. Randall, ed. *Beyond Nationalism: The Social Thought of Emily Greene Balch* (New York: Twayne Publishers, 1972), 15–32.

53. Claire H. Hammond, *Women and the Professionalization of Economics*, 33.

54. Claire H. Hammond, "Helen Frances Page Bates: The First American Woman Ph.D. in Economics," *CSWEP Newsletter* (Winter 1991): 9.

55. The AEA listed every candidate for a doctoral degree in political economy in every year from 1904 to 1940. Lewis A. Froman compiled a list of all such candidates, so that each candidate's name appeared only once. He composed several tables, including students listed by field of study and institution by five year periods ("Graduate Students in Economics, 1904–1928," *American Economic Review* 20 [1930]: 236–47). I followed the same procedure, but only listed women students (to the degree they could be identified by name). Froman used the procedure again when he updated his study for the years 1928–1940, "Graduate Students in Economics, 1904–1940," *American Economic Association* 32 (1942): 817–26.

56. Rossiter, *Women Scientists in America*, 112.

57. *Publications of the American Economic Association, Third Series* 8, no. 1 (Feb 1907): 260–62; Crystal Eastman, "The American Way of Distributing Industrial Accident Losses," *Publications of the American Economic Association, Third Series* 10 (1909): 119–34.

58. Hammond, *Women and the Professionalization of Economics*, 44.

59. Haskell, *The Emergence of Professional Social Science*, 183.

60. Barbara Libby found that 28.5 percent of all the women to receive doctorates in economics between 1900 and 1940 earned their baccalaureate degree at one of the women's colleges, "A Statistical Analysis of Women in the Economics Profession, 1900–1940," 190.

61. The study was based on data collected from the catalogs from around 60 coeducational colleges and universities and 9 women's colleges reported in 1918 in the *Journal of the Association of Collegiate Alumnae* (the precursor to American Association of University Women). See Helen Sard Hughes, "The Academic Chance," *Journal of the Association of Collegiate Alumnae* 12, no. 2 (January 1919): 79–82.

62. This count is based on looking at the list of members and deciding whether they were male or female on the basis of first name and appellation ("Miss" or "Mrs."). American Economic Association, "List of members, 1905" *Publication of the American Economic Association, Third Series* 6, no. 1–2, 201–65. This list was the first published by the AEA to include addresses and affiliations of all members.

63. See Hammond, *Women and the Professionalization of Economics*, 31–36.

64. Frederick Olsen, "Helen Laura Sumner Woodbury," in *Notable American Women 1607–1950*, ed. by Edward T. James (Cambridge: Harvard University Press, 1971), 651.

65. Thomas D. Boston, "W. E. B. DuBois and the Historical School of Economics" *American Economic Association* 81, no. 2 (May 1991): 306.

66. "Sadie Alexander," in *The Black Women's Oral History Project*, Volume 2 edited by Ruth Edmonds Hill, (Cambridge, Mass.: Schlesinger Library, 1991), 70–85; and Julianne Malveaux, "Missed Opportunity: Sadie Tanner Mossell Alexander and the Economics Profession," *American Economic Review* 81, no. 2 (May 1991): 307–10.

67. Malveaux, "Missed Opportunity," 308.

68. Rossiter, *Women Scientists in America*, 220.

69. Ibid., 221.

70. Feminists face this dilemma in many academic disciplines. Any discipline that argues that its mission is the objective study of natural or social phenomena will likely see feminist theorists as charlatans. For example, Rosemarie Tong, in the introduction to her book on feminist theories, tells of her colleagues' reactions to developing a course on the introduction to feminist theory at Williams College in the early 1980s. One called it "a political polemic"; another claimed he could see "nothing theoretical about feminist theory at all." *Feminist Thought: A Comprehensive Introduction* (Boulder, Colo.: Westview Press, 1989), 1.

71. Silva and Slaughter, *Serving Power*, 142.

72. Rossiter, *Women Scientists in America*, 232.

73. Information on Abbott is from Ellen Fitzpatrick, *Endless Crusade: Women Social Scientists and Progressive Reform* (New York: Oxford University Press, 1990).

74. Rossiter, *Women Scientists in America*, 164.

75. Rossiter, *Women Scientists in America*, 313.

76. By the mid-1970s, none of the tenured staff were women.

77. Mary E. Cookingham, "Social Economists and Reform: Berkeley, 1906–1961," *History of Political Economy* 19, no. 1 (1987): 47–63.

78. "After World War II, several of the women's colleges made a deliberate effort to increase the number of men on their faculties, presumably in the hope that this was a sign of improved quality, or at least status." Patricia Albjerg Graham, "Expansion and Exclusion: A History of Women in American Higher Education," *Signs* 3, no. 4 (Summer 1978): 768.

79. This quote is one of only two minor mentions of women, despite their rather extensive survey research: Theodore Caplow and Reece McGee, *The Academic Marketplace* (New York: Basic Books, 1958), 194.

80. Irma Adelman, "My Life Philosophy" *The American Economist* 34, no. 2 (Fall 1990): 11.

81. Daniel Orr, "Reflections on the Hiring of Faculty," *American Economic Review*, 83, no. 2 (May 1993): 42–43.

Chapter 3

1. For a good summary of the history of as well as the divisions within the modern women's movement see Barbara Ryan, *Feminism and the Women's Movement* (London: Routledge, 1992).

2. These include anthropology, literature, psychology, sociology, education, history, and philosophy.

3. CSWEP data received from Elizabeth Hoffman, 1992. These data were reported in graph form (Hoffman, *American Economic Review* 82, no. 2 [May 1992]: 612), compiled by Shulamit Kahn using NSF data.

4. John J. Siegfried and Charles Scott, "Recent Trends in Undergraduate Economics Degrees," *Journal of Economic Education* 25, no. 3 (Summer 1994): 281–86.

5. See Anne Krueger et al., "Report of the Commission on Graduate Education in Economics," *Journal of Economic Literature* 29, no. 3 (September 1991): 1035–53 and W. Lee Hansen, "The Education and Training of Economics Doctorates: Major Findings of the American Economic Association's Commission on Graduate Education in Economics," *Journal of Economic Literature* 29, no. 3 (September 1991): 1054–88.

6. Isabel Sawhill, "Report of the Committee on the Status of Women in the Economics Profession," *American Economic Review* 77, no. 2 (May 1987): 402.

7. National Research Council, *Doctoral Recipients United States Universities, Summary Report 1991* (Washington, D.C.: National Academy Press, 1992) and National Research Council, *Doctoral Recipients United States Universities, Summary Report 1981* (Washington, D.C.: National Academy Press, 1982).

8. Debra Barbezat, "The Market for New Ph.D. Economists," *Journal of Economic Education* 23, no. 3 (Summer 1992): 262–76.

9. *CSWEP Newsletter* (Winter 1995), 9.

10. Since 1972 the AEA has annually surveyed a set of graduate degree-granting and undergraduate economics departments. In its annual reports to the AEA (published in the *American Economic Review* and the *CSWEP Newsletter*), CSWEP tabulates information on female faculty from the survey.

11. Carolyn Shaw Bell (one of the founding mothers of CSWEP) in CSWEP's first report to the AEA refers to the 43 universities that grant about two-thirds of all doctorates in economics as: " . . . making up what is euphemistically referred to as the chairman's group, but is otherwise known as the cartel." Carolyn Shaw Bell, "Report of the Committee on the Status of Women in the Economics Profession," *American Economic Review* 63, no. 2 (May 1973): 509.

12. Elizabeth Bailey, "The Committee on the Status of Women in the Economics Profession," *American Economic Review* 71, no. 2 (May 1981): 470–71, 473.

13. *CSWEP Newsletter* (Winter 1995): 8–9.

14. See Hansen "The Education and Training of Economics Doctorate," 1055.

15. Ivy Broder's results of a telephone survey to the top graduate schools were incorrectly reproduced in a *New York Times* article (Louis Uchitelle, "In Economics, a Subtle Exclusion," *New York Times*, 11 January 1993, D3–4). The numbers cited here are corrected numbers from Broder.

16. Ibid.

17. Myra Strober, "Women Economists: Career Aspirations, Education, and Training" *American Economic Review* 65, no. 2 (May 1975): 96.

18. Debra Barbezat, "The Market for New Ph.D. Economists," 266.

19. Ferber's results were published in the *IAFFE Newsletter* 5, no. 2 (1995): 14.

20. Shulamit Kahn, "Gender Differences in Academic Paths of Economists," *American Economic Review* 83, no. 2 (May 1993): 52–56.

21. Ivy Broder, "Professional Achievements and Gender Differences Among Academic Economists," *Economic Inquiry* 31, no. 1 (January 1993): 116–27.

22. Larry Singell Jr. and Joe A. Stone, "Gender Differences in Ph.D. Economists' Careers," *Contemporary Policy Issues* 11, no. 4 (October 1993): 95–106.

23. Shulamit Kahn, "Women in the Economics Profession," *Journal of Economic Perspectives* 9, no. 4 (Fall 1995): 193–205.

24. Robin Bartlett, "A Conversation with Carolyn Shaw Bell," *CSWEP Newsletter* (Fall 1993): 7–9.

25. Barbara Reagan. "Report of the Committee on the Status of Women in the Economics Profession," *American Economic Review* 67, no. 1 (May 1977): 460.

26. Ibid., 461–62.

27. Myra Strober and Barbara B. Reagan. "Sex Differences in Economists' Fields of Specialization," in *Women in the Workplace: The Implications of Occupational Segregation*, ed. Martha Blaxall and Barbara B. Reagan (Chicago: University of Chicago Press, 1976), 303–17; Myra Strober, "Women Economists: Career Aspirations, Education, and Training"; and Alice Amsden and Collete Moser, "Job Search and Affirmative Action," *American Economic Review* 66, no. 2 (May 1976): 83–91.

28. Elizabeth Bailey, "The Committee on the Status of Women in the Economics Profession," *American Economic Association* 72, no. 2 (May 1982): 431.

29. Isabel Sawhill, "CSWEP Annual Report, 1985," *CSWEP Newsletter* (Winter 1986): 2–5.

30. *IAFFE Membership Directory* (June 1994): 1.

31. Current officers and executive committee members of the AEA are listed in each issue of *American Economic Review*.

32. Counts do not include those in President-Elect position. The list of officers from 1886–1948 comes from the *American Economic Review* 39, no. 1 (1949): 295–304. All others come from front material in *American Economic Review* (various years).

33. Mary Fish and Jean Gibbons, "A Comparison of the Publications of Female and Male Economists," *Journal of Economic Education* (Winter 1989): 93–105.

34. Rebecca Blank, "The Effect of Double-Blind versus Single-Blind Reviewing: Experimental Evidence for the *American Economic Review*," *American Economic Review* 81, no. 5 (1991): 1041–67.

35. Van W. Kolpin and Larry D. Singell Jr., "The Gender Composition and Scholarly Performance of Economics Departments: A Test for Employment Discrimination," *Industrial and Labor Relations Review* 49, no. 3 (1996): 408–23.

36. Marshall H. Medoff, "The Ranking of Economists" *Journal of Economic Education* (Fall 1989): 409, 411.

37. Ibid., 413.

38. Marianne Ferber, "Citations and Networking," *Gender and Society* 2, no. 1 (March 1986): 82–89.

39. Susan F. Feiner and Barbara A. Morgan, "Women and Minorities in Introductory Economics Textbooks: 1974–1984," *Journal of Economic Education* 18 (Fall 1987): 376–92.

40. Susan F. Feiner, "Introductory Textbook and the treatment of Issues Related to Women and Minorities, 1984 and 1991," *Journal of Economic Education* (Spring 1993): 145–62.

41. Tara Gray, "Women in Labor Economics Textbooks," *Journal of Economic Education* (Fall 1992): 362–73.

42. Nancy Burnett, *Gender and the Liberal Arts Curriculum*, (Mimeo, Department of Economics, Claremont McKenna College, 1994). Burnett's sample includes the top 25 percent of colleges ranked by *U.S. News & World Report, America's Best Colleges* 1993.

43. Anne O. Krueger et al. "Report on the Commission of Graduate Education in Economics," 1035-55.

44. Ibid., 1040.

Chapter 4

1. Marianne Ferber and Michelle L. Teiman, "The Oldest, the Most Established, the Most Quantitative of the Social Sciences—and the Most Dominated by Men: The Impact of Feminism on Economics," in *Men Studies Modified,* ed. Dale Spender (New York: Pergamon Press, 1981), 125.

2. Arjo Klamer and David Colander, *The Making of an Economist* (Boulder, Colo.: Westview Press, 1990).

3. Debra Barbezat "The Market for New Ph.D. Economists," *Journal of Economic Education* 23, no. 3 (1992): 262–76.

4. Marsha R. Shelburn and Patsy G. Lewellyn, "Gender Bias in Doctoral Programs in Economics," *Journal of Economic Education* 26, no. 4 (Fall 1995): 373–83.

5. Richard M. Alston, J. R. Kearl, and Michael B. Vaughan, "Is There a Consensus Among Economists in the 1990s?" *American Economic Review* 82, no. 2 (1992): 203–9.

6. Myra Strober, "Women Economists: Career Aspirations, Education, and Training," *American Economic Review* 65, no. 2 (1975): 92–99.

7. The most prominent of these authors is Sandra Harding. Others scholars besides feminists have used this line of reasoning extensively in their understanding of the development of ideas, notably Marxists. For an early treatment see Antonio Gramsci, *Selections from the Prison Notebooks* (New York: International Publishers, 1971).

8. The respondent had moved with no forwarding address or the survey was returned from an administrative aide or spouse indicating that the respondent was out of the country, had died, or was incapacitated in some way, making completion of the survey impossible.

9. Of these 10, 8 felt they were not knowledgeable enough on the topic to provide useful answers (had been retired for many years, were non-U.S. citizens temporarily in the United States, or had been outside of the mainstream of economics for a long time), and two refused to answer because they thought the survey was biased.

10. Strober's survey of the Committee on the Status of Women in the Economics Profession members in 1974 had a response rate of 55 percent ("Women Economists: Career Aspirations, Education, and Training"). In a stratified random sample of 1,350 economists employed in the United States in 1990, Richard M. Alston, J. R. Kearl, and Michael B. Vaughan had an overall response rate of 34.4 percent ("Is There a Consensus Among Economists in the 1990s?"). Debra Barbezat had 291 usable surveys of 600 (49%) graduate students polled ("The Market for New Ph.D. Economists").

11. Elizabeth Hoffman, "Report of the Committee on the Status of Women in the Economics Profession," *American Economic Review* 82, no. 2 (May 1992): 612.

12. Table 2 in Nancy Gordon, "Report of the Committee on the Status of Women in the Economics Profession," *American Economic Review* 79, no. 2 (May 1989): 422–25; and Daniel P. McMillan and Larry. D. Singell Jr. "Gender Differences in First Jobs for Economists," *Southern Economic Journal* 60 (January 1994): 701–14.

13. Using a chi-squared test, the distribution of marital status was significantly different for men and women (at the 9% level).

14. The t-statistic on the dummy coefficient for gender was not significant (at the 10% level) in an ordered probit regression on income levels among those with Ph.D.s.

15. U.S. Department of Commerce, Census Bureau, *Money Income of Household, Families and Persons in 1991* (Washington, D.C.: Government Printing Office, 1992).

16. National Research Council, *Doctoral Recipients United States Universities, Summary Report 1991* (Washington, D.C.: National Academy Press, 1992), 78–79.

17. However, it should be noted that the previous year, CSWEP reported that 22 percent of jobs went to women—so the 1992 numbers may not be particularly representative of the trends in economics. See Elizabeth Hoffman, "Report of the Committee on the Status of Women in the Economics Profession," *American Economic Review* 83, no. 2 (1993): 509; and Hoffman, "Report of the Committee on the Status of Women in the Economics Profession," *American Economic Review* 82, no. 2 (May 1992): 611.

18. Possible explanations might be that junior women change jobs more often than men, and that agencies and departments are seeking to replace them. Alternatively, employers may feel that if there is a high (low) percentage of senior females, there is no (considerable) need or pressure to hire new female economists.

19. In 1981, 63.1 percent of all males and 71.3 percent of all females receiving Ph.D.s were U.S. citizens. In 1991 those percentages dropped to 38.9 percent for male recipients and 53.4 of female recipients. (National Research Council, *Doctoral Recipients United States Universities, Summary Report 1981* [Washington, D.C.: National Academy Press, 1982], 34–37; National Research Council, *Summary Reports, 1991*, 76–79.)

20. See, for example, Sandra Harding, *Whose Science? Whose Knowledge?: Thinking from Women's Lives* (Ithaca: Cornell University Press, 1991) and Nancy Hartsock, "The Feminist Standpoint: Developing the Ground for a Specifically Feminist Historical Materialism," in *Discovering Reality*, ed. Sandra Harding and Merrill Hintikka (Boston: Reidel Publishing Co., 1983), 283–310.

21. Sandra Harding, "Rethinking Standpoint Epistemology," in *Feminist Epistemologies*, ed. Linda Alcott and Elizabeth Potter (London: Routledge, 1993), 54.

22. Patricia Hill Collins, *Black Feminist Thought* (London: Routledge, 1991).

Chapter 5

1. These include: *Cambridge Journal of Economics, Review of Radical Political Economics, Journal of Social Economics, Journal of Post-Keynesian Economics, Rethinking Marxism, Science and Society, World Development*, and *Journal of Economic Issues*.

2. The *American Economic Review*, published five times a year, includes academic articles, written almost exclusively from a neoclassical theoretic position. (The May issue is the proceedings from the annual AEA meetings.) The *Journal of Economic Literature* includes review articles, book reviews, and a listing of newly published books and articles and is published quarterly. The *Journal of Economic Perspectives* publishes articles that could be read by advanced undergraduate economic majors. And although this journal was intended to be more inclusive of alternative perspectives, it is still weak on this measure. As neoclassically trained economist and former AEA board member Donald McCloskey notes, "When I recently proposed at a meeting of the Executive Committee of the American Economic Association that the *Journal of Economic Perspectives* examine some perspectives beyond the present gamut from M to N, another member of the committee com-

plained to me in private that this would make the magazine into 'political rubbish.' " ("The Discreet Charm of the Bourgeoisie," *Feminist Economics* 1, no. 3 (1995): 119).

3. David Colander, Douglas North, and Amartya Sen are three prominent economists who actively critique neoclassical economics and pose alternative understandings that increasingly recognize the importance of institutions and power in economic modeling.

4. Those unfamiliar with regression analysis may choose to skip the results of the ordered probit regressions.

5. The results for each of the 25 regressions are not included here since so few of the differences in responses are statistically significant. They are available from the author.

6. Using a scale where 1 is substantial negative impact, 2 is some negative impact, 3 is little or no impact, 4 is some positive impact, and 5 is substantial positive impact, the coefficient on the sex dummy in the equation measuring the impact of feminism on neoclassical economics was .7373, with a standard error of .445 and a t-statistic of 1.66. For the equation measuring feminism's impact on the number of female graduate students, the coefficient on the sex dummy was –.4907, with a standard error of .254 and a t-statistic of 1.93.

7. Using the same scale referred to in footnote 6, the coefficients (with standard error in the parenthesis) on the age variable for ordered probit equations concerning the impact of feminism on neoclassical economics, theory of the firm, and international trade and finance are as follows: .0213 (.012); .0235 (.012); and .0276 (.013). Each were significant at the 10 percent level with t-statistics on the coefficient for the age variable for neoclassical economics at 1.80 and 1.93 for theory of the firm. The age coefficient for the ordered probit on responses concerning feminism's impact on international trade and finance was significant at the 5 percent level with a t-statistic of 2.07.

8. In a survey of 23 journals representing the most prestigious, most likely to include labor issues, and those which are more inclusive of non-neoclassical methods, Jean Shackelford ("Perspectives on Diversity in Economic Education: The College Experience," Mimeo, December 1992) found that 2.9 percent of over 26,000 articles published between 1969 and 1990 examined issues of race or gender as identified by key words in article titles.

9. For example, on the volumes listed, the mostly Marxist *Review of Radical Political Economics*, *Science and Society*, and *Cambridge Journal of Economics* had no articles on gender nor did the primarily Institutionalist *Journal of Economic Perspectives*. The *Review of Black Political Economy* did have two of its five articles focusing on gender issues. Conversely, 5 of the 17 articles listed in the rather conservative, neoclassical Chicago-based *Journal of Political Economy* were in one of these 11 topics.

10. Yana van der Meulen Rodgers, "The Prevalence of Gender Topics in U.S. Economics Journals" *Feminist Economics* 2, no. 2 (1996): 129–35.

Chapter 6

1. The survey included room at the end for comments. Fewer than half the respondents wrote any comments.

2. A probit regression confirmed there were no statistical differences.

Chapter 7

1. "A Theory of Marriage," *Journal of Political Economy* 81, no. 4 (July/Aug. 1973): 814.

2. Becker really *reopened* the door. For the first four decades of the twentieth century economists, especially women economists, were very interested in household time and budget studies. The pioneering work was by Margaret Reid, *Economics of Household Production* (New York: J. Wiley & Sons, 1934).

3. For these very same reasons, neoclassical economics is also ill equipped to handle explanations of inequality based on race or economic class. This book is primarily concerned with neoclassical's relationship to feminism and explanations of gender inequality.

4. This section is only a cursory introduction to the neoclassical model. Readers with economics background may wish to skip ahead to the next section. Readers who want more lengthy discussions of the model (as well as problems with it) can find them in Daniel Hausman, *The Inexact and Separate Science of Economics* (Cambridge: Cambridge University Press, 1992) and Stephen Resnick and Richard Wolff, *Economics: Marxian versus Neoclassical* (Baltimore: Johns Hopkins University Press, 1987). For an excellent introduction to the neoclassical model, for those with no economics background, from one of its finest adherents, see Milton and Rose Friedman, *Free to Choose* (New York: Harcourt Brace Jovanovich, 1979), especially chapter 1.

5. Mark Blaug, *Economic Theory in Retrospect,* 4th ed. (Cambridge: Cambridge University Press, 1988), 4.

6. Philip Mirowski argues convincingly that economics does not evolve from Newtonian physics, as is often argued by historians of economic thought (see Blaug), but instead has its "hard core" mid-nineteenth-century physics. (Philip Mirowski, *Against Mechanism: Protecting Economics from Science* [Totowa, N.J.: Rowman and Littlefield, 1988]). In addition, Mirowski and Cook have recently cast doubt on Leon Walras as the originator of economics as "science." (See Philip Mirowski and Pamela Cook, "Walras' 'Economics and Mechanics': Translation, Commentary, Context" in *Economics as Discourse: An Economic Analysis of the Language of Economists,* ed. Warren J. Samuels [Boston, Mass.: Kluwer Academic Publishers, 1990], 189–215.)

7. This is not to say that all the actors are participating in these markets. Some consumers will be "priced out" of the market; that is, the equilibrium price is just too high for them to purchase the good based on their tastes. Similarly, at the equilibrium price, some producers will not find it profitable to produce any goods.

8. There is no such thing as "the market." There are interactions between individuals that take place at stores, business offices, and factories, but there is not one market where all consumers meet.

9. Corry Azzi and Ronald Ehrenberg, "Household Allocation of Time and Church Attendance," *Journal of Political Economy* 83 (February 1975): 27–53; Daniel Hammermesh and Neal M. Soss, "An Economic Theory of Suicide," *Journal of Political Economy* 82 (Jan/Feb 1974): 83–98; and Robert Willis, "A New Approach to the Economic Theory of Fertility," *Journal of Political Economy* 81, no. 2 (March/April 1973): S14–64.

10. Francine D. Blau and Marianne Ferber's *The Economics of Women, Men and Work,* 2d ed. (Englewood Cliffs, N.J.: Prentice-Hall, 1992) provides a very thorough presentation of neoclassical economics' explanations of women's wages, occupational distribution, and allocation of household time.

11. Gary Becker, *The Economics of Discrimination* (Chicago: University of Chicago Press, 1957).

12. *The Economic Approach to Human Behavior* (Chicago: University of Chicago Press, 1976), 15.

13. For a thorough review of neoclassical theories of discrimination see Glen Cain, "The Economic Analysis of Labor Market Discrimination: A Survey," in *Handbook of Labor Economics, Volume I,* ed. Orley Ashenfelter and R. Layard (New York: North Holland, 1986), 693–785.

14. Kenneth Arrow, "The Theory of Discrimination," in *Discrimination in the Labor Market,* ed. Orley Ashenfelter and Albert Rees (Princeton, N.J.: Princeton University Press, 1973), 10.

15. See Dennis J. Aigner and Glen G. Cain, "Statistical Theories of Discrimination in Labor Markets," *Industrial and Labor Relations Review* 30, no. 2 (January 1977): 175–87.

16. For an excellent unraveling of neoclassical discrimination theories as they apply to blacks, see William Darity Jr., "The Human Capital Approach to Black-White Earnings Inequality: Some Unsettled Questions," *Journal of Human Resources* 17, no. 1 (1982): 72–93.

17. Theodore Schultz, "Investment in Human Capital," *American Economic Review* 51, no. 1 (1960): 1–17, and Gary Becker, *Human Capital: A Theoretical and Empirical Analysis*, 2d ed. (New York: Columbia University Press for the National Economic Research Bureau, 1975). The first edition was published in 1964.

18. See chapters 3 and 4 of Blau and Ferber's *The Economics of Women, Men and Work* for an excellent discussion of neoclassical economic theories of household production.

19. Marianne Ferber and Julie Nelson, eds. *Beyond Economic Man: Feminist Theory and Economics* (Chicago: University of Chicago Press, 1993), 6. The articles referred to in the quote are: Carolyn Shaw Bell, "Economics, Sex, and Gender," *Social Science Quarterly* 55, no. 3 (1974): 615–31; Marianne Ferber and Bonnie Birnbaum, "The 'New Home Economics': Retrospects and Prospects," *Journal of Consumer Research* 4 (1977):19–28; and Isabel Sawhill, "Economic Perspectives on the Family," *Daedalus* 106 (1977):115–25.

20. For more recent feminist critiques of Becker's model of the family see Barbara Bergmann, "Becker's Theory of the Family: Preposterous Conclusions," *Feminist Economics* 1, no. 1 (Spring 1995): 141–50; Paula England, "The Separative Self: Androcentric Bias in Neoclassical Assumptions," in *Beyond Economic Man: Feminist Theory and Economics,* ed. Marianne A. Ferber and Julie A. Nelson (Chicago: University of Chicago Press, 1993), 37–53; Frances R. Woolley, "The Feminist Challenge to Neoclassical Economics," *Cambridge Journal of Economics* 17 (1993): 485–500; Elaine McCrate, "Trade Merger and Employment: Economic Theory on Marriage," *Review of Radical Political Economics* 19, no. 1 (1987): 73–89; and Lisa Jo Brown, "Neoclassical Economics and the Sexual Division of Labor," *Eastern Economic Journal* 10 (Oct./Nov. 1984): 367–79.

21. Mark Blaug, *The Methodology of Economics* (Cambridge: Cambridge University Press, 1980), 2.

22. Milton Friedman, *Essays in Positive Economics* (Chicago: University of Chicago Press, 1953).

23. The essay is reproduced in Bruce Caldwell, ed. *Appraisal and Criticism in Economics: A Book of Readings* (Boston: Allen and Unwin, 1984), 138–78.

24. Becker, *The Economic Approach to Human Behavior*, 5.

25. People concerned with class and race are also painted with the same brush!

26. Joseph Persky, "The Ethnology of *Homo Economicus*," *Journal of Economic Perspectives* 9, no. 2 (1995): 221.

27. The disagreement is best exemplified by the well-worn phrase attributed to George Bernard Shaw: "Even if you lined up all the economists in the world from end to end, you still wouldn't reach a conclusion."

28. These authors include Donald McCloskey, Jonathan Elster, Amartya Sen, Bruce Caldwell, Arjo Klamer, and David Colander. Each have written extensively on the problems with neoclassical methodology, making their works too numerous to cite here.

29. Authors include Sandra Harding, Helen Longino, Elizabeth Anderson, Susan Bordo, and Donna Hardaway. Also see Linda Alcott and Elizabeth Potter, eds. *Feminist Epistemologies* (London: Routledge, 1993).

30. For discussions of feminism, objectivity, and economics see Sandra Harding, "Can Feminist Thought Make Economics More Objective?" *Feminist Economics* 1, no. 1 (Spring 1995): 7–32; Janet Seiz, "Epistemology and the Tasks of Feminist Economics," *Feminist Economics* 1, no. 3 (Fall 1995): 110–18; Diana Straussmann and Livia Polanyi, "The Economist as Storyteller: What the Texts Reveal," in *Out of the Margins: Feminist Perspectives on Economics*, ed. Edith Kuiper and Jolande Sap (London: Routledge, 1995), 129–45; and Julie A. Nelson, *Feminism, Objectivity and Economics* (London: Routledge, 1996).

31. Janet Seiz, "Feminism and the History of Thought," *History of Political Economy* 25, no. 1 (1993): 190.

32. Nancy Folbre and Heidi Hartmann, "The Rhetoric of Self-interest: Ideology and Gender in Economic Theory" in *The Consequences of Rhetoric,* ed. Arjo Klamer, Donald McCloskey, and Robert Solow (Cambridge: Cambridge University Press, 1988): 187.

33. Hausman, *The Inexact and Separate Science of Economics*, 95.

34. Amartya Sen, "Rational Fools: A Critique of the Behavioral Foundations of Economic Theory," *Philosophy and Public Affairs* 6 (Summer 1977): 318–44; Nancy Folbre and Heidi Hartmann, "The Rhetoric of Self-Interest: Ideology and Gender in Economic Theory," 184–203; Julie Nelson, "Gender, Metaphor, and the Definition of Economics," *Economics and Philosophy* 8 (1992):103–25; and Paula England, "The Separative Self: Androcentric Bias in Neoclassical Assumptions."

35. For a critique see Elaine McCrate, "Trade Merger and Employment: Economic Theory on Marriage," 73–89.

36. This point is the basis of Samuel Bowles and Herbert Gintis's book *Capitalism and Democracy* (New York: Basic Books, 1986).

37. For discussion of liberal feminist theory see chapters 3 and 7 of Alison Jaggar, *Feminist Politics and Human Nature* (Totowa, N.J.: Rowman and Allanheld, 1983); chapter 1 of Rosemarie Tong, *Feminist Thought: A Contemporary Introduction* (Boulder, Colo.: Westview Press, 1989) and chapter 1 of Josephine Donovan, *Feminist Theory: The Intellectual Traditions of American Feminism* (New York: Continuum Publishing Co., 1991).

38. Yana van der Meulen Rodgers, "The Prevalence of Gender Topics in U.S. Economics Journals" *Feminist Economics* 2, no. 2 (1996): 129–35.

39. Ferber and Nelson, eds., *Beyond Economic Man* and Edith Kuiper and Jolande Sap, eds. (with Susan Feiner, Notburga Ott, and Zafiris Tzannatos), *Out of the Margins: Feminist Perspectives on Economics* (London: Routledge, 1995).

40. Two feminist economists who have made several important contributions and who use neoclassical tools and assumption (e.g., profit- and utility-maximizing behavior) in their work are Francine Blau and Rebecca Blank.

41. See, for example: Rebecca Blank and Patricia Ruggles, "Short-term Recidivism among Public-Assistance Recipients," *American Economic Review* 84, no. 2 (May 1994): 49–53, and Arline Geronimus and Sanders Korenman, "The Socioeconomic Consequences of Teen Childbearing Reconsidered," *Quarterly Journal of Economics* 107 (1992): 1187–1214.

42. *Understanding the Gender Gap: An Economic History of American Women* (New York: Oxford University Press, 1990).

43. For a summary of the literature on wage differences see Francine Blau, "Discrimination Against Women: Theory and Evidence," in *Labor Economics: Modern Views*, ed. William Darity Jr. (Boston: Kluwer-Nijhoff, 1984). For a feminist critique of human capital and occupational segregation see Paula England, "The Failure of Human Capital Theory to Explain Occupational Sex Segregation," *Journal of Human Resources* 17, no. 3 (Summer 1982): 358–70.

44. See, for example, Notburga Ott, "Fertility and Division of Work in the Family: A Game Theoretic Model of Household Decisions," in *Out of the Margins: Feminist Perspectives on Economics,* ed. Edith Kuiper and Jolande Sap (London: Routledge, 1995): 80–99.

45. For example, Paula England, "The Failure of Human Capital Theory to Explain Occupational Segregation."

46. See, for example, M. Kim and Solomon Polachek, "Panel Estimates of Male-Female Earnings Functions," *Journal of Human Resources* 29, no. 2 (1994): 406–28.

47. *Whose Science, Whose Knowledge: Thinking from Women's Lives* (Ithaca N.Y.: Cornell University Press, 1991). Feminist empiricism is discussed on pages 105–55 of chapter 5.

Chapter 8

1. Heidi Hartmann, "The Unhappy Marriage of Marxism and Feminism," in *Women and Revolution: A Discussion of the Unhappy Marriage of Marxism and Feminism*, ed. Lydia Sargent (Boston: South End Press, 1981), 2. Earlier drafts of this essay were circulated as early as 1975 (those drafts were coauthored by Amy Bridges), and a similar version appeared in 1979 in the journal *Capital and Class*. The essay has been reproduced in several anthologies and edited volumes and is one of the "classic" articles discussing the role of feminism in Marxist analysis.

2. The term socialist feminist is used throughout this chapter to refer to those who identified themselves with people and groups fighting class-based and gender-based inequalities.

3. See, for example, Meredith Tax, *The Rising of the Women: Feminist Solidarity and Class Conflict, 1880–1917* (New York: Monthly Review Press, 1980) and Mari Jo Buhle, *Women and American Socialism 1870–1920* (Urbana, Ill.: University of Illinois Press, 1983).

4. See, for example, Josephine Donovan, *Feminist Theory: The Intellectual Traditions of American Feminism* (New York: Continuum Publishing Co., 1991); Rosemarie Tong, *Feminist Thought: A Contemporary Introduction* (Boulder, Colo.: Westview Press, 1989); and Alison Jaggar and Paula Rothenberg Struhl, *Feminist Frameworks: Alternative Theoretical Accounts of the Relations Between Men and Women* (New York: McGraw-Hill, 1978).

5. David Gordon, Richard Edwards, and Michael Reich provide a contemporary analysis of the social structures that are built around the process of accumulation

in *Segmented Work, Divided Workers* (Cambridge: Cambridge University Press, 1982).

6. For a review of Marxian theories of the state see Martin Carnoy, *The State and Political Theory* (Princeton, N.J.: Princeton University Press, 1984).

7. Nancy Folbre, "Socialism, Feminist and Scientific," in *Beyond Economic Man: Feminist Theory and Economics*, ed. Marianne Ferber and Julie Nelson (Chicago: University of Chicago Press 1993), 106.

8. August Bebel, *Women Under Socialism* (New York: Schocken Books, 1971), 5. This version of Bebel's classic was translated from the original German of the 33rd edition by Daniel DeLeon in 1909. (Note: English versions were published using this title.)

9. Seyla Benhabib and Drucilla Cornell, "Introduction: Beyond the Politics of Gender," in *Feminism as Critique: On the Politics of Gender*, ed. Seyla Benhabib and Drucilla Cornell (Minneapolis: University of Minnesota Press, 1987), 2.

10. Frederick Engels, *The Origin of the Family, Private Property and the State* (New York: International Publishers, 1972).

11. Ibid., 71.

12. Ibid., 125.

13. Eleanor Leacock discusses Morgan's anthropological work at length in her introduction to the 1972 edition of Engels's *The Origin of the Family*, 7–67.

14. Engels, *The Origins*, 137.

15. Ibid., 153.

16. Ibid., 139.

17. Karl Marx, *Capital: A Critical Analysis of Capitalist Production*, Volume 1 (New York: International Publishers, 1967), 351.

18. Ibid., 395.

19. V. I. Lenin from a speech at the First All-Russian Congress of Women Workers, November 19, 1918. Reproduced in *The Woman Question: Selections from the Writings of Karl Marx, Frederick Engels, V. I. Lenin and Joseph Stalin* (New York: International Publishers, 1975), 43.

20. From *Conditions of the Working Class in England, 1844* and reproduced in *The Woman Question*, 33.

21. Joan Landes, "Marxism and the Woman Question," in *Promissory Notes: Women in the Transition to Socialism*, ed. Sonia Kruks, Rayna Rapp, and Marilyn B. Young (New York: Monthly Review Press, 1989), 17.

22. Nancy Folbre, "Socialism, Feminist and Scientific."

23. Engels and Marx were very concerned with making their theories as rigorous and scientific as competing theories. Engels writes, "These two great discoveries, the materialist conception of history and the revelation of the secret of capitalist production through surplus value, we owe to Marx. With these great discoveries socialism became a science." From "Socialism: Utopian and Scientific," published in French in 1880 originally part of a larger work *Anti-Duhring*, which came out in 1878. (*Marx-Engels Reader*, 2d. ed., ed. Robert C. Tucker [New York: W. W. Norton, 1978], 700.)

24. See Folbre, "Socialism, Feminism, and Scientific."

25. Ibid., 102.

26. Many socialist feminists have criticized Marxist treatments of the "Woman Question." A good review of those critiques can be found in Lise Vogel, *Marxism and the Oppression of Women: Toward a Unitary Theory* (New Brunswick: Rutgers University Press, 1983).

27. For a more thorough investigation of this point see Linda Nicholson, "Feminism and Marxism: Integrating Kinship and the Economic" in *Feminism as Critique*, ed. Benhabib and Cornell, 16–30.

28. Landes, "Marxism and the Woman Question," 23.

29. See Heidi Hartmann, "Capitalism, Patriarchy, and Job Segregation by Sex," *Signs* 1, no. 3, pt. 2 (1976): 137–70 and Jane Humphries, "Class Struggle and the Persistence of the Working-Class Family," *Cambridge Journal of Economics* 1 (1977): 241–58.

30. Alison Jaggar, *Feminist Politics and Human Nature* (Totawa, N.J.: Rowman and Allanheld, 1983), 78.

31. Ibid., 78.

32. For an excellent discussion of Marx's conception of human nature, see chapter 4 of Jaggar, *Feminist Politics and Human Nature*, 51–82.

33. Gayle Rubin, "The Traffic of Women: Notes on the 'Political Economy' of Sex," in *Toward an Anthropology of Women*, ed. Rayna Rapp Reiter (New York: Monthly Review Press, 1976), 157–210.

34. See Antonio Gramsci, *Selections from the Prison Notebooks* (New York: International Publishers, 1971).

35. Jane Flax, in *Building Feminist Theory: Essays from Quest* ed. the Quest Book Committee (New York: Longman, 1981), 184. (The article first appeared in *Quest: A Feminist Quarterly* 2, no. 1 [Summer 1976].)

36. See Sara Evans, *Personal Politics: The Roots of Women's Liberation in the Civil Rights Movement and the New Left* (New York: Knopf, 1979) on women's dissatisfaction with the New Left.

37. For a concise history of the development of socialist feminism in the United States, see Karen V. Hansen and Irene J. Philipson's introduction to their edited volume *Women, Class, and the Feminist Imagination: A Socialist-Feminist Reader* (Philadelphia: Temple University Press, 1990), 3–40. The pivotal areas of the disagreements between socialist feminists and radical feminists were the role of men in eliminating women's oppression and the role of other forms of oppression—notably class—in defining and eliminating gender-based domination.

38. Lise Vogel, *Marxism and the Oppression of Women* and Michèle Barrett, *Women's Oppression Today: Problems in Marxist Feminist Analysis* (London: Verso Books, 1980).

39. Sandra Morgen, "Conceptualizing and Changing Consciousness: Socialist-Feminist Perspectives," in *Women, Class, and the Feminist Imagination: A Socialist-Feminist Reader*, ed. Karen V. Hansen and Irene J. Philipson (Philadelphia: Temple University Press, 1990), 278.

40. For more on this development see Herbert Gintis, "The Reemergence of Marxian Economics in America," in *The Left Academy: Marxist Scholarship on American Campuses*, ed. Bertell Ollman and Edward Vernoff (New York: McGraw-Hill, 1982), 53–81.

41. Adam Przeworski, "Marxism and Rational Choice," *Politics and Society*, 14 (1986): 383.

42. Juliet Mitchell, "Women: The Longest Revolution," in *The Feminist Imagination*, 43–73. The article was originally published in *New Left Review* 40 (1966).

43. These journals included British publications *New Left Review*, *Capital and Class*, and *Cambridge Journal of Economics* and U.S. publications *Socialist Revolution* (later to be called *Socialist Review*), *Review of Radical Political Economics*, and *Radical America*.

44. Shulamith Firestone, *The Dialectic of Sex: The Case for Feminist Revolution* (New York: Bantam, 1971) and Kate Millett, *Sexual Politics* (New York: Avon, 1971).

45. Mitchell, "Women: The Longest Revolution," 49.

46. Margaret Bentson, "The Political Economy of Women's Liberation," *Monthly Review* 21, no. 4 (Sept. 1969): 24.

47. The number is cited in Maxine Molyneux, "Beyond the Domestic Labour Debate," *New Left Review* 116 (July/Aug. 1979): 3.

48. Ibid.

49. Christine Delphy, "The Main Enemy," chapter 4 of *Close to Home: A Materialist Analysis of Women's Oppression* (Amherst, Mass.: University of Massachusetts Press, 1984), 57–77 (published originally in 1970 in *Partisans*); John Harrison, "The Political Economy of Housework," *Bulletin of the Conference of Socialist Economics* 3, no. 1 (1973): 35–52; and Jean Gardiner, Susan Himmelweit, and Maureen Mackintosh, "Women's Domestic Labour," *Bulletin of the Conference of Socialist Economics* 4, no. 2 (1975).

50. Mariarosa Dalla Costa, "Women and the Subversion of the Community" translated by Selma James, *Radical America* 6, no. 1 (Jan. 1972): 62–102.

51. Susan Himmelweit, "Domestic Labor," in *The New Palgrave: Social Economics*, ed. John Eatwell, Murray Milgate and Peter Newman (New York: W. W. Norton, 1989), 38.

52. Nancy Folbre, "Exploitation Comes Home: a Critique of the Marxian Theory of Family Labor," *Cambridge Journal of Economics* 6 (1982): 318.

53. Hartmann, "The Unhappy Marriage," 3.

54. For example, Teresa Amott and Julie Matthaei use a form of the dual systems approach as the basis for their historical survey of women and work in the United States in *Gender, Race and Work: A Multicultural Economic History of Women in the United States* (Boston: South End Press, 1991).

55. Barrett, *Women's Oppression Today*, 97.

56. Ibid., 98.

57. Julie Matthaei, *An Economic History of Women in America: Women's Work, the Sexual Division of Labor and the Development of Capitalism* (New York: Schocken Books, 1982) and Harriet Fraad, Stephen Resnick, and Richard Wolff, *Bringing It All Home: Class, Gender and Power in the Modern Household* (Boulder, Colo.: Pluto Press, 1994).

58. Lourdes Benería, "Reproduction, Production and the Sexual Division of Labor," *Cambridge Journal of Economics* 3 (1979): 207.

59. A good early example is a 1970 article written about integrating radical economics into the college curriculum in which destruction of the environment, imperialism, racism, and the subjugation of women are included as important topics. Richard C. Edwards, Arthur MacEwan, and the Staff of Social Science 125 at Harvard University, "A Radical Approach to Economics: Basis for a New Curriculum," *American Economic Review* 60, no. 2 (May 1970): 352–63.

60. See pages 85–87 in *Beyond the Wasteland: A Democratic Alternative to Economic Decline* (Garden City, N.J.: Anchor Press/Doubleday, 1983). For a more thorough discussion of the problem of gender in this work, see Randy Albelda and Chris Tilly, "Toward a Broader Vision: Race, Gender and Labor Market Segmentation in the Social Structure of Accumulation Framework," in *Social Structures of Accumulation: The Political Economy of Growth and Crisis*, ed. David Kotz, Terrence McDonough, and Michael Reich (Cambridge: Cambridge University Press, 1994): 212–30.

61. John Roemer, *Analytical Foundations of Marxian Economic Theory* (Cambridge: Cambridge University Press, 1981); Michio Morishima, *Marx's Economics* (Cambridge: Cambridge University Press, 1973); and Ian Steedman, *Marx After Sraffa* (London: New Left Books, 1977).

62. Robert Paul Wolff, "The Resurrection of Karl Marx Political Economist," *Social Research* 53, no. 3 (Autumn 1986): 508.

63. John Eatwell, Murray Milgate, and Peter Newman, eds., *The New Palgrave: A Dictionary of Economics* (New York: Stockton Press, 1987).

64. M. C. Howard and J. E. King, *A History of Marxian Economics* (Princeton, N.J.: Princeton University Press, 1992).

65. Gintis, "The Reemergence of Marxian Economics in America."

66. Richard C. Edwards, Michael Reich, and Thomas Weisskopf, *The Capitalist System*, 3d ed. (Englewood Cliffs, N.J.: Prentice-Hall, 1986).

67. Samuel Bowles and Richard Edwards, *Radical Political Economy* (Brookfield, Vt.: Edward Elgar, 1990).

68. Howard J. Sherman, "Methodology of Critical Marxian Economic Theory," in *The Role of Economic Theory*, ed. Philip A. Klein (Boston, Mass.: Kluwer Academic Publishers, 1994), 77–95.

69. Julie Matthaei, "Marxist-Feminist Contributions to Radical Economics," and Jane Humphries, "Method, Materialism, and Marxist-Feminism: A Comment on Matthaei"; both appear in *Radical Economics*, ed. Bruce Roberts and Susan Feiner (Norwell, Mass.: Kluwer Academic Publishers, 1992), 117–54.

70. Three books that make this argument are Nancy Folbre, *Who Pays for the Kids?: Gender and the Structure of Constraints* (London: Routledge, 1994); Chris Beasley, *Sexual Economyths: Conceiving a Feminist Economics* (New York: St. Martin's Press, 1994); and Judith Grant, *Fundamental Feminism: Contesting the Core Concepts of Feminist Theory* (London: Routledge, 1993).

Chapter 9

1. Rebecca Blank, "A Female Perspective on Economic Man?" in *Revolution in Knowledge: Feminism in Social Science*, ed. Sue Rosenberg Zalk and Janice Gordon-Kelton (Boulder, Colo.: Westview Press, 1992), 114.

2. Janet Seiz, "Gender and Economic Research," in *Post-Popperian Methodology of Economics*, ed. Neil de Marchi (Boston: Kluwer Academic Publishers, 1992), 300.

3. It would be unfair to lay the lack of feminist advances solely at the feet of neoclassical economics. For although neoclassical economics is very resistant to most feminist approaches, it is not alone in presenting fundamental theoretical impasses for feminists.

4. Those interested in IAFFE can contact Jean Shackelford, Economics Department, Bucknell University, Lewisberg, PA 17837. Those interested in subscribing to FEMECON-L should send an E-mail to listserv@bucknell.edu with the message: subscribe femecon-l.

5. Daniel Hausman, "Introduction" in *The Philosophy of Economics: An Anthology* ed. Daniel Hausman (Cambridge: Cambridge University Press, 1984), 30.

6. Nancy Folbre, "The Unproductive Housewife: Her Evolution in Nineteenth-Century Economic Thought," *Signs* 16, no. 3 (1991): 463–84.

7. United Nations Development Programme, *Human Development Report, 1995* (New York: Oxford University Press, 1995): 6.

8. Two recent articles address this problem in detail: Nancy Folbre, " 'Holding Hands at Midnight': The Paradox of Caring Labor," *Feminist Economics* 1, no. 1 (Spring 1995): 73–93; and Susan Himmelweit, "The Discovery of Unpaid Work," *Feminist Economics* 1, no. 2 (Summer 1995): 1–19.

9. See, for example, Heidi Hartmann, "The Family as the Locus of Gender, Class, and Political Struggle: The Example of Housework," *Signs* 6, no. 3 (1981): 366–94.

10. See Chris Tilly and Randy Albelda, "Family Structure and Family Earnings: The Determinants of Earnings Differences among Family Types," *Industrial Relations* 33, no. 2 (1994): 151–67.

11. U.S. Department of Commerce, Bureau of the Census, *Income, Poverty, and Valuation of Noncash Benefits: 1994* (Washington D.C.: Government Printing Office, 1995), B-22.

12. See, for example, Lourdes Benería, "Toward a Greater Integration of Gender in Economics," *World Development* 23, no. 11 (November 1995): 1839–50 and Carmen Diana Deere, "What Difference Does Gender Make? Rethinking Peasant Studies," *Feminist Economics* 1, no. 1 (Spring 1995): 53–72.

13. There is a large literature on household bargaining models. For some feminist treatments see: Shelley Phipps and Peter Burton, "Social/Institutional Variables and Behavior Within Households: An Empirical Test Using the Luxembourg Income Study," *Feminist Economics* 1, no. 1 (Spring 1995): 151–74; Lynn Duggan, "Restacking the Deck: Family Policy and Women's Fall-Back Position in Germany Before and After Unification," *Feminist Economics* 1, no. 1 (Spring 1995): 175–94; Shelley Lundberg and Robert Pollack, "Separate Spheres Bargaining and the Marriage Market," *Journal of Political Economy* 101, no. 6 (1993): 988–1010; Notburga Ott, *Interfamily Bargaining and Household Decisions* (New York: Springer-Verlag, 1992); Amartya Sen, "Gender and Cooperative Conflicts, in *Persistent Inequalities*, ed. Irene Tinker (New York: Oxford University Press, 1990), 123–79; and Marjorie McElroy and Mary Jean Horney, "Nash-Bargained Household Decisions: Toward a Generalization of the Theory of Demand," *International Economic Review* 22, no. 2 (1981): 333–49. For a feminist critique of bargaining models see Janet Seiz, "The Bargaining Approach and Feminist Methodology," *Review of Radical Political Economics* 23, no. 1–2 (1991): 22–29.

14. See Folbre, "Holding Hands at Midnight"; Himmelweit, "The Discovery of Unpaid Work"; and Maria Sagrario Floro, "Women's Well-Being, Poverty, and Work Intensity," *Feminist Economics* 1, no. 3 (Fall 1995): 1–25.

15. Marilyn Waring, *If Women Counted: A New Feminist Economics* (San Francisco: Harper and Row, 1988). See also, Lourdes Benería, "Accounting for Women's Work: The Progress of Two Decades," *World Development* 20, no. 11 (1992): 1547–60 and United Nations Development Programme, *Human Development Report, 1995*.

16. See, for example, Elaine McCrate, "Trade Merger and Employment: Economic Theory on Marriage," *Review of Radical Political Economics* 19, no. 1 (1987): 73–89; Nancy Folbre and Heidi Hartmann, "The Rhetoric of Self-Interest: Ideology and Gender in Economic Theory," in *The Consequences of Rhetoric,* ed. Arjo Klamer, Donald McCloskey, and Robert Solow (Cambridge: Cambridge University Press, 1988), 184–203; Julie Nelson, "Gender, Metaphor, and the Definition of Economics," *Economics and Philosophy* 8 (1992): 103–25; and Paula England, "The Separative Self: Androcentric Bias in Neoclassical Assumptions," in *Beyond Economic Man: Feminist Theory and Economics,* ed. Marianne A. Ferber and Julie A. Nelson (Chicago: University of Chicago Press, 1993), 37–53.

17. Diana Straussmann and Livia Polanyi, "The Economist as Storyteller: What the Texts Reveal," in *Out of the Margins: Feminist Perspectives on Economics*, ed. Edith Kuiper and Jolande Sap (London: Routledge, 1995), 129–45; Ulla Grapard, "Robinson Crusoe: The Quintessential Economic Man?" *Feminist Economics* 1, no. 1 (Spring 1995): 33–52; and Julie Nelson, "The Study of Choice or the Study of Provisioning? Gender and the Definition of Economics," in *Behind Economic Man: Feminist Theory and Economics,* ed. Marianne Ferber and Julie Nelson (Chicago: University of Chicago Press, 1993), 23–36.

18. See, for example, Sandra Harding, "Can Feminist Thought Make Economics More Objective?" *Feminist Economics* 1, no. 1 (Spring 1995): 7–32; Julie Nelson, "Value-Free or Valueless? Notes on the Pursuit of Detachment in Economics," *History of Political Economy* 25, no. 1 (Spring 1993): 121–45; and Ann Jennings, "Public or Private? Institutional Economics and Feminism," in *Beyond Economic Man: Feminist Theory and Economics*, ed. Marianne Ferber and Julie Nelson (Chicago: University of Chicago Press, 1993), 111–29.

19. *World Development* 23, no. 11 (November 1995).

20. Diane Elson, ed., *Male Bias in the Development Process* (Manchester, U.K.: Manchester University Press. 1991); Nancy Folbre, Barbara Bergmann, Bina Agarwal, and Maria Floro, eds., *Women's Work in the World Economy* (New York: New York University Press, 1992); Lourdes Benería and Shelley Feldman, eds., *Unequal Burden: Economic Crises, Persistent Poverty, and Women's Work* (Boulder, Colo.: Westview Press, 1992); and Nahid Aslanbeigui, Steven Pressman, and Gale Summerfield, eds., *Women in the Age of Economic Transformation* (London: Routledge, 1994). In addition, Benería edited a volume on women and development in 1982 (Lourdes Benería, ed., *Women and Development: The Sexual Division of Labor in Rural Societies* [New York: Preager Press, 1982]).

21. Naila Kabeer, *Reversed Realities: Gender Hierarchies in Development Thought* (London: Verso, 1994); two books by Isabella Bakker: *The Strategic Silence: Gender and Economic Policy* (London: Zed Books, 1994) and *Engendering Macroeconomic Policy Reform in the Era of Adjustment and Restructuring: A Conceptual Overview* (Ottawa: North-South Institute, 1992); Carmen Diana Deere, *Household and Class Relations: Peasants and Landlords in Northern Peru* (Berkeley: University of California Press, 1990); and Marjorie Cohen, *Free Trade and the Structure of Women's Work* (Ottawa: Garamond Press, 1987).

22. Some of the earlier feminist contributions in this area include: Juanita Kreps, *Sex in the Marketplace: American Women at Work* (Baltimore: Johns Hopkins Press, 1971); Janice Madden, *The Economics of Sex Discrimination* (Lexington, Mass.: Lexington Books, 1973); Barbara Bergmann, "Occupational Segregation, Wages and Profits When Employers Discriminate by Race or Sex," *Eastern Economic Journal* 1 (April–July 1974): 103–10; Cynthia B. Lloyd, ed., *Sex Discrimination, and the Division of Labor* (New York: Columbia University Press, 1975); Martha Blaxall and Barbara Reagan, eds., *Women and the Workplace: The Implications of Occupational Segregation* (Chicago: University of Chicago Press, 1976); Cynthia B. Lloyd and Beth T. Niemi, *The Economics of Sex Differentials* (New York: Columbia University Press, 1979); Cynthia B. Lloyd, Emily Andrews, and Curtis L. Gilroy, eds., *Women in the Labor Market* (New York: Columbia University Press, 1979); Francine Blau and Wallace Hendricks, "Occupational Segregation by Sex: Trends and Prospects," *Journal of Human Resources* 14, no. 2 (1979): 197–210; Phyllis Wallace with Linda Datcher and Julianne Malveaux, *Black Women in the Labor Force* (Cambridge: MIT Press, 1980); Donald Treiman and Heidi Hartmann, eds., *Women, Work, and Wages: Equal Pay for Jobs of Equal Value* (Washington,

D.C.: National Academy Press, 1981); and Paula England, "The Failure of Human Capital Theory to Explain Occupational Segregation," *Journal of Human Resources* 17, no. 3 (1982): 358–70.

23. Teresa Amott and Julie Matthaei, *Race, Gender and Work: A Multicultural History of Women in the United States* (Boston: South End Press, 1991); Jane Humphries, "The Working Class Family, Women's Liberation, and Class Struggle: The Case of Nineteenth Century British History," *Review of Radical Political Economics* 9, no. 3 (Fall 1977): 25–41; and Jane Humphries, "Enclosures, Common Rights, and Women: The Proletarianization of Families in the Late 18th and Early 19th Centuries," *Journal of Economic History* 50, no. 1 (1990): 17–42.

24. See, for example, recent publications: Emily P. Hoffman, ed., *Essays on the Economics of Discrimination* (Kalamazoo, Mich.: W. E. Upjohn Institute for Employment Research, 1991); Francine Blau and Andrea Beller, "Black-White Earnings Over the 1970s and 1980s: Gender Differences in Trends," *Review of Economics and Statistics* 74 (1992): 276–86; Francine Blau and Lawrence Kahn, "The Gender Gap: Learning from International Comparisons," *American Economic Review* 82, no. 2 (May 1992): 533–38; Elaine Sorensen, *Comparable Worth: Is It a Worthy Policy?* (Princeton: Princeton University Press, 1994); Elaine McCrate and Laura Leete, "Black-White Wage Differences among Young Women," *Industrial Relations* 33, no. 2 (April 1994): 168–83; Mary King, "Human Capital and Black Women's Occupational Mobility," *Industrial Relations* 34, no. 2 (April 1995): 282–98; and Michael Greene and Emily Hoffnar, "Gender Earnings Inequality in the Service and Manufacturing Industries in the U.S.," *Feminist Economics* 1, no. 3 (Fall 1995): 82–95.

25. Antonella Picchio, *Social Reproduction: The Political Economy of the Labor Market* (Cambridge: Cambridge University Press, 1992); Randy Albelda and Chris Tilly, "All in the Family: Family Types, Access to Income, and Implications for Family Income Policies," *Policy Studies Journal* 20 (1992): 388-404; and Deborah Figart and June Lapidus, "A Gender Analysis of U.S. Labor Market Policies for the Working Poor," *Feminist Economics* 1, no. 3 (Fall 1995): 60–81.

26. Lee Badgett is the pioneer in this area. Two recently published articles by her are: "The Wage Effects of Sexual Orientation Discrimination," *Industrial and Labor Relations Review* 48, no. 4 (Summer 1995): 726–39 and "Gender, Sexuality, and Sexual Orientation: All in the Feminist Family?" *Feminist Economics* 1, no. 1 (Spring, 1995): 121–39.

27. See M. V. Lee Badgett and Rhonda Williams, "The Economics of Sexual Orientation: Establishing a Research Agenda," *Feminist Studies* 18, no. 3 (Fall 1992): 649–57 and Julie Matthaei, "The Sexual Division of Labor, Sexuality, and Lesbian/Gay Liberation: Toward a Marxist-Feminist Analysis of Sexuality in U.S. Capitalism," *Review of Radical Political Economics* 27, no 2 (June 1995): 1–37.

28. See Lee Levin, "Toward a Feminist, Post-Keynesian Theory of Investment: A Consideration of the Socially and Emotionally Constituted Nature of Agent Knowledge," in *Out of the Margins: Feminist Perspectives on Economics*, ed. Edith Kuiper and Jolande Sap (London: Routledge, 1995), 100–129.

29. Esther Redmount, "Toward a Feminist Econometrics," in *Out of the Margins: Feminist Perspectives on Economics*, ed. Edith Kuiper and Jolande Sap (London: Routledge, 1995), 216–22.

30. Mary Ann Dimand, Robert W. Dimand, and Evelyn L. Forget, *Women of Value: Feminist Essays on the History of Women in Economics* (Brookfield, Vt.: Edward Elgar, 1995).

31. Jean Shackelford, "Mabel Newcomer and the Economics Profession: 1917–1957" Paper presented at the 6th Annual International Conference on Socio-

Economics (1994); Mary Hirschfeld, "Antecedents of the New Home Economics," Paper presented at 1994 ASSA Meetings (1994); and Julianne Malveaux, "Missed Opportunity: Sadie Tanner Mossell Alexander and the Economics Profession," *American Economic Review* 81, no. 2 (May 1991): 307–10.

32. Michèle Pujol, *Feminism and Anti-Feminism in Early Economic Thought* (Brookfield, Vt.: Edward Elgar, 1992).

33. See Folbre, "The Unproductive Housewife"; Margo Anderson, "The History of Women and the History of Statistics," *Journal of Women's History* 4, no. 1 (Spring 1992): 14–36; Claudia Goldin, *Understanding the Gender Gap* (Chicago: University of Chicago Press, 1990); Nancy Folbre and Marjorie Abel, "Women's Work and Women's Households: Gender Bias in the U.S. Census," *Social Research* 56, no. 3 (1989): 545–69; and Penelope Ciancanelli, "Reestimation of the Labor Force Participation of Married Women from 1900 to 1930" (Ph.D. diss., New School for Social Research, 1983).

34. See, for example, Martha MacDonald, "The Empirical Challenges of Feminist Economics: The Example of Economic Restructuring," in *Out of the Margins: Feminist Perspectives on Economics,* ed. Edith Kuiper and Jolande Sap (London: Routledge, 1995): 175–97.

BIBLIOGRAPHY

Adelman, Irma. "My Life Philosophy." *The American Economist* 34, no. 2 (Fall 1990): 3–14.

Aigner, Dennis, and Glen G. Cain. "Statistical Theories of Discrimination in Labor Markets." *Industrial and Labor Relations Review* 30, no. 2 (January 1977): 175–77.

Albelda, Randy, and Chris Tilly. "All in the Family: Family Types, Access to Income, and Implications for Family Income Policies." *Policy Studies Journal* 20 (1992): 388–404.

———. "Toward a Broader Vision: Race, Gender and Labor Market Segmentation in the Social Structure of Accumulation Framework." In *Social Structures of Accumulation: The Political Economy of Growth and Crisis*, edited by David Kotz, Terrence McDonough, and Michael Reich, 212–30. Cambridge: Cambridge University Press, 1994.

Alcott, Linda, and Elizabeth Potter, eds. *Feminist Epistemologies*. London: Routledge, 1993.

Alston, Richard M., J. R. Kearl, and Michael B. Vaughan. "Is There a Consensus Among Economists in the 1990s?" *American Economic Review* 82, no. 2 (May 1992): 203–9.

Amott, Teresa, and Julie Matthaei. *Race, Gender and Work: A Multicultural History of Women in the United States*. Boston: South End Press, 1991.

Amsden, Alice, and Collete Moser. "Job Search and Affirmative Action." *American Economic Review* 65, no. 2 (May 1976): 83–91.

Anderson, Margo. "The History of Women and the History of Statistics." *Journal of Women's History* 4, no. 1 (Spring 1992): 14–36.

Arrow, Kenneth. "The Theory of Discrimination." In *Discrimination in the Labor Market*, edited by Orley Ashenfelter and Albert Rees, 3–33. Princeton, N.J.: Princeton University Press, 1973.

Aslanbeigui, Nahid, Steven Pressman, and Gale Summerfield, eds. *Women in the Age of Economic Transformation*. London: Routledge, 1994.

Azzi, Corry, and Ronald Ehrenberg. "Household Allocation of Time and Church Attendance." *Journal of Political Economy* 83 (February 1975): 27–53.

Badgett, M. V. Lee. "Gender, Sexuality, and Sexual Orientation: All in the Feminist Family?" *Feminist Economics* 1, no. 1 (Spring 1995): 121–39.

———. "The Wage Effects of Sexual Orientation Discrimination." *Industrial and Labor Relations Review* 48, no. 4 (Summer 1995): 726–39.

Badgett, M. V. Lee, and Rhonda Williams. "The Economics of Sexual Orientation: Establishing a Research Agenda." *Feminist Studies* 18, no. 3 (Fall 1992): 649–57.

Bailey, Elizabeth. "The Committee on the Status of Women in the Economics Profession." *American Economic Review* 71, no. 2 (May 1981): 470–77.

———. "The Committee on the Status of Women in the Economics Profession." *American Economic Review* 72, no. 2 (May 1982): 431–41.

Bakker, Isabella. *Engendering Macroeconomic Policy Reform in the Era of Adjustment and Restructuring: A Conceptual Overview.* Ottawa: North-South Institute, 1992.

———. *The Strategic Silence: Gender and Economic Policy.* London: Zed Books, 1994.

Balch, Emily. "Public Assistance of the Poor in France." *Publications of the American Economic Association* 8, no. 4–5 (July and Sept. 1893): 263–45.

Barbezat, Debra. "The Market for New Ph.D. Economists." *Journal of Economic Education* 23, no. 3 (Summer 1992): 262–76.

Barrett, Michele. *Women's Oppression Today: Problems in Marxist Feminist Analysis.* London: Verso Books, 1980.

Bartlett, Robin. "A Conversation with Carolyn Shaw Bell." *CSWEP Newsletter* (Fall 1993): 7–9.

Beasley, Chris. *Sexual Economyths: Conceiving a Feminist Economics.* New York: St. Martin's Press, 1994.

Bebel, August. *Women Under Socialism.* New York: Schocken Books, 1971

Becker, Gary. *The Economics of Discrimination.* Chicago: University of Chicago Press, 1957.

———. "A Theory of Marriage." *Journal of Political Economy* 81, no. 4 (July/Aug. 1973): 813–46.

———. *Human Capital: A Theoretical and Empirical Analysis*, 2d ed. New York: Columbia University Press for the National Economic Research Bureau, 1975. (The first edition was published in 1964.)

———. *The Economic Approach to Human Behavior.* Chicago: University of Chicago Press, 1976.

Bell, Carolyn Shaw. "Report of the Committee on the Status of Women in the Economics Profession." *American Economic Review* 63, no. 2 (May 1973): 508–11.

———. "Economics, Sex, and Gender." *Social Science Quarterly* 55, no. 3 (1974): 615–31.

Benería, Lourdes. "Reproduction, Production and the Sexual Division of Labor." *Cambridge Journal of Economics* 3 (1979): 203–25.

———. "Accounting for Women's Work: The Progress of Two Decades." *World Development* 20, no. 11 (1992):1547–60.

———. "Toward a Greater Integration of Gender in Economics." *World Development* 23, no. 11 (November 1995): 1839–50.

Benería, Lourdes, ed. *Women and Development: The Sexual Division of Labor in Rural Societies.* New York: Praeger Press, 1982.

Benería, Lourdes, and Shelley Feldman, eds. *Unequal Burden: Economic Crises, Persistent Poverty, and Women's Work.* Boulder, Colo.: Westview Press, 1992.

Benhabib, Seyla, and Drucilla Cornell. "Introduction: Beyond the Politics of Gender." In *Feminism as Critique: On the Politics of Gender*, edited by Seyla Benhabib and Drucilla Cornell, 1–15. Minneapolis: University of Minnesota Press, 1987.

Benston, Margaret. "The Political Economy of Women's Liberation." *Monthly Review* 21, no. 4 (September 1969): 13–27.

Bergmann, Barbara. "Occupational Segregation, Wages and Profits When Employers Discriminate by Race or Sex." *Eastern Economic Journal* 1 (April–July 1974): 103–10.

————. "Becker's Theory of the Family: Preposterous Conclusions." *Feminist Economics* 1, no. 1 (Spring 1995): 141–50.

Bernard, Jessie. *Academic Women.* University Park, Pa.: Pennsylvania State University Press, 1964.

Blank, Rebecca. "The Effect of Double-Blind versus Single-Blind Reviewing: Experimental Evidence for the *American Economic Review.*" *American Economic Review* 81, no. 5 (1991): 1041–67.

————. "A Female Perspective on Economic Man?" In *Revolution in Knowledge: Feminism in Social Science*, edited by Sue Rosenberg Zalk and Janice Gordon-Kelton, 111–24. Boulder, Colo.: Westview Press, 1992.

Blank, Rebecca, and Patricia Ruggles. "Short-Term Recidivism Among Public-Assistance Recipients." *American Economic Review* 84, no. 2 (May 1994): 49–53.

Blau, Francine. "Discrimination Against Women: Theory and Evidence." In *Labor Economics: Modern Views,* edited by William Darity Jr., 53–89. Boston: Kluwer-Nijhoff, 1984.

Blau, Francine, and Andrea Beller. "Black-White Earnings Over the 1970s and 1980s: Gender Differences in Trends." *Review of Economics and Statistics* 74 (1992): 276–86.

Blau, Francine D., and Marianne Ferber. *The Economics of Women, Men and Work*, 2d ed. Englewood Cliffs, N.J.: Prentice-Hall, 1992.

Blau, Francine, and Wallace Hendricks. "Occupational Segregation by Sex: Trends and Prospects." *Journal of Human Resources* 14, no. 2 (1979): 197–210.

Blau, Francine, and Lawrence Kahn. "The Gender Gap: Learning from International Comparisions." *American Economic Review* 82, no. 2 (May 1992): 533–38.

Blaug, Mark. *The Methodology of Economics.* Cambridge: Cambridge University Press, 1980.

————. *Economic Theory in Retrospect*, 4th ed. Cambridge: Cambridge University Press, 1988.

Blaxall, Martha, and Barbara Reagan, eds. *Women and the Workplace: The Implications of Occupational Segregation*. Chicago: University of Chicago Press, 1976.

Boston, Thomas D. "W. E. B. DuBois and the Historical School of Economics." *American Economic Association* 81, no. 2 (May 1991): 303–6.

Bowles, Samuel, and Richard C. Edwards, eds. *Radical Political Economy.* Brookfield, Vt.: Edward Elgar, 1990.

Bowles, Samuel, and Herbert Gintis. *Capitalism and Democracy.* New York: Basic Books, 1986.

Bowles, Samuel, David Gordon, and Thomas Weisskopf. *Beyond the Wasteland: A Democratic Alternative to Economic Decline.* Garden City, N.J.: Anchor Press/Doubleday, 1983.

Broder, Ivy. "Professional Achievements and Gender Differences Among Academic Economists." *Economic Inquiry* 31, no. 1 (January 1993): 116–27.

Brown, Lisa Jo. "Neoclassical Economics and the Sexual Division of Labor." *Eastern Economic Journal* 10 (Oct./Nov. 1984): 367–79.

Buhle, Mari Jo. *Women and American Socialism 1870–1920.* Urbana, Ill.: University of Illinois Press, 1983.

Burnett, Nancy. "Gender and the Liberal Arts Curriculum." Mimeo, Department of Economics, Claremont McKenna College, 1994.

Cain, Glen. "The Economic Analysis of Labor Market Discrimination: A Survey." In *Handbook of Labor Economics, Volume I,* edited Orley Ashenfelter and R. Layard, 693–785. New York: North Holland, 1986.

Caplow, Theodore, and Reece McGee. *The Academic Marketplace.* New York: Basic Books, 1958.

Carnoy, Martin. *The State and Political Theory.* Princeton, N.J: Princeton University Press, 1984.

Church, Robert L. "Economists as Experts: The Rise of an Academic Profession in the United States, 1870–1920." In *The University in Society, Volume 2: Europe, Scotland and the United States*, edited by Lawrence Stone, 571–609. Princeton: Princeton University Press, 1974.

Ciancanelli, Penelope. "Reestimation of the Labor Force Participation of Married Women from 1900 to 1930." Ph.D. diss., New School for Social Research, 1983.

Ciancanelli, Penelope, and Bettina Berch. "Gender and GNP." In *Analyzing Gender: A Handbook of Social Science Research*, edited by Beth D. Hess and Myra Marx Ferree, 244–266. Newbury Park, Calif.: Sage Publications, 1987.

Clark, John Bates. *The Distribution of Wealth: A Theory of Wages, Interest and Profits.* New York: Augustus M. Kelly Bookseller, 1965. (Originally published in 1898.)

Coats, A. W. "The Educational Revolution and the Professionalization of American Economics." In *Breaking the Mould: Higher Learning in the Nineteenth Century*, edited by William J. Barber, 340–75. Middletown, Conn.: Wesleyan University Press, 1988.

Cohen, Marjorie. "The Razor's Edge Invisible: Feminism's Effect on Economics." *International Journal of Women Studies* 8, no. 3 (May/June 1985): 286–98.

———. *Free Trade and the Structure of Women's Work.* Ottawa: Garamond Press, 1987.

Collins, Patricia Hill. *Black Feminist Thought.* London: Routledge, 1991.

Cookingham, Mary E. "Social Economists and Reform: Berkeley, 1906–1961." *History of Political Economy* 19, no. 1 (1987): 47–63.

Dalla Costa, Mariarosa. "Women and the Subversion of the Community." Translated by Selma James. *Radical America* 6, no. 1 (January 1972): 62–102.

Darity, William Jr. "The Human Capital Approach to Black-White Earnings Inequality: Some Unsettled Questions." *Journal of Human Resources* 17, no. 1 (1982): 72–93.

Davis, Allen F. "Katharine Coman." In *Notable American Women*, edited by Edward T. James, 365–367. Cambridge: Harvard University Press, 1971.

Deere, Carmen Diana. *Household and Class Relations: Peasants and Landlords in Northern Peru.* Berkeley: University of California Press, 1990.

———. "What Difference Does Gender Make? Rethinking Peasant Studies." *Feminist Economics* 1, no. 1 (Spring 1995): 53–72.

de Graffenried, Clare. "Child Labor." *Publication of the American Economic Association, First Series* 5, no. 2 (1890): 73–149.

Delphy, Christine. "The Main Enemy." Chapter 4 of *Close to Home: A Materialist Analysis of Women's Oppression*, 57–77. Amherst, Mass.: University of Massachusetts Press, 1984.

Dimand, Mary Ann, Robert W. Dimand, and Evelyn L. Forget. *Women of Value: Feminist Essays on the History of Women in Economics.* Brookfield, Vt.: Edward Elgar, 1995.

Donovan, Josephine. *Feminist Theory: The Intellectual Traditions of American Feminism.* New York: Continuum Publishing Co., 1991.

Duggan, Lynn. "Restacking the Deck: Family Policy and Women's Fall-Back Position in Germany before and after Unification." *Feminist Economics* 1, no. 1 (Spring 1995): 175–94.

Eastman, Crystal. "The American Way of Distributing Industrial Accident Losses." *Publications of the American Economic Association, Third Series* 10 (1909): 119–34.

Eatwell, John, Murray Milgate, and Peter Newman, eds. *The New Palgrave: A Dictionary of Economics.* New York: Stockton Press, 1987.

Edwards, Richard C., Arthur MacEwan, and the Staff of Social Science 125 at Harvard University. "A Radical Approach to Economics: Basis for a New Curriculum." *American Economic Review* 60, no. 2 (1970): 352–63.

Edwards, Richard C., Michael Reich, and Thomas Weisskopf, eds. *The Capitalist System,* 3d ed. Englewood Cliffs, N.J.: Prentice-Hall, 1986.

Eells, Walter Crosby. *American Association of University Professors Bulletin* 42 (1956): 644–51.

Elson, Diane, ed. *Male Bias in the Development Process.* Manchester, U.K.: Manchester University Press, 1991.

Ely, Richard T. *Report of the Organization of the American Economic Association* 1, no. 1 (March 1886): 40–41.

———. *Ground Under My Feet: An Autobiography.* New York: Macmillan, 1938.

Engels, Frederick. *The Origin of the Family, Private Property and the State.* New York: International Publishers, 1972.

England, Paula. "The Separative Self: Androcentric Bias in Neoclassical Assumptions." In *Beyond Economic Man: Feminist Theory and Economics,* edited by Marianne A. Ferber and Julie A. Nelson, 37–53. Chicago: University of Chicago Press, 1993.

———. "The Failure of Human Capital Theory to Explain Occupational Segregation." *Journal of Human Resources* 17, no. 3 (1982): 358–70.

Evans, Sara. *Personal Politics: The Roots of Women's Liberation in the Civil Rights Movement and the New Left.* New York: Knopf, 1979.

Feiner, Susan F. "Introductory Textbook and the Treatment of Issues Related to Women and Minorities, 1984 and 1991." *Journal of Economic Education* 24, no. 2 (Spring 1993): 145–62.

Feiner, Susan F., and Barbara A. Morgan. "Women and Minorities in Introductory Economics Textbooks: 1974–1984." *Journal of Economic Education* 18 (Fall 1987): 376–92.

Ferber, Marianne. "Citations and Networking." *Gender and Society* 2, no. 1 (March 1986): 82–89.

Ferber, Marianne, and Bonnie Birnbaum. "The 'New Home Economics': Retrospects and Prospects." *Journal of Consumer Research* 4 (1977): 19–28.

Ferber, Marianne, and Julie A. Nelson, eds. *Beyond Economic Man: Feminist Theory and Economics.* Chicago: University of Chicago Press, 1993.

Ferber, Marianne, and Michelle L. Teiman. "The Oldest, the Most Established, the Most Quantitative of the Social Sciences—and the Most Dominated by Men: The Impact of Feminism on Economics." In *Men Studies Modified,* edited by Dale Spender, 125–39. New York: Pergamon Press, 1981.

Figart, Deborah, and June Lapidus. "A Gender Analysis of U.S. Labor Market Policies for the Working Poor." *Feminist Economics* 1, no. 3 (Fall 1995): 60–81.

Firestone, Shulamith. *The Dialectic of Sex: The Case for Feminist Revolution.* New York: Bantam, 1971.

Fish, Mary, and Jean Gibbons. "A Comparison of the Publications of Female and Male Economists." *Journal of Economic Education* 20, no. 1 (Winter 1989): 93–105.

Fitzpatrick, Ellen. *Endless Crusade: Women Social Scientists and Progressive Reform.* New York: Oxford University Press, 1990.

Flax, Jane. "Does Feminism Need Marxism?" In *Building Feminist Theory: Essays from Quest,* edited by the Quest Book Committee, 174–85. New York: Longman, 1981.

Floro, Maria Sagrario. "Women's Well-Being, Poverty, and Work Intensity." *Feminist Economics* 1, no. 3 (Fall 1995): 1–25.

Folbre, Nancy. "Exploitation Comes Home: A Critique of the Marxian Theory of Family Labor." *Cambridge Journal of Economics* 6 (1982): 317–29.

———. "The Unproductive Housewife: Her Evolution in Nineteenth-Century Economic Thought." *Signs* 16, no. 3 (1991): 463–84.

———. "Socialism, Feminist and Scientific." In *Beyond Economic Man: Feminist Theory and Economics,* edited by Marianne Ferber and Julie Nelson, 94–110. Chicago: University of Chicago Press, 1993.

———. *Who Pays for the Kids?: Gender and the Structure of Constraints.* London: Routledge, 1994.

———. " 'Holding Hands at Midnight': The Paradox of Caring Labor." *Feminist Economics* 1, no. 1 (Spring 1995): 73–93.

Folbre, Nancy, and Majorie Abel. "Women's Work and Women's Households: Gender Bias in the U.S. Census." *Social Research* 56, no. 3 (1989): 545–69.

Folbre, Nancy, Barbara Bergmann, Bina Agarwal, and Maria Floro, eds. *Women's Work in the World Economy.* New York: New York University Press, 1992.

Folbre, Nancy, and Heidi Hartmann. "The Rhetoric of Self-Interest: Ideology and Gender in Economic Theory." In *The Consequences of Rhetoric,* edited by Arjo Klamer, Donald McCloskey, and Robert Solow, 184–203. Cambridge: Cambridge University Press, 1988.

Fraad, Harriet, Stephen Resnick, and Richard Wolff. *Bringing It All Home: Class, Gender and Power in the Modern Household.* Boulder, Colo.: Pluto Press, 1994.

Friedman, Milton. *Essays in Positive Economics.* Chicago: Chicago University Press, 1953.

Friedman, Milton, and Rose Friedman. *Free to Choose.* New York: Harcourt Brace Jovanovich, 1979.

Froman, Lewis A. "Graduate Students in Economics, 1904–1928." *American Economic Review* 20 (1930): 236–47.

———. "Graduate Students in Economics, 1904–1940." *American Economic Association* 32 (1942): 817–26.

Furner, Mary O. *Advocacy and Objectivity: A Crisis in the Professionalization of American Social Science, 1865–1905.* Lexington, Ky.: The University Press of Kentucky, 1975.

———. "Knowing Capitalism: Public Investigation and the Labor Question in the Long Progressive Era." In *The State and Economic Knowledge: The American and British Experiences,* edited by Mary O. Furner and Barry Supple, 241–86. Cambridge: Cambridge University Press, 1990.

Gardiner, Jean, Susan Himmelweit, and Maureen Mackintosh. "Women's Domestic Labour." *Bulletin of the Conference of Socialist Economics* 4, no. 2 (1975).

Geronimus, Arline, and Sanders Korenman. "The Socioeconomic Consequences of Teen Childbearing Reconsidered." *Quarterly Journal of Economics* 107 (1992): 1187–214.

Gintis, Herbert. "The Reemergence of Marxian Economics in America." In *The Left Academy: Marxist Scholarship on American Campuses,* edited by Bertell Ollman and Edward Vernoff, 53–81. New York: McGraw-Hill, 1982.

Goldin, Claudia. *Understanding the Gender Gap: An Economic History of American Women.* New York: Oxford University Press, 1990.

Gordon, Nancy. "Report of the Committee on the Status of Women in the Economics Profession." *American Economic Review* 79, no. 2 (May 1989): 422–25.

———. "Report of the Committee on the Status of Women in the Economics Profession." *CSWEP Newsletter* (Winter 1990).

Gordon, David, Richard Edwards, and Michael Reich. *Segmented Work, Divided Workers*. Cambridge: Cambridge University Press, 1982.

Graham, Patricia Albjerg. "Expansion and Exclusion: A History of Women in American Higher Education." *Signs* 3, no. 4 (Summer 1978): 759–73.

Gramsci, Antonio. *Selections from the Prison Notebooks*. New York: International Publishers, 1971.

Grant, Judith. *Fundamental Feminism: Contesting the Core Concepts of Feminist Theory*. London: Routledge, 1993.

Grapard, Ulla. "Robinson Crusoe: The Quintessential Economic Man?" *Feminist Economics* 1, no. 1 (Spring 1995): 33–52.

Gray, Tara. "Women in Labor Economics Textbooks." *Journal of Economic Education* 23, no. 4 (Fall 1992): 362–73.

Greene, Michael, and Emily Hoffnar. "Gender Earnings Inequality in the Service and Manufacturing Industries in the U.S." *Feminist Economics* 1, no. 3 (Fall 1995): 82–95.

Hammermesh, Daniel, and Neal M. Soss. "An Economic Theory of Suicide." *Journal of Political Economy* 82, no. 1 (Jan./Feb. 1974): 83–98.

Hammond, Claire H. "Helen Frances Page Bates: The First American Woman Ph.D. in Economics." *CSWEP Newsletter* (Winter 1991): 9.

———. *Women and the Professionalization of Economics*. Winston-Salem, NC: Wake Forest University, Working Paper Series No. 90.2, 1990.

Hansen, W. Lee. "The Education and Training of Economics Doctorates: Major Findings of the American Association's Commission on Graduate Education in Economics." *Journal of Economic Literature* 29, no. 3 (Sept. 1991): 1054–88.

Hansen, Karen V., and Irene J. Philipson. *Women, Class, and the Feminist Imagination: A Socialist-Feminist Reader*. Philadelphia: Temple University Press, 1990.

Harding, Sandra. *Whose Science? Whose Knowledge?: Thinking from Women's Lives*. Ithaca: Cornell University Press, 1991.

———. "Rethinking Standpoint Epistemology." In *Feminist Epistemologies,* edited by Linda Alcott and Elizabeth Potter, 49–82. London: Routledge, 1993.

———. "Can Feminist Thought Make Economics More Objective?" *Feminist Economics* 1, no. 1 (Spring 1995): 7–32.

Harrison, John. "The Political Economy of Housework." *Bulletin of the Conference of Socialist Economics* 3, no. 1 (1973): 35–52.

Hartmann, Heidi. "Capitalism, Patriarchy and Job Segregation by Sex." *Signs* 3, no. 2 (1976): 137–69.

———. "The Unhappy Marriage of Marxim and Feminism." In *Women and Revolution: A Discussion of the Unhappy Marriage of Marxism and Feminism,* edited by Lydia Sargent, 1–41. Boston, Mass.: South End Press, 1981.

———. "The Family as the Locus of Gender, Class, and Political Struggle: The Example of Housework." *Signs* 6, no. 3 (1981): 366–94.

Hartsock, Nancy. "The Feminist Standpoint: Developing the Ground for a Specifically Feminist Historical Materialism." In *Discovering Reality,* edited by Sandra Harding and Merrill Hintikka, 283–310. Boston: Reidel Publishing Co., 1983.

Haskell, Thomas. *The Emergence of Professional Social Science: The American Social Science Association and the Nineteenth Century Crisis of Authority*. Urbana: University of Illinois Press, 1977.

Hausman, Daniel. *The Inexact and Separate Science of Economics*. Cambridge: Cambridge University Press, 1992.

Hausman, Daniel, ed. *The Philosophy of Economics: An Anthology*. Cambridge: Cambridge University Press, 1984.

Hill, Ruth Edmonds, ed. "Sadie Alexander." In *The Black Women's Oral History Project. Volume 2*, 70–85. Cambridge, Mass.: Schlesinger Library, 1991.

Himmelweit, Susan. "Domestic Labor." In *The New Palgrave: Social Economics*, edited by John Eatwell, Murray Milgate, and Peter Newman, 35–39. New York: W. W. Norton, 1989.

———. "The Discovery of Unpaid Work." *Feminist Economics* 1, no. 2 (Summer 1995): 1–19.

Hirschfeld, Mary. "Antecedents of the New Home Economics." Paper presented at ASSA Meetings, 1994.

Hoffman, Elizabeth. "Report of the Committee on the Status of Women in the Economics Profession." *American Economic Review* 82, no. 2 (May 1992): 610–14.

———. "Report of the Committee on the Status of Women in the Economics Profession." *American Economic Review* 83, no. 2 (May 1993): 508–11.

Hoffman, Emily P. ed. *Essays on the Economics of Discrimination*. Kalamazoo, Mich.: W. E. Upjohn Institute for Employment Research, 1991.

Howard, M. C., and J. E. King. *A History of Marxian Economics*. Princeton, N.J.: Princeton University Press, 1992.

Hughes, Helen Sard. "The Academic Chance." *Journal of the Association of Collegiate Alumnae* 12, no. 2 (January 1919): 79–82.

Humphries, Jane. "Class Struggle and the Persistence of the Working-Class Family." *Cambridge Journal of Economics* 1 (1977): 241–58.

———. "The Working Class Family, Women's Liberation, and Class Struggle: The Case of Nineteenth Century British History." *Review of Radical Political Economics* 9, no. 3 (Fall 1977): 25–41.

———. "Enclosures, Common Rights, and Women: The Proletarianization of Families in the Late 18th and early 19th Centuries." *Journal of Economic History* 50, no. 1 (1990): 17–42.

———. "Method, Materialism, and Marxist-Feminism: A Comment on Matthaei." In *Radical Economics*, edited by Bruce Roberts and Susan Feiner, 145–54. Norwell, Mass.: Kluwer Academic Publishers, 1992.

Jaggar, Alison. *Feminist Politics and Human Nature*. Totawa, N.J.: Rowman and Allanheld, 1983.

Jaggar, Alison, and Paula Rothenberg Struhl, eds. *Feminist Frameworks: Alternative Theoretical Accounts of the Relations Between Men and Women*. New York: McGraw-Hill, 1978.

Jennings, Ann. "Public or Private? Institutional Economics and Feminism." In *Beyond Economic Man: Feminist Theory and Economics*, edited by Marianne Ferber and Julie Nelson, 111–29. Chicago: University of Chicago Press, 1993.

Kabeer, Naila. *Reversed Realities: Gender Hierarchies in Development Thought*. London: Verso, 1994.

Kahn, Shulamit. "Gender Differences in Academic Paths of Economists." *American Economic Review* 83, no. 2 (May 1993): 52–6.

———. "Women in the Economics Profession." *Journal of Economic Perspectives* 9, no. 4 (Fall 1995): 193–205.

Kessler-Harris, Alice. *Out to Work: A History of Wage-Earning Women in the United States*. New York: Oxford University Press, 1982.

Kim, M., and Solomon Polachek. "Panel Estimates of Male-Female Earnings Functions." *Journal of Human Resources* 29, no. 2 (1994): 406–28.

King, Mary. "Human Capital and Black Women's Occupational Mobility." *Industrial Relations* 34, no. 2 (April 1995): 282–98.

Klamer, Arjo, and David Colander. *The Making of an Economist.* Boulder, Colo.: Westview Press, 1990.

Kolpin, Van W., and Larry D. Singell Jr. "The Gender Composition and Scholarly Performance of Economics Departments: A Test for Employment Discrimination." *Industrial and Labor Relations Review* 49, no. 3 (1996): 408–23.

Kreps, Juanita. *Sex in the Marketplace: American Women at Work.* Baltimore: Johns Hopkins Press, 1971.

Krueger, Anne et al. "Report of the Commission on Graduate Education in Economics." *Journal of Economic Literature* 29, no. 3 (Sept. 1991): 1035–53.

Kuhn, Thomas. *The Structure of Scientific Revolutions,* 2d ed. Chicago: University of Chicago Press, 1970.

Kuiper, Edith, and Jolande Sap, eds. with Susan Feiner, Notburga Ott, and Zafiris Tzannatos. *Out of the Margins: Feminist Perspectives on Economics.* London: Routledge, 1995.

Landes, Joan. "Marxism and the Woman Question." In *Promissory Notes: Women in the Transition to Socialism,* edited by Sonia Kruks, Rayna Rapp, and Marilyn B. Young, 15–28. New York: Monthly Review Press, 1989.

Levin, Lee. "Toward a Post-Keynesian Theory of Investment: A Consideration of the Socially and Emotionally Constituted Nature of Agent Knowledge." In *Out of the Margins: Feminist Perspectives on Economics,* edited by Edith Kuiper and Jolande Sap, 100–29. London: Routledge, 1995.

Libby, Barbara. "Women in Economics Before 1940." *Essays in Business and Economic History* 2 (1984): 272–90.

———. "A Statistical Analysis of Women in the Economics Profession, 1900–1940." *Essays in Business and Economics History* 5 (1987): 180–201.

———. "Women in the Economics Profession, 1900–1940: Factors in Their Declining Visibility." *Essays in Business and Economics History* 8 (1990): 121–29.

Lloyd, Cynthia B. ed. *Sex Discrimination, and the Division of Labor.* New York: Columbia University Press, 1975.

Lloyd, Cynthia B., Emily Andrews, and Curtis L. Gilroy, eds. *Women in the Labor Market.* New York: Columbia University Press, 1979.

Lloyd, Cynthia B., and Beth T. Niemi. *The Economics of Sex Differentials.* New York: Columbia University Press, 1979.

Lundberg, Shelley, and Robert Pollak. "Separate Spheres Bargaining and the Marriage Market." *Journal of Political Economy* 101, no. 6 (1993): 988–1010.

MacDonald, Martha. "Economics and Feminism: The Dismal Science?" *Studies in Political Economy* 15 (Fall 1984): 151–178.

———. "The Empirical Challenges of Feminist Economics: The Example of Economic Restructuring." In *Out of the Margins: Feminist Perspectives on Economics,* edited by Edith Kuiper and Jolande Sap, 175–97. London: Routledge, 1995.

Madden, Janice. *The Economics of Sex Discrimination.* Lexington, Mass.: Lexington Books, 1973.

Malveaux, Julianne. "Missed Opportunity: Sadie Tanner Mossell Alexander and the Economics Profession." *American Economic Review* 81, no. 2 (May 1991): 307–10.

Mancias, Peter T. *A History and Philosophy of the Social Sciences.* Oxford: Basil Blackwell, 1987.

Marx, Karl. *Capital: A Critical Analysis of Capitalist Production*, Volume 1. New York: International Publishers, 1967.

Mason, Edward S. "The Harvard Department of Economic from the Beginning to WWII." *Quarterly Journal of Economics* 97, no. 3 (August 1982): 383–433.

Matthaei, Julie. *An Economic History of Women in America: Women's Work, the Sexual Division of Labor and the Development of Capitalism*. New York: Schocken Books, 1982.

———. "Marxist-Feminist Contributions to Radical Economics." In *Radical Economics*, edited by Bruce Roberts and Susan Feiner, 117–44. Norwell, Mass.: Kluwer Academic Publishers, 1992.

———. "The Sexual Division of Labor, Sexuality, and Lesbian/Gay Liberation: Toward a Marxist-Feminist Analysis of Sexuality in U.S. Capitalism." *Review of Radical Political Economics* 27, no. 2 (June 1995): 1–37.

McCloskey, Donald. "The Discreet Charm of the Bourgeoisie." *Feminist Economics* 1, no. 3 (Fall 1995): 119–24.

McCrate, Elaine. "Trade Merger and Employment: Economic Theory on Marriage." *Review of Radical Political Economics* 19, no. 1 (1987): 73–89.

McCrate, Elaine, and Laura Leete. "Black-White Wage Differences among Young Women." *Industrial Relations* 33, no. 2 (April 1994): 168–83.

McElroy, Marjorie, and Mary Jean Horney. "Nash-Bargained Household Decisions: Toward a Generalization of the Theory of Demand." *International Economic Review* 22, no. 2 (1981): 333–49.

McMillan, Daniel P., and Larry D. Singell Jr. "Gender Differences in First Jobs for Economists." *Southern Economic Journal* 60 (January 1994): 701–14.

Medoff, Marshall H. "The Ranking of Economists." *Journal of Economic Education* 20, no. 4 (Fall 1989): 405–15.

Millett, Kate. *Sexual Politics*. New York: Avon, 1971.

Mirowski, Philip. *Against Mechanism: Protecting Economics from Science*. Totowa, N.J.: Rowman and Littlefield, 1988.

Mirowski, Philip, and Pamela Cook. "Walras' 'Economics and Mechanics': Translation, Commentary, Context." In *Economics as Discourse: An Economic Analysis of the Language of Economists*, edited by Warren J. Samuels, 189–215. Boston, Mass.: Kluwer Academic Publishers, 1990.

Mitchell, Juliet. "Women: The Longest Revolution." In *Women, Class, and the Feminist Imagination: A Socialist-Feminist Reader*, edited by Karen V. Hansen and Irene J. Philipson, 43–78. Philadelphia: Temple University Press, 1990.

Molyneux, Maxine. "Beyond the Domestic Labour Debate." *New Left Review* 116 (July/Aug. 1979): 3–27.

Morgen, Sandra. "Conceptualizing and Changing Consciousness: Socialist-Feminist Perspectives." In *Women, Class, and the Feminist Imagination: A Socialist-Feminist Reader*, edited by Karen V. Hansen and Ilene J. Philipson, 277–91. Philadelphia: Temple University Press, 1990.

Morishima, Michio. *Marx's Economics*. Cambridge: Cambridge University Press, 1973.

National Research Council. *Doctoral Recipients United States Universities, Summary Report 1981*. Washington, D.C.: National Academy Press, 1982.

———. *Doctoral Recipients United States Universities, Summary Report 1991*. Washington, D.C.: National Academy Press, 1992.

National Science Foundation. *Women and Minorities in Science and Engineering: An Update*, prepared by Patricia E. White. Washington, D.C., January 1992.

Nelson, Julie A. "Gender, Metaphor, and the Definition of Economics." *Economics and Philosophy* 8 (1992): 103–25.

———. "The Study of Choice or the Study of Provisioning? Gender and the Definition of Economics." In *Behind Economic Man: Feminist Theory and Economics,* edited by Marianne Ferber and Julie Nelson, 23–36. Chicago: University of Chicago Press, 1993.

———. "Value-free or Valueless? Notes on the Pursuit of Detachment in Economics." *History of Political Economy* 25, no. 1 (Spring 1993): 121–45.

———. "Feminism and Economics." *Journal of Economic Perspectives* 9, no. 2 (Spring 1995): 131–48.

———. *Feminism, Objectivity and Economics.* London, Routledge, 1996.

Nicholson, Linda. "Feminism and Marxism: Integrating Kinship and the Economic." In *Feminism as Critique: On the Politics of Gender,* edited by Seyla Benhabib and Drucilla Cornell, 16–30. Minneapolis: University of Minnesota Press, 1987.

Olsen, Frederick. "Helen Laura Sumner Woodbury." In *Notable American Women 1607–1950,* edited by Edward T. James, 651. Cambridge: Harvard University Press, 1971.

Orr, Daniel. "Reflections on the Hiring of Faculty." *American Economic Review* 83, no. 2 (May 1993): 39–43.

Ott, Notburga. "Fertility and Division of Work in the Family: A Game Theoretic Model of Household Decisions." In *Out of the Margins: Feminist Perspectives on Economics,* edited by Edith Kuiper and Jolande Sap, 80–99. London: Routledge, 1995.

———. *Interfamily Bargaining and Household Decisions.* New York: Springer-Verlag, 1992.

Persky, Joseph. "The Ethology of *Homo Economicus.*" *Journal of Economic Perspectives* 9, no. 2 (Spring 1995): 221–31.

Peterson, Janice, and Doug Brown, eds. *The Economic Status of Women Under Capitalism: Institutional Economics and Feminist Thought.* Brookfield, Vt.: Edward Elgar, 1994.

Phipps, Shelley, and Peter Burton. "Social/Institutional Variables and Behavior Within Households: An Empirical Test Using the Luxembourg Income Study." *Feminist Economics* 1, no. 1 (Spring 1995): 151–74.

Picchio, Antonella. *Social Reproduction: The Political Economy of the Labor Market.* Cambridge: Cambridge University Press, 1992.

Przeworski, Adam. "Marxism and Rational Choice." *Politics and Society* 14 (1986): 379–409.

Pulol, Michèle. *Feminism and Anti-Feminism in Early Economic Thought.* Brookfield, Vt.: Edward Elgar, 1992.

Randall, Mercedes M., ed. *Beyond Nationalism: The Social Thought of Emily Greene Balch.* New York: Twayne Publishers, 1972.

Reagan, Barbara. "Report on the Committee on the Status of Women in the Economics Profession." *American Economic Review* 66, no. 2 (May 1976): 490–501.

———. "Report of the Committee on the Status of Women in the Economics Profession." *American Economic Review* 67, no. 1 (February 1977): 460–64.

Redmount, Esther. "Toward a Feminist Econometrics." In *Out of the Margins: Feminist Perspectives on Economics,* edited by Edith Kuiper and Jolande Sap, 216–22. London: Routledge, 1995.

Reid, Margaret. *Economics of Household Production.* New York: John Wiley & Sons, 1934.

Resnick, Stephen, and Richard Wolff. *Economics: Marxian Versus Neoclassical.* Baltimore: Johns Hopkins University Press, 1987.

Roemer, John. *Analytical Foundations of Marxian Economic Theory.* Cambridge: Cambridge University Press, 1981.

Ross, Dorothy. *The Origins of American Social Science.* Cambridge: Cambridge University Press, 1991.

Rossiter, Margaret W. *Women Scientists in America: Struggles and Strategies to 1940.* Baltimore: Johns Hopkins University Press, 1982.

Rubin, Gayle. "The Traffic of Women: Notes on the 'Political Economy' of Sex." In *Toward an Anthropology of Women,* edited by Rayna Rapp Reiter, 157–210. New York: Monthly Review Press, 1976.

Ryan, Barbara. *Feminism and the Women's Movement.* London: Routledge, 1992.

Sawhill, Isabel. "Economic Perspectives on the Family." *Daedalus* 106 (1977): 115–25.

———. "Report of the Committee on the Status of Women in the Economics Profession." *CSWEP Newsletter* (Winter 1986): 2–5.

———. "Report of the Committee on the Status of Women in the Economics Profession." *American Economic Review* 77, no. 2 (May 1987): 401–3.

Schram, Sanford. *Words of Welfare: The Poverty of Social Science and the Social Science of Poverty.* Minneapolis: University of Minesota Press, 1995.

Schultz, Theodore. "Investment in Human Capital." *American Economic Review* 51, no. 1 (1960): 1–17

Seiz, Janet. "The Bargaining Approach and Feminist Methodology." *Review of Radical Political Economics* 23, no. 1–2 (1991): 22–29.

———. "Gender and Economic Research." In *Post-Popperian Methodology of Economics,* edited by Neil de Marchi, 273–319. Boston: Kluwer Academic Publishers, 1992.

———. "Feminism and the History of Thought." *History of Political Economy* 25, no. 1 (1993): 185–201.

———. "Epistemology and the Tasks of Feminist Economics." *Feminist Economics* 1, no. 3 (Fall 1995): 110–18.

Sen, Amartya. "Gender and Cooperative Conflicts." In *Persistent Inequalities,* edited by Irene Tinker, 123–79. New York: Oxford University Press, 1990.

———. "Rational Fools: A Critique of the Behavioral Foundations of Economic Theory." *Philosophy and Public Affairs* 6 (Summer 1977): 318–44.

Shackelford, Jean. "Perspectives on Diversity in Economic Education: The College Experience." Mimeo, December 1992.

———. "Mabel Newcomer and the Economics Profession: 1917–1957." Paper presented at the 6th Annual International Conference on Socio-Economics, 1994.

Shelburn, Marsha R., and Patsy G. Lewellyn. "Gender Bias in Doctoral Programs in Economics." *Journal of Economic Education* 26, no. 4 (Fall 1995): 373–83.

Sherman, Howard J. "Methodology of Critical Marxian Economic Theory." In *The Role of Economic Theory,* edited by Philip A. Klein, 77–95. Boston, Mass.: Kluwer Academic Publishers, 1994.

Siegfried, John, and Charles Scott. "Recent Trends in Undergraduate Economics Degress." *Journal of Economic Education* 25, no. 3 (Summer 1994): 281–26.

Silva, Edward T., and Shelia A. Slaughter. *Serving Power: The Making of the Academic Social Science Expert.* Westport, Conn.: Greenwood Press, 1984.

Singell, Larry Jr., and Joe A. Stone. "Gender Differences in Ph.D. Economists' Careers." *Contemporary Policy Issues* 11, no. 4 (October 1993): 95–106.

Sorensen, Elaine. *Comparable Worth: Is It a Worthy Policy?* Princeton: Princeton University Press, 1994.

Steedman, Ian. *Marx After Sraffa*. London: New Left Books, 1977.

Straussmann, Diana, and Livia Polanyi. "The Economist as Storyteller: What the Texts Reveal." In *Out of the Margins: Feminist Perspectives on Economics,* edited by Edith Kuiper and Jolande Sap, 129–45. London: Routledge, 1995.

Strober, Myra. "Women Economists: Career Aspirations, Education, and Training." *American Economic Review* 65, no. 2 (May 1975): 92–99.

Strober, Myra, and Barbara B. Reagan. "Sex Differences in Economists' Fields of Specialization." In *Women in the Workplace: The Implications of Occupational Segregation,* edited by Martha Blaxall and Barbara B. Reagan, 303–17. Chicago: University of Chicago Press, 1976.

Tax, Meredith. *The Rising of the Women: Feminist Solidarity and Class Conflict, 1880–1917*. New York: Monthly Review Press, 1980.

The Woman Question: Selections from the Writings of Karl Marx, Frederick Engels, V. I. Lenin and Joseph Stalin. New York: International Publishers, 1975.

Tilly, Chris, and Randy Albelda. "Family Structure and Family Earnings: The Determinants of Earnings Differences among Family Types." *Industrial Relations* 33, no. 2 (1994): 151–67.

Tong, Rosemarie. *Feminist Thought: A Contemporary Introduction*. Boulder, Colo.: Westview Press, 1989.

Treiman, Donald, and Heidi Hartmann, eds. *Women, Work, and Wages: Equal Pay for Jobs of Equal Value*. Washington, D.C.: National Academy Press, 1981.

Uchitelle, Louis. "In Economics, a Subtle Exclusion." *New York Times* 11 January 1993, D3–4.

United Nations Development Programme. *Human Development Report, 1995*. New York: Oxford University Press, 1995.

U.S. Department of Commerce, Census Bureau. *Historical Statistics of the United States*. Washington, D.C.: Government Printing Office, 1975.

———. *Marital Status and Living Arrangements, 1991*. Washington, D.C.: Government Printing Office, 1992.

———. *Money Income of Household, Families and Persons in 1991* P60–184. Washington, D.C.: Government Printing Office, 1992.

———. *Statistical Abstract of the United States, 1994*. Washington, D.C.: Government Printing Office, 1994.

U.S. Department of Education. *Digest of Educational Statistics*. Washington, D.C.: Government Printing Office, 1971.

U.S. Department of Education, National Center for Educational Statistics. *Digest of Educational Statistics*. Lantham, MD: National Center for Educational Statistics, 1994.

van der Meulen Rodgers, Yana. "The Prevalence of Gender Topics in U.S. Economics Journals." *Feminist Economics* 2, no. 2 (1996): 129–35.

Vogel, Lise. *Marxism and the Oppression of Women: Toward a Unitary Theory*. New Brunswick, N.J.: Rutgers University Press, 1983.

Wallace, Phyllis with Linda Datcher and Julianne Malveaux. *Black Women in the Labor Force*. Cambridge: MIT Press, 1980.

Waring, Marilyn. *If Women Counted: A New Feminist Economics*. San Francisco: Harper and Row, 1988.

Willis, Robert. "A New Approach to the Economic Theory of Fertility." *Journal of Political Economy* 81, no. 2 (March/April 1973): S14–64.

Wolff, Robert Paul. "The Resurrection of Karl Marx Political Economist." *Social Research* 53, no. 3 (Autumn 1986): 475–512.

Woolley, Frances R. "The Feminist Challenge to Neoclassical Economics." *Cambridge Journal of Economics* 17 (1993): 485–500.

INDEX

Abbott, Edith, 29–30

academic economists, 36; early history of, 15, 17–20, 24–26, 31–33; percentage of female, 41–46, 60–61. *See also* CSWEP, data on women in economics; female economists, academics

academic freedom, 19, 27, 184n. 30

Adelman, Irma, 32, 51

AEA. *See* American Economic Association

affirmative action, 84, 86, 91, 119

African-Americans, 14, 22, 26–27, 62, 115, 119

Aid to Families with Dependent Children (AFDC), 84–85, 125

Alexander, Sadie Tanner Mossell, 26, 168

alienation, 132, 137

Althussar, Louis, 151

altruism, 122–23, 163

American Economic Association (AEA), 7; journals, 50, 71, 73, 77, 190n. 2; membership, 23, 26; officers, 18, 23, 31, 49–50; origins, 13, 18–19, 21, 23–25; role in forming CSWEP, 7, 47–49; Universal Academic Questionnaire, 41–44, 65, 187nn. 10, 11

American Historical Association, 18, 20

American Social Science Association (ASSA), 15–18

Balch, Emily Greene, 24, 185n. 52

bargaining theory, 128

Barrett, Michèle, 145, 151

Bates, Helen Francis Page, 24, 26

Bebel, August, 134, 139, 147

Becker, Gary, 9, 105–6, 113, 115–17, 121, 127

Bell, Carolyn Shaw, 119

Benería, Lourdes, 151–52

Bentson, Margaret, 147

blacks. *See* African-Americans

Blank, Rebecca, 50, 157

Blau, Francine, 51

Blaug, Mark, 107, 120

Breckinridge, Sophonisba, 29–30

Broder, Ivy, 44–45, 182n. 15, 187n. 15

Brown, Doug, 167

capitalism. *See* capitalist production

THE AUTHOR

Randy Albelda is an associate professor of economics in the College of Arts and Sciences at the University of Massachusetts-Boston. In addition to her work on feminism and economics, Albelda has researched and taught on women's economic status, income inequality, family structure, labor markets, and state and local finance. Albelda is widely involved with Boston and Massachusetts groups concerned with women's economic well-being, economics education efforts, and tax reform. She has written extensively for academic and popular audiences. She is an editorial board member of *Dollars and Sense* magazine and the journal *Feminist Economics*. She is coauthor of *Glass Ceilings and Bottomless Pits: Women's Work, Women's Poverty* (1997), *Unlevel Playing Fields: Understanding Wage Inequality and Discrimination* (1997), and *The War on the Poor: A Defense Manual* (1996). Albelda received her Ph.D. in economics from the University of Massachusetts–Amherst in 1983.

THE EDITOR

Claire Sprague is Professor Emerita of the Department of English, Brooklyn College of the City University of New York. She has also taught at New York University, John Jay College, the University of Zaragoza, Reed College, and the University of Wisconsin. Her publications include *In Pursuit of Doris Lessing: Nine Nations Reading* (1990), *Rereading Doris Lessing: Narrative Patterns of Doubling and Repetition* (1987), *Van Wyck Brooks: The Early Years* (1968, 1993), and *Virginia Woolf* (1970). She was the first president of the Doris Lessing Society and an editor of the *Doris Lessing Newsletter* (1979–1986). She is the coproducer of *Sister Talk,* a radio program aired over WOMR, Provincetown, and WTJU, Charlottesville. Her current work in progress is a study of five artist and writer couples in twentieth-century America.